The Campus History Series

THE LATIN/GREEK INSTITUTE AT THE CITY UNIVERSITY OF NEW YORK

On the Front Cover: Pictured is the August 13, 1982, end of the summer celebration of the Latin/Greek Institute held at the famed Rainbow Room. (Courtesy of the Office of Building Design and Exhibitions, Graduate Center of the City University of New York.)

On the Back Cover: This is an image of the New York Public Library and Bryant Park by photographer Angelo Rizzuto. (Courtesy of Library of Congress.)

The Campus History Series

The Latin/Greek Institute at the City University of New York

Lucas G. Rubin

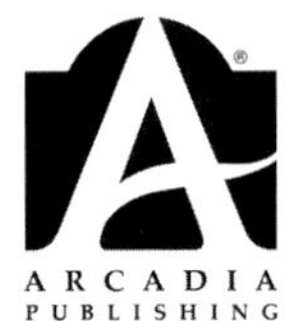

ISBN 978-1-4671-6115-2

Published by Arcadia Publishing
Charleston, South Carolina

Printed in the United States of America

Library of Congress Control Number: 2024934679

For all general information, please contact Arcadia Publishing:
Telephone 843-853-2070
Fax 843-853-0044
E-mail sales@arcadiapublishing.com

Visit us on the Internet at www.arcadiapublishing.com

To Floyd Moreland, Rita Fleischer, Hardy Hansen, and Gerry Quinn:

datur haec venia antiquitati
ut miscendo humana divinis primordia . . .
augustiora faciat

Contents

Acknowledgments 6

Introduction 7

1. *Prolegomena*: Brooklyn College and the Classics 11
2. *In Principio*: The CUNY Latin Institute, 1973–1977 31
3. The Latin/Greek Institute, 1978–1999 51
4. *Monumentum Aere Perennius*:
   The New Millennium, 2000–2023 75
5. *Ἀλωτὰ γίγνεται ἐπιμελείᾳ καὶ πόνῳ ἅπαντα*:
   The Curriculum 89
6. *Nil Adsuetudine Maius*: Institute Traditions 103

Bibliography 127

Acknowledgments

This book is the work of the entire Latin/Greek Institute community: the faculty, alumni, staff, and friends who, over the past five decades, photographed, documented, and recorded various moments in the Institute's history. My role in this endeavor was minor and limited to sourcing, collecting, and organizing.

Nevertheless, some specific recognitions are in order. First and foremost, my deepest thanks to Floyd L. Moreland, *creator, conditor et paterfamilias*, with whom I exchanged dozens of emails and texts (plus a good number of calls and the occasional Zoom). Rita Fleischer and Hardy Hansen were as indispensable to putting this together as they were in building the LGI. All three received and answered dozens of inquiries a week. Their recollection of people, places, and events was formidable, something that would come as little surprise to any of their former students and colleagues.

Also at the Institute, my thanks to every current and former faculty member and alumnus/a mentioned herein (many of whom eagerly shared, along with information on their post-program dénouement, a story or recollection of their time at the LGI). Alan Fishbone, Michelle Kwintner, Bill Pagonis, and Stephanie Russell are owed special thanks in this regard; all four helped fill in many gaps.

Among my colleagues at Brooklyn College, my gratitude to: Marianne LaBatto, associate archivist, and Joe Fodor, BC history enthusiast; David Paré, my spring 2023 research assistant; Lauren Mancia, associate professor of history, my cocurator for 2023's *Magisterial Feminae* exhibition; and all of my colleagues in the Department of Classics who caretake and add their own unique contributions to the department's formidable legacy (especially John Van Sickle, member of the LGI faculty in 1982). Finally, my predecessor at the LGI, Katherine Hsu, was the first—and most enthusiastic—supporter of the project.

At the Graduate Center, a special thanks to Ray Ring and his folks in the Office of Building Design and Exhibitions, especially Faythe Weaver, who've preserved much of the GC's—and a portion of the LGI's—history. Amy Jarvis, my editor at Arcadia, was helpful at every turn and generous in providing the time that I needed to complete the work. And, finally, to Simona and Itai: *super omnia, carissimi mihi estis.*

Unless otherwise noted, all images appear courtesy of the Brooklyn College Archives and Special Collections.

Introduction

In the first 50 years since its 1973 foundation, the Latin/Greek Institute (LGI) at the City University of New York (CUNY) has trained almost 3,000 students in the classical languages. The LGI's total-immersion programs facilitate a degree of language acquisition without peer: after 50 days of highly choreographed study in the Institute's basic Latin or Greek programs, students—who enter with little or no prior knowledge—return to their home institutions ready to take advanced reading courses and/or sit for graduate language exams.

A summer at the LGI is almost impossible to describe; rather, the intensity and rigor are something that can only be experienced. The pace and pedagogy—and their effectiveness—are perhaps best demonstrated by the following: on Day 8 of the Summer Latin Institute (SLI), students begin to read, at sight, the poetry of Catullus; on Day 29, students in Basic Greek (SGI) engage Plato's *Ion*, which they'll complete in its entirety in nine days. Facilitating student learning at this pace requires exacting precision from the faculty, extraordinary commitment on the part of students, and significant endurance from both.

In its first half century, the Institute has become an essential part of the ecosystem of classical studies. It has helped mitigate the nationwide decline in Latin and (especially) Greek instruction, provided a mechanism for current and aspiring scholars outside of the classics who require Latin or Greek for their research and inquiry, and has helped jumpstart the careers of those who came late to the study of the ancient world. For the past three decades, it has also helped diversify advanced study in the humanities: the number of students from historically underrepresented groups attending the Institute doubled in the decade beginning in 1998 and again after 2009. Today, Institute students hail from across the country and, increasingly, worldwide. Their reasons for attending vary and, for those whose motivations are academic, represent a broad range of fields and disciplines.

The impact of the Institute is perhaps best demonstrated by the success of its graduates, for whom there is (as of 2023) information for about 60 percent. Of these, around 20% have gone on to complete a PhD in the humanities, with philosophy, classics, English, art history, and history constituting the top five most represented fields. An even larger number have completed terminal MAs (or "MPhils") in an array of subjects in the humanities and social sciences, while another 20 percent or so hold a JD or other advanced professional degree (MBA, MEd, or a career/industry-focused MS). This includes a good number of MDs. Many alumni hold multiple degrees, including several joint PhD and JD holders (and at least four who also hold an additional graduate degree); one with a PhD, MD, and an MA; at least one with two PhDs (history and classics); and finally, one with an MD, JD, MPH, and MA. The Institute can also count one MacArthur Fellow among the ranks of its alumni. For the curious, the youngest student to complete an LGI program was 14 (several, in fact), and the oldest was 78; in addition, the LGI can take responsibility for at least four marriages.

Many graduates go on to the ranks of full-time faculty or K–12 teaching, though alumni are found in almost every sector and industry. Regardless of their chosen path, nearly all would acknowledge that their Institute summer was simultaneously one of the most rigorous but also rewarding experiences of their academic careers. For many, completion of the Institute was critical—the *sine qua non*—to their subsequent professional success. For those who pursued careers elsewhere, their experience at the Institute equipped them with the confidence to master a significant amount of material in a limited time.

If often seen as a standalone enterprise at CUNY's midtown Manhattan Graduate Center, the LGI is actually the convergence of two distinct histories: the first, that of classical studies at Brooklyn College, a public liberal arts college founded in 1930, and the second—three and a half decades later and some 2,500 miles away—the consequence of a challenge faced by the humanities at the University of California at Berkeley. Of these, that at Brooklyn College requires a somewhat longer investigation and one that lends itself to a photographic retrospective. Consequently, our history opens on the West Coast in the mid-1960s.

The study of Latin (and, to a lesser extent, ancient Greek) had been a staple of American education from the founding of the Republic. Though it had experienced periods of greater or lesser emphasis, by the 1960s an unprecedented and seemingly sustained decline had set in, a process accelerated by the rapid socioeconomic changes of the postwar period. The reasons are (and remain) manifold, but two are illustrative: the increased focus on science and technology in education, an emphasis of the 1958 National Defense Education Act, and the codification of Vatican II in 1963, which all but removed regular exposure to the language for many.

In a range of disciplines, however, competency in Latin and/or Greek was essential to advanced study, and otherwise qualified students began entering graduate programs un- or underprepared to engage the languages at a necessary level of competence. At the graduate level, remediation is especially challenging, with few effective options and generally insufficient time to gain the necessary level of facility.

By the mid-1960s, the Department of Comparative Literature at the University of California at Berkeley had reached a crisis point with its students' inability to pass their obligatory Latin proficiency exam. The faculty considered the language essential and, averse to eliminating its requirement, approached the classics department about finding a solution. The department suggested that this was an ideal challenge for one of their graduate students, Floyd L. Moreland, who had established a reputation as a talented Latinist and a dynamic teacher—and one with a lot of novel ideas about language instruction.

Though only a few years into graduate study himself, Moreland was energized by the challenge. Joined by his Berkeley classmate Mary-Kay Gamel, he developed a basic curriculum and assembled a patchwork of study materials drawn from multiple sources: textbooks were carved up and reorganized, and a range of handouts—which remain a staple at the Institute—were developed (many of these prototypes of the materials that remain in use to the present day).

The Berkeley intensive Latin program was first offered in the summer of 1967. Though purposeful and well planned, some of the details and many of its materials were initially *ad hoc* assemblages; most importantly, its novel pedagogy was largely untested. At the summer's end, however, it had proved a success, achieving the department's objectives for enrolled students, and providing proof of concept for Moreland and Gamel's model of rapid language acquisition. The program was subsequently broadened in scope and formalized into the Berkeley Summer Latin Workshop, which, though later modified, remains in operation to the present day—very much the progenitor of the LGI.

As Moreland's graduate studies were concluding and his PhD within reach, his search for a full-time faculty position began in earnest. Though he entertained offers from several schools, only one expressed specific interest in his work with the Latin Workshop: Brooklyn College's Ethyle Wolfe, then chair of its Department of Classics and Comparative Literature—and a rising star in the college's administration. Wolfe was interested in starting a similar program at CUNY, which, given the right institutional support, might reach a larger audience. Moreland was interviewed in January 1971, and an offer of a tenure track position at Brooklyn College followed soon thereafter.

That the Latin/Greek Institute should take root at Brooklyn College should come, in retrospect, as little surprise. As a traditional field of study, classics was central to the college's earliest curriculum and, over the decades, home to many leading classical and premodern scholars. At the same time, the college has always had a fiercely independent streak. This dichotomy is evident in the LGI itself: a traditional field of study manifested as a *sui generis* enterprise. If the subject matter was as traditional as possible, the way in which it would be taught was not: in the context of the early (and tumultuous) 1970s, it was positively cutting-edge.

What follows is an illustrated history of the CUNY Latin / Greek Institute, from its origins through its first 50 years. It is very much a ἱστορία (*historia*) in the fullest meaning of the Greek term: inquiry, history, and story. Context is important, and the LGI's history begins with its prehistory. Here, Brooklyn College's Department of Classics is essential to the story, not least as it has played an outsized role in its contribution to Latin pedagogy (Chapter 1). In this regard, Moreland—and the LGI—would prove a natural fit.

After two years of planning and preparing, the CUNY Latin Institute was launched in 1973 (Chapter 2). Its establishment was aided by several factors: the Berkeley Workshop had provided invaluable information about the instructional model; Wolfe, in the year of Moreland's hire, was appointed the college's dean of humanities, beginning an ascendancy to its eventual academic leadership. Finally, Moreland found himself surrounded by several colleagues, many also recruited by Wolfe. One of these, though only a part-time appointment, would become integral to the founding, maturation, and character of the Institute and another would be essential to expanding the Institute to encompass both classical languages.

In the decades that followed, new programs would be added—most significantly, that in intensive Greek (1978)—as well as various iterations of programs designed for more advanced students (Chapters 3–5). All of these have adhered to Moreland's foundational concepts for intensive teaching and learning, a core set of practices essential to the LGI's pedagogy and central to the success of its students (detailed in Chapter 5). Finally, as the Institute grew in enrollment and found itself on surer footing, an array of customs and traditions became woven into its fabric, some by design and others arising organically or by circumstance (Chapter 6).

Within the limited confines of this book, it is impossible to mention every member of the faculty, staff, or institutional colleague who has contributed to, supported, and helped advance the Institute over the past half century. It is also impossible to mention any but a fraction of the thousands of students who have attended, many of whom have gone on to extraordinary careers in academia and elsewhere. Each one of them, however, is just as essential to and part of the LGI's history. In addition, as this is an illustrated history, there are some years for which photographic evidence is entirely lacking. Finally, illustrations themselves are often limited in their ability to explain complex phenomena; this is especially true of such essential and detailed topics as curriculum and pedagogy. Nonetheless, the hope and intent of this book is to convey, at a minimum, something of the essence and spirit of this truly unique academic enterprise.

This work contains abbreviations. Though defined in context, here's a guide:

BC Brooklyn College

CUNY The City University of New York

GC The Graduate School and University Center of the City University of New York (CUNY Graduate Center). Both BC and the GC are part of CUNY.

LGI Latin/Greek Institute

SLI The Summer Latin Institute (also known as the Basic Latin program)

SGI The Summer Greek Institute (also known as the Basic Greek program)

L, G When written with a number next to a name, this refers to the year in which the individual completed a specific program: Latin or Greek

AL, AG When written with a number next to a name, this refers to the year in which the individual completed a specific program: Advanced Latin or Advanced Greek

UL, UG When written with a number next to a name, this refers to the year in which the individual completed a specific program: Upper Latin or Upper Greek

At the Institute, faculty and students have always been on a first name basis. Floyd Moreland believed this was essential to help reduce psychological barriers between students and teachers and to foster a spirit of camaraderie, the summer is a marathon run together. Finally, in most LGI materials, faculty are designated by their full initials: FLM = Floyd L. Moreland, Rita M. Fleischer = RMF, Hardy Hansen = HH, et al. To align with the publisher's standards, this text uses last names.

One

Prolegomena
Brooklyn College and the Classics

As early as 1861, the City of Brooklyn sought to establish a public college. The Civil War intervened and the postwar period, with its explosive growth in population and industry, forestalled any such movement. In 1898, Brooklyn was absorbed by the metropolis just across the East River, becoming one of the five boroughs of New York City.

Although Brooklyn was already home to several private colleges (including the Brooklyn Collegiate and Polytechnic Institute [now New York University Tandon School of Engineering], founded in 1854; St. Francis College, 1884; and Pratt Institute, 1887), its first public college was a men-only evening extension school opened by City College in 1910. A satellite campus of Hunter College (for women) followed soon thereafter. Enrollment far exceeded capacity and on April 22, 1930, the Board of Higher Education authorized the creation of an independent college through the consolidation of the two satellite campuses. The new Brooklyn College was the first coeducational public college in New York City, and its initial faculty was largely drawn from the City College and Hunter extension campuses. The new college remained in downtown Brooklyn until a permanent campus was opened in 1937.

Classics was considered essential to a well-rounded education, and a dedicated department was established concurrently with that of the new college. At its inception, it had the largest student registration in the country. In 1957, the department was reconfigured as "Classics and World Literature" and (Biblical) Hebrew—previously considered one of the classical languages—was migrated to the Department of Modern Languages. In 1962, the department was again reorganized as the Department of Classics and Comparative Literature, an emphasis it retained until 1974, when it reverted to classics.

Beyond the department, the college has been home to many premodern scholars, whose research overlapped that of the classics. Of special note is the number of prominent female faculty across these fields, at a time when women were far less represented and faced numerous challenges in higher education. Brooklyn College honored their illustrious history in a 2023 exhibition, *Magisterial Feminae: How Women Who Studied the Ancient World Innovated Brooklyn College, the Latin/Greek Institute, and Beyond.*

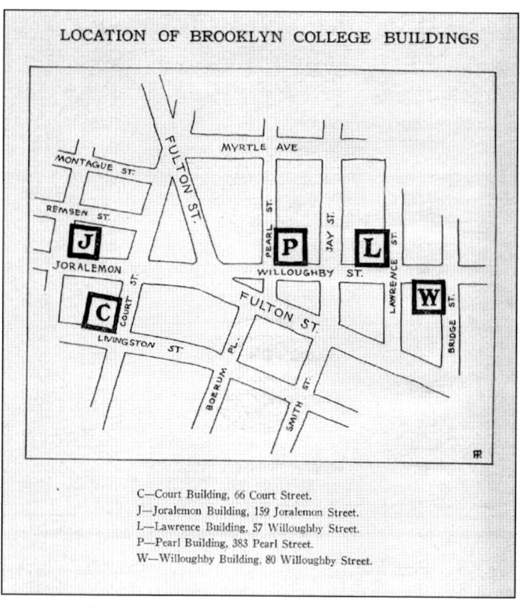

In 1933, the *Brooklyn College Bulletin* included a guide to the various buildings in downtown Brooklyn that comprised the nascent college's campus, several of which were holdovers from the original City and Hunter College extension campuses. Enrollments in the new institution were strong and growing, but the busy civic and business district limited typical college activities. Consequently, the search for a suitable campus was paramount.

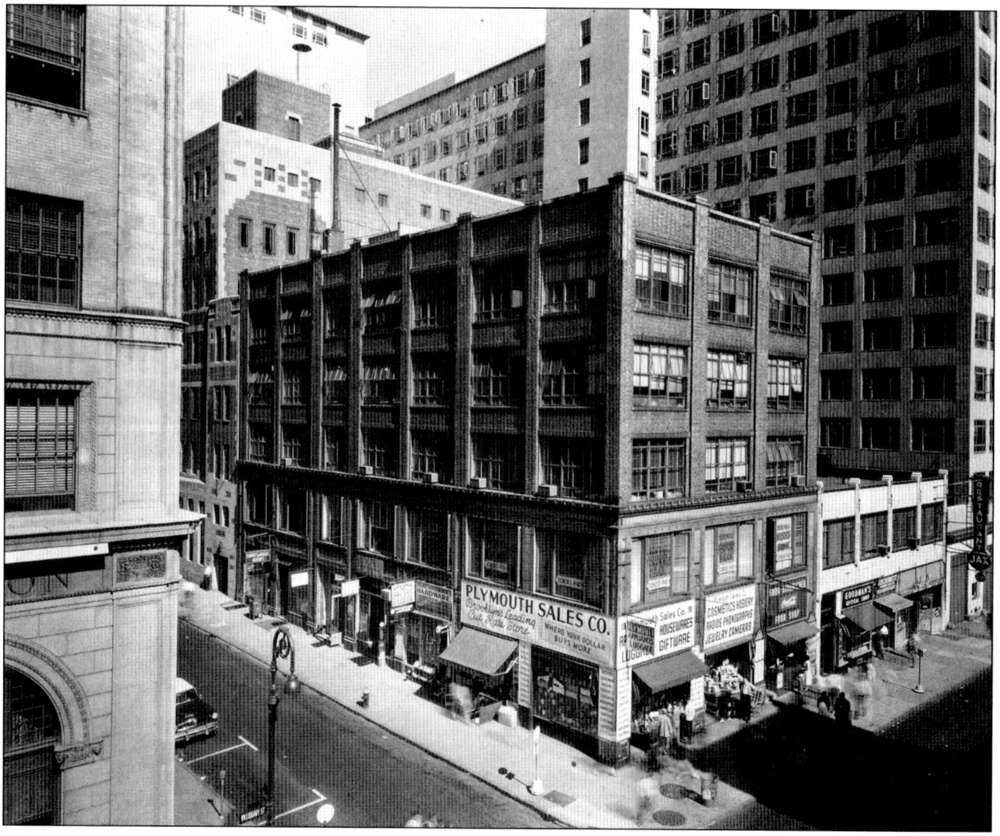

Each of the college's downtown buildings was identified by its adjoining thoroughfare; that at 383 Pearl Street, the Pearl Building, housed the college's administrative offices. Located adjacent to the original Brooklyn Law School building (now the Brooklyn Friends School), the building later housed another college: the for-profit ASA College, which closed in 2023 following the loss of its accreditation.

Hunter College rented several floors at 66 Court Street, the Brooklyn Chamber of Commerce Building, in 1927. Designed by the architect Abraham J. Simberg as an office tower, the 30-story building is a Neo-Gothic edifice with setbacks of brick, limestone, and granite, finished with terra-cotta revetments. In 1981, the building was converted into cooperative apartments, and in 2011, now known as 75 Livingston, it was landmarked as part of the Borough Hall Skyscraper Historic District. The 21 buildings included in this designation reflect the importance of this area as Brooklyn's center of business, government, and civic life from the opening of the Brooklyn Bridge (1883) through the Great Depression.

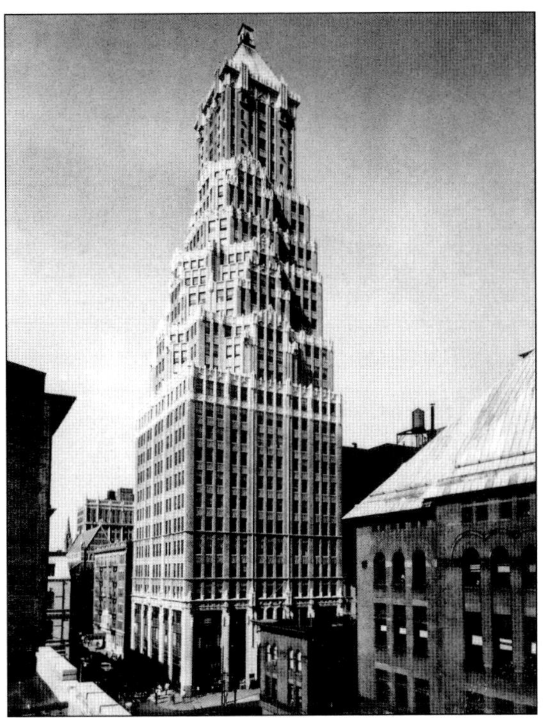

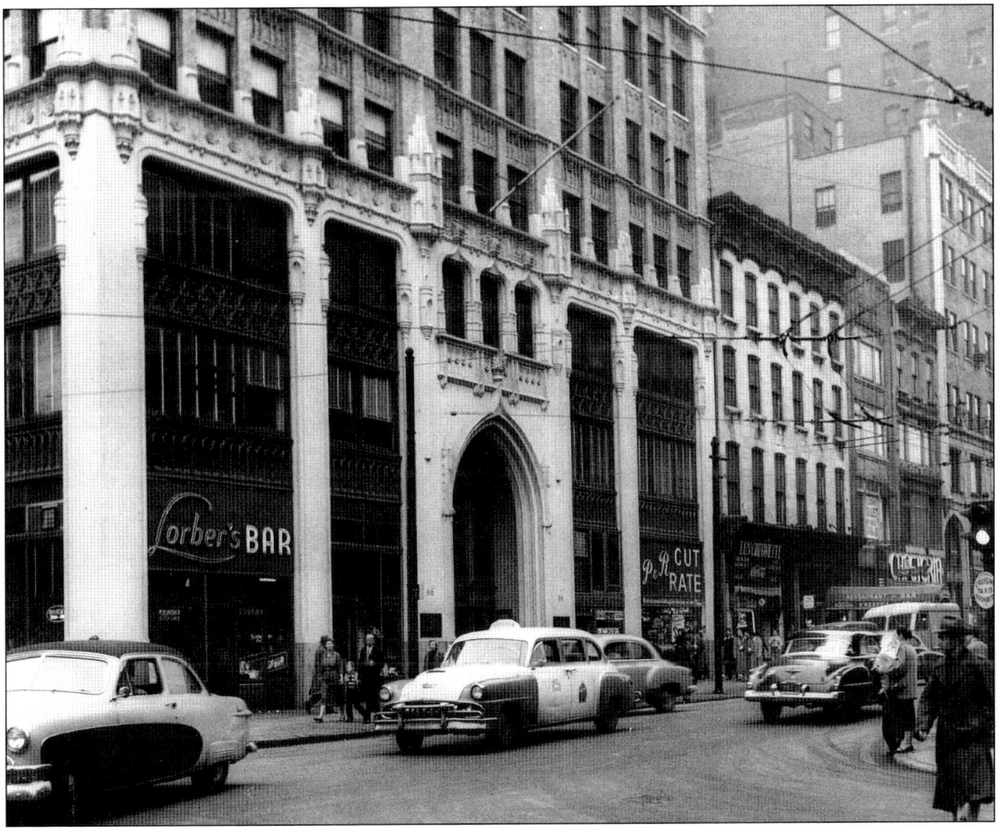

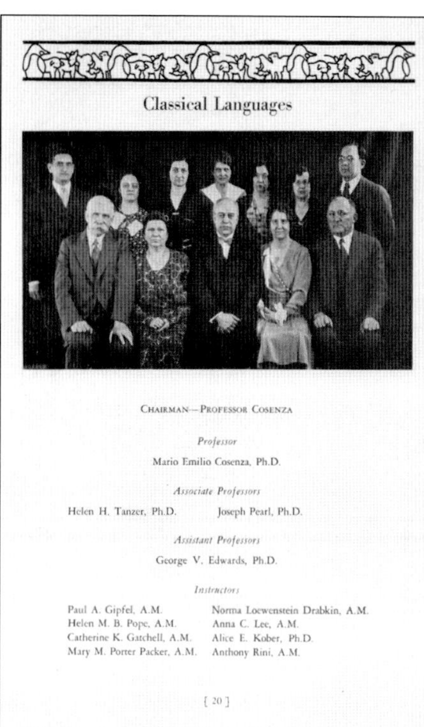

Classical Languages

CHAIRMAN—PROFESSOR COSENZA

Professor

Mario Emilio Cosenza, Ph.D.

Associate Professors

Helen H. Tanzer, Ph.D. Joseph Pearl, Ph.D.

Assistant Professors

George V. Edwards, Ph.D.

Instructors

Paul A. Gipfel, A.M. Norma Loewenstein Drabkin, A.M.
Helen M. B. Pope, A.M. Anna C. Lee, A.M.
Catherine K. Gatchell, A.M. Alice E. Kober, Ph.D.
Mary M. Porter Packer, A.M. Anthony Rini, A.M.

[20]

The Department of Classical Languages was one of 13 academic units formed from the merger of the extension faculties of City College and Hunter College in 1930. The 1933 *Broeklundian* provides the earliest known picture of the department. The yearbook title, inspired by the original Dutch hamlet of Breukelen, remains in use to the present day, having replaced its predecessors *Town and Gown* (1931) and *Skyscrapers* (1932).

Helen Tanzer (1876–1961) earned an AB from Barnard College in 1903 and began teaching classics at Hunter College immediately thereafter. This early photograph captures her class on Roman life. After service in World War I at the Division of Foreign Language Publications, she returned to Hunter, completed her PhD at Johns Hopkins, and joined Brooklyn College's newly organized classics department. She retired as a full professor in 1937.

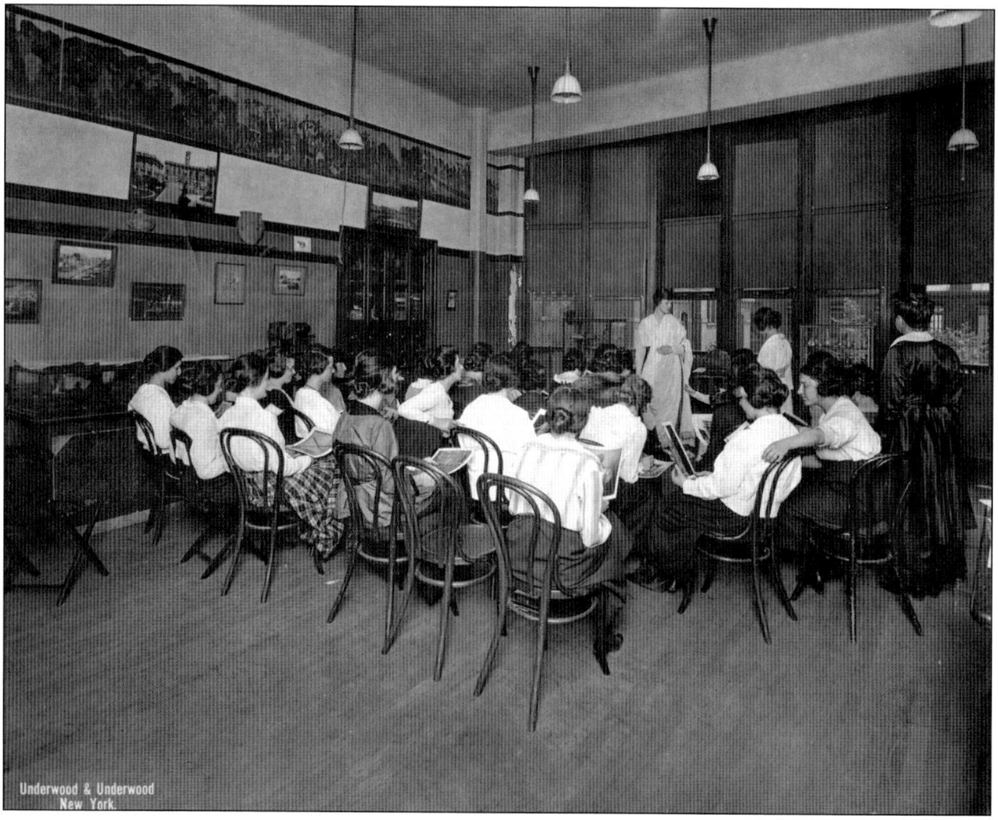

Underwood & Underwood
New York.

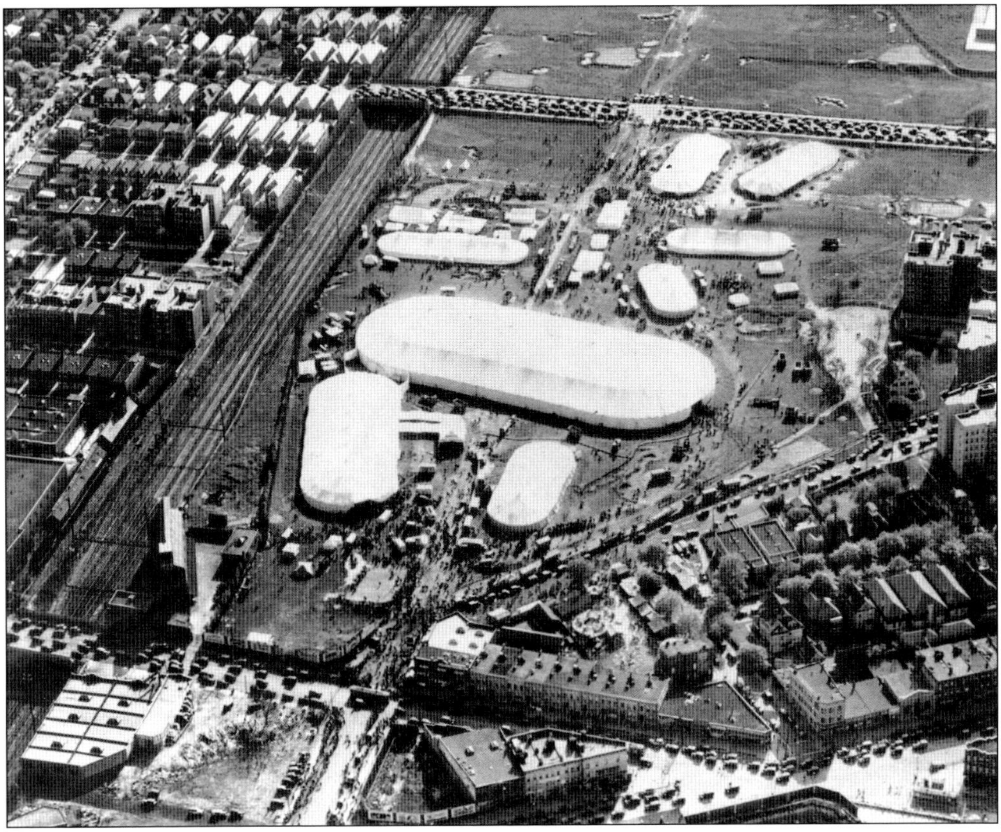

Given the urgency to build a permanent campus, a large and suitable plot of land was identified in the Midwood section of Brooklyn. At the time, the parcel was used for public recreation, most notably as a staging area for the Barnum and Bailey Circus. In December 1934, the city's Board of Estimate approved the purchase of the land for $1,625,528 and, after a direct appeal by Mayor Fiorello La Guardia to Pres. Franklin Delano Roosevelt, the Public Works Administration (PWA) allocated $5 million for the campus's construction. The campus's present environs are evident in the aerial photograph of the circus.

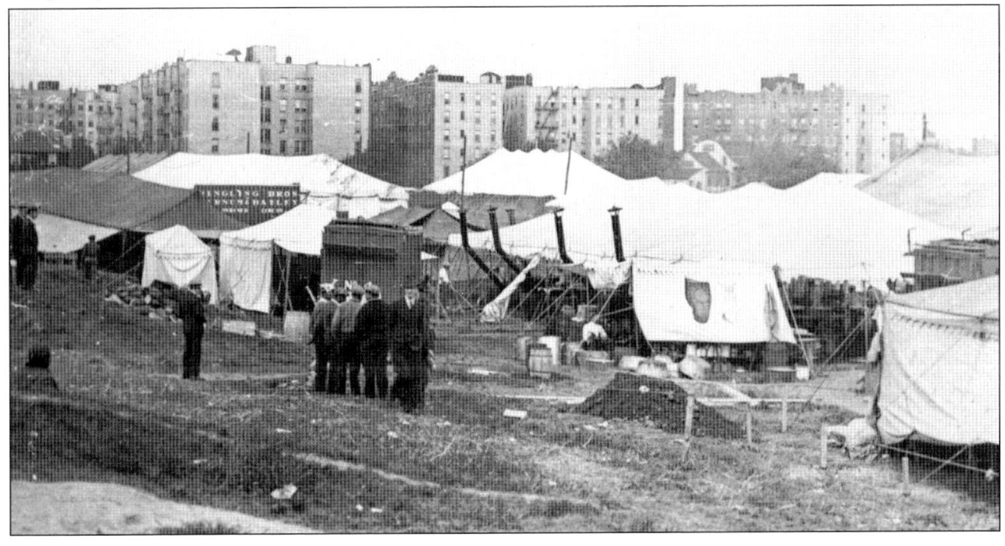

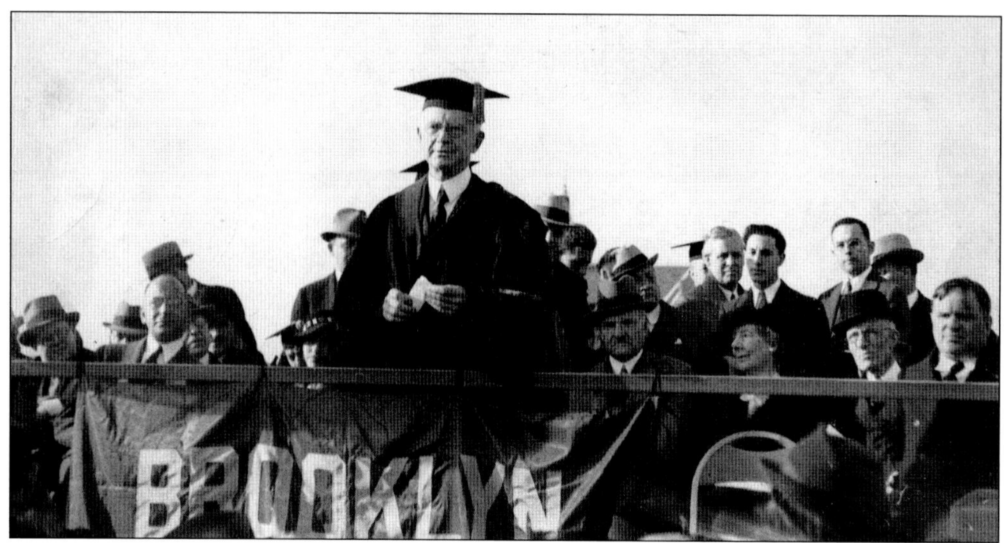

On October 2, 1935, Mayor La Guardia, borough president Raymond Ingersoll, and college president William Boylan (1869–1940) inaugurated the construction of the new campus (all three would have buildings named in their honor). Here, President Boylan addresses the crowd. La Guardia followed, breaking ground with a silver-plated shovel (on permanent display in the Brooklyn College library).

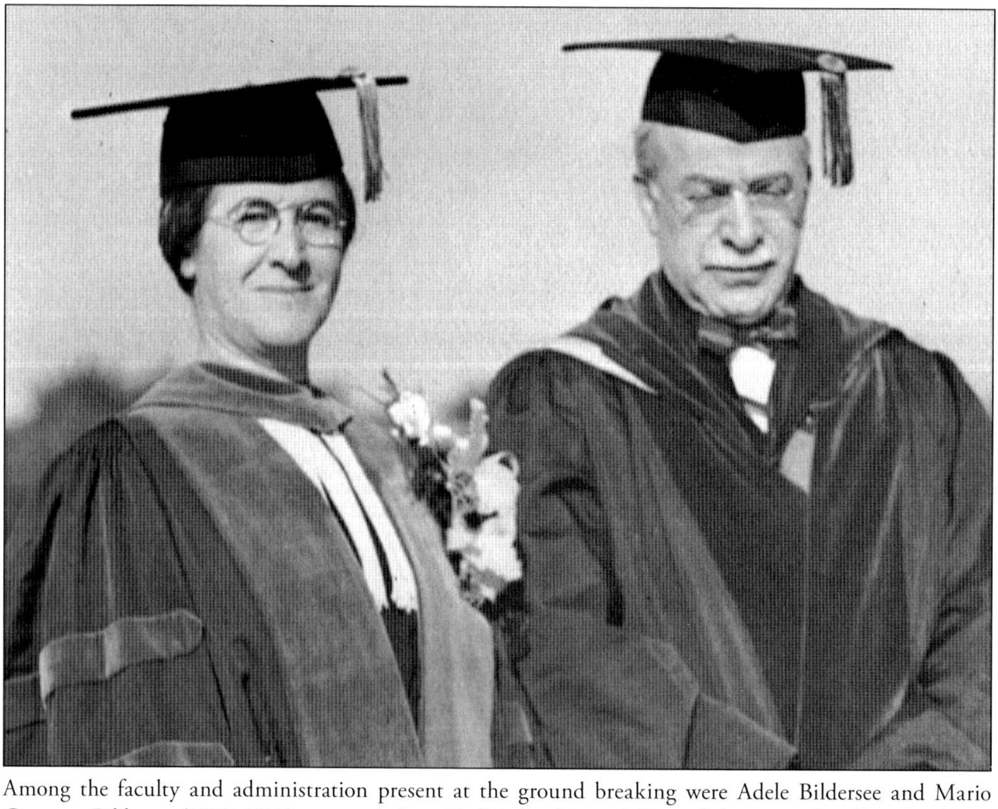

Among the faculty and administration present at the ground breaking were Adele Bildersee and Mario Cosenza. Bildersee (1883–1971) was a scholar of Judaic Studies and dean of the women's college (and later dean of admissions). Cosenza (1880–1966) was a classicist, founding member of the department, dean of the men's college, the college's first provost, and briefly acting president (in 1939). He retired in 1949.

The campus was designed by Randolph Evans, whose employer, the Wood-Harmon Corporation, at the time owned the land. Inspired by the University of Virginia, the Georgian-style campus is shaped around a central quadrangle flanked by identical buildings of red brick oriented toward a library with a tower. Evans's original plan, shown here, was more ambitious than what was eventually constructed.

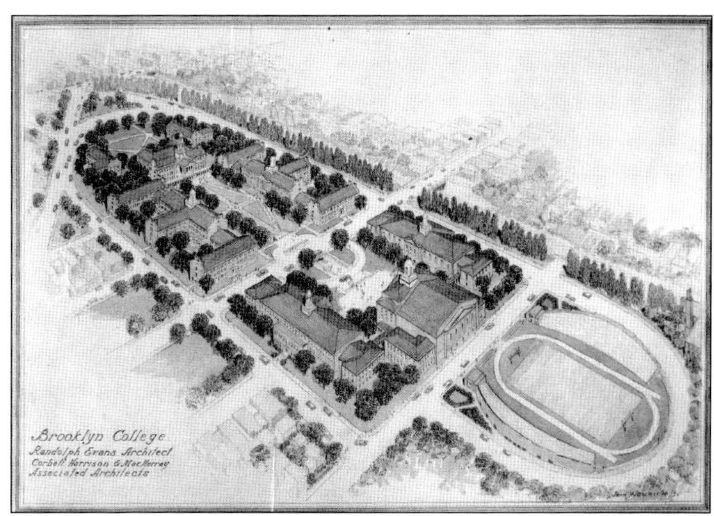

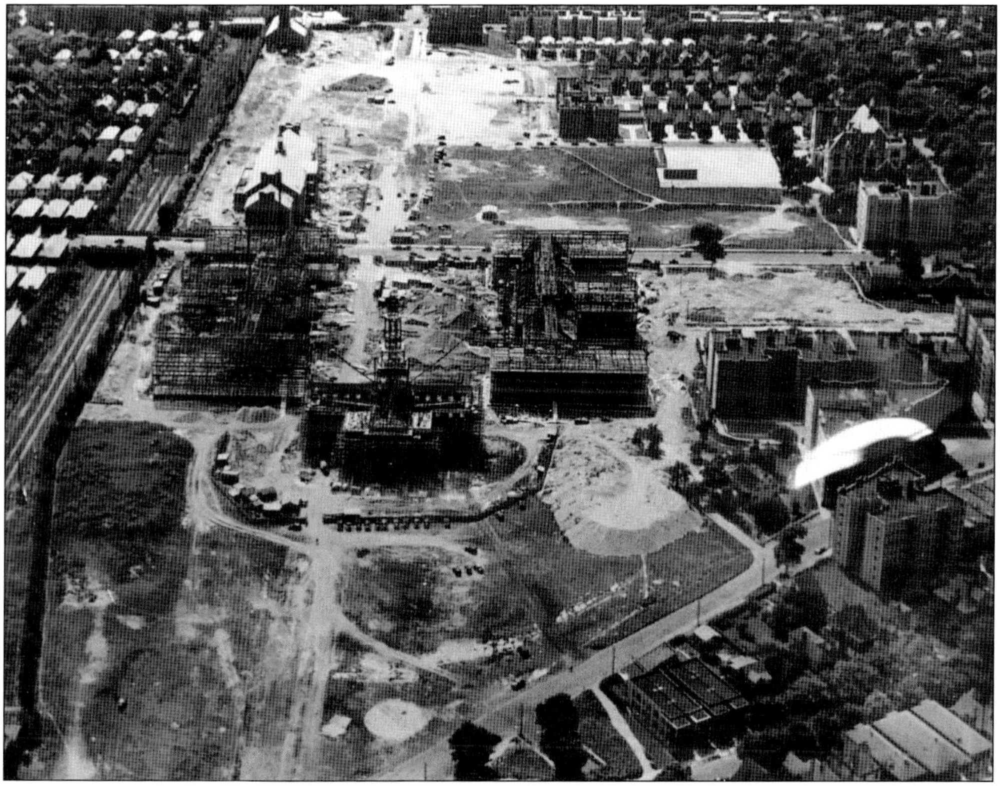

In addition to the funds provided by the PWA, the Works Progress Administration (WPA) supplied the labor. The construction of the core buildings and the basic landscaping were completed in only two years at a cost of $5,847,776. Although much of the campus to the west of Bedford Avenue was initially left unfinished, the east quad has been likened to that of an Ivy League campus; fitting, in that the College has been sometimes termed the "poor man's Harvard."

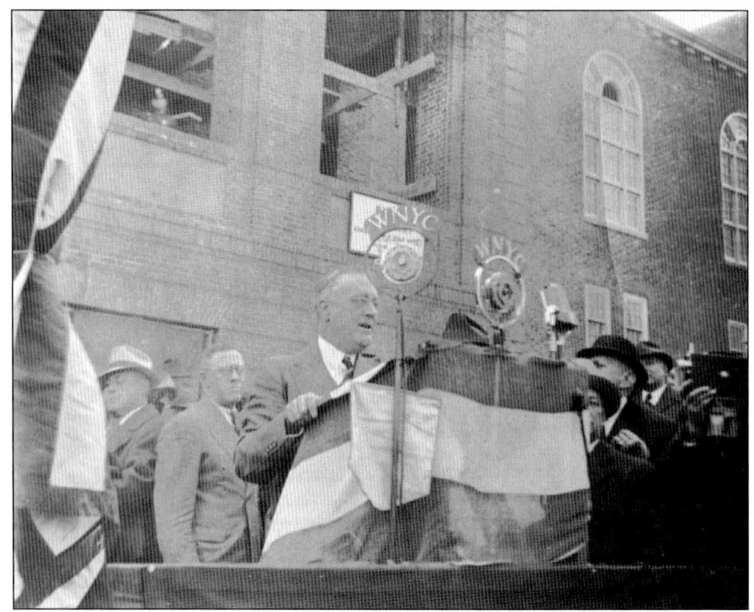

On October 28, 1936, Pres. Franklin D. Roosevelt came to Brooklyn College to lay the cornerstone for the gymnasium (appropriately named Roosevelt Hall). On the occasion, public schools were granted a half-day holiday and crowds lined the streets to welcome the presidential motorcade.

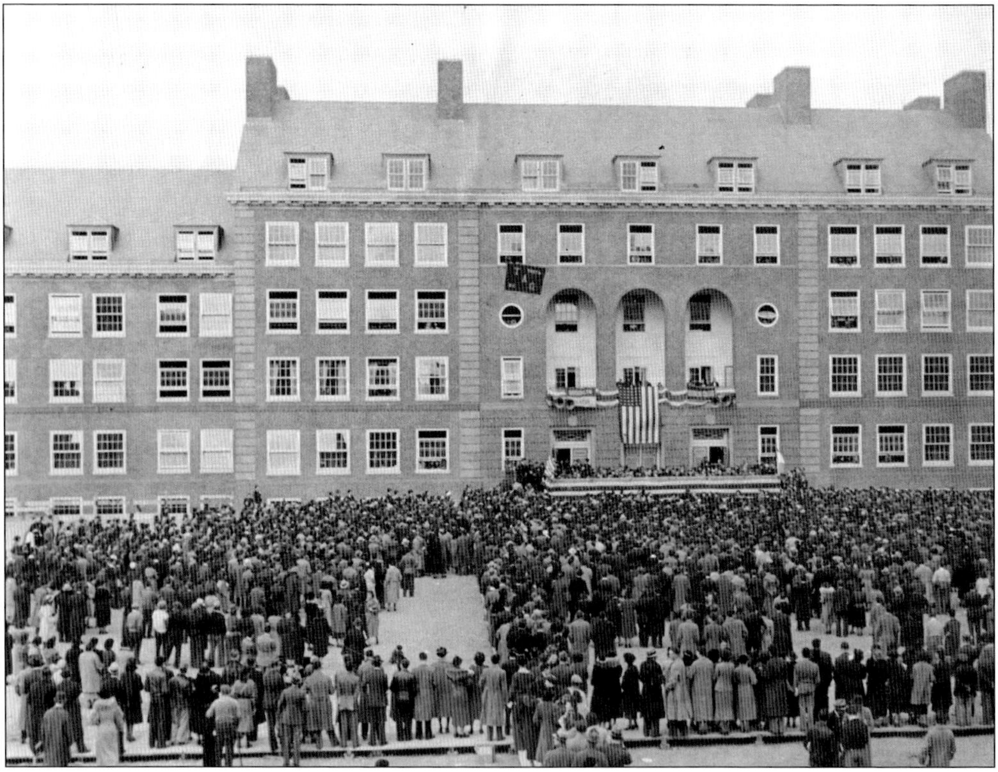

The new campus was dedicated on October 18, 1937. Some 7,000 spectators gathered in the quad before the Academic Building, posthumously renamed for Boylan. A scholar of education and pedagogy (PhD from Fordham), Boylan was an adept administrator who nurtured the college's creation, construction of its campus, and commitment to high academic standards. Appointed in 1930, he retired due to illness in 1938 and passed away in 1940.

Boylan Hall has functioned as the college's primary administrative building since its completion in 1937. The president's office, immediately above the main entranceway, includes a prominent loggia that overlooks the quad (obscured here by trees). The building has been home to the Department of Classics since its completion.

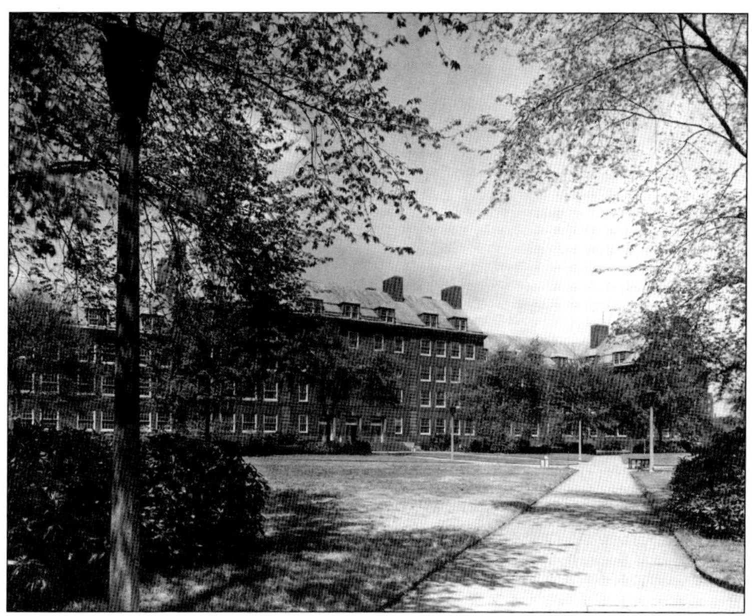

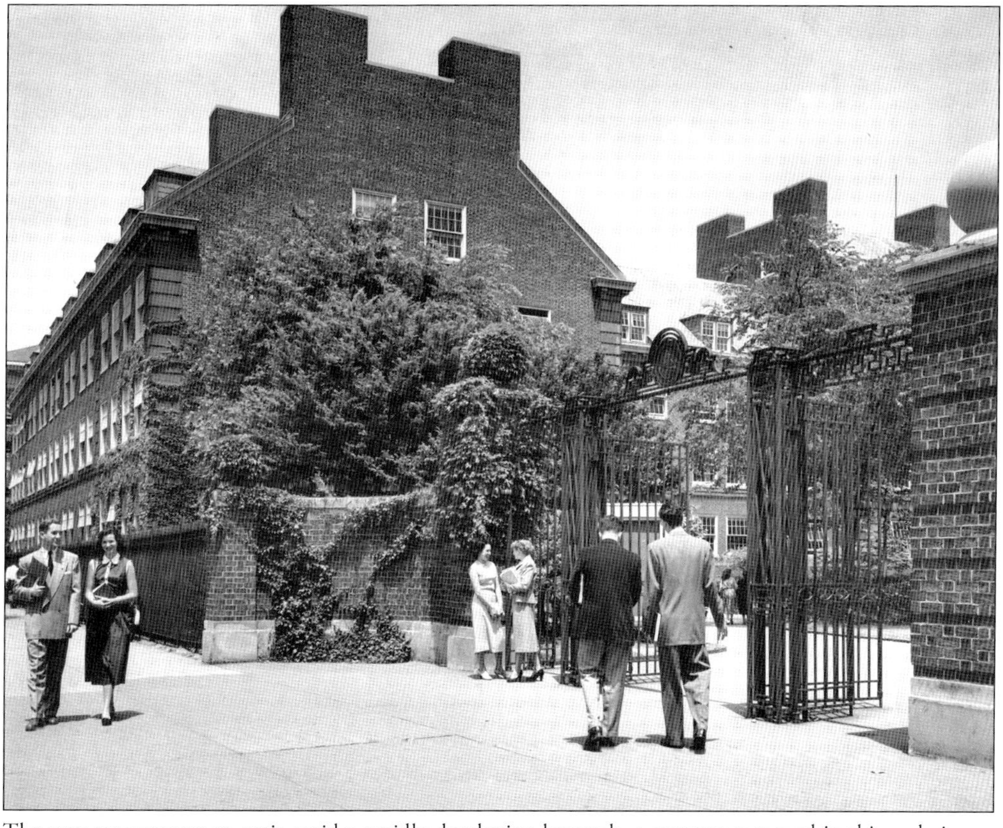

The new campus was an oasis amid a rapidly developing borough, a contrast conveyed in this early image of its Bedford Avenue entrance. The campus continues to receive awards and recognition for its beauty and environmental sustainability. Its tranquil Lily Pond, adjacent to the library, contains a memorial plaque for Gladys Shoemaker (1926–1982), a classics professor and a pioneer in the use of Latin to teach remedial English.

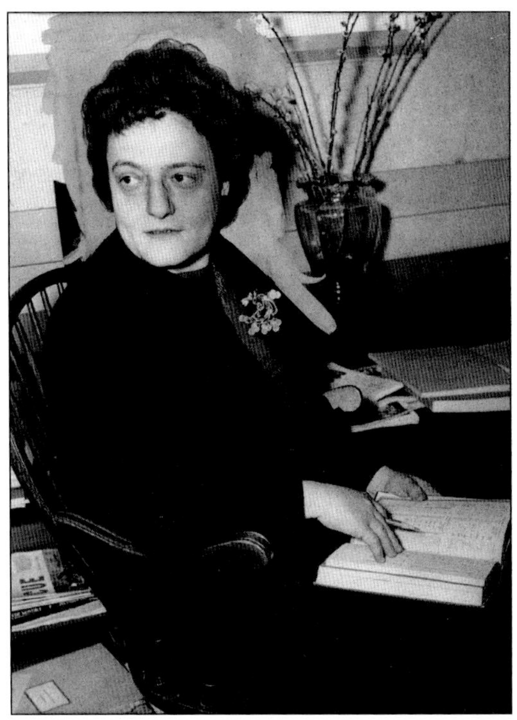

Alice Kober (born 1904) joined Brooklyn College in its inaugural year, where she remained until her untimely death in 1950. She played a seminal role in the decipherment of Linear B, most significantly demonstrating that it was an inflected language—essential to its eventual translation. A gifted linguist, she taught herself Braille and translated exams for sight-impaired students. (Courtesy of Thomas Palaima, Garrett Bruner, and the Program in Aegean Scripts and Prehistory, University of Texas at Austin.)

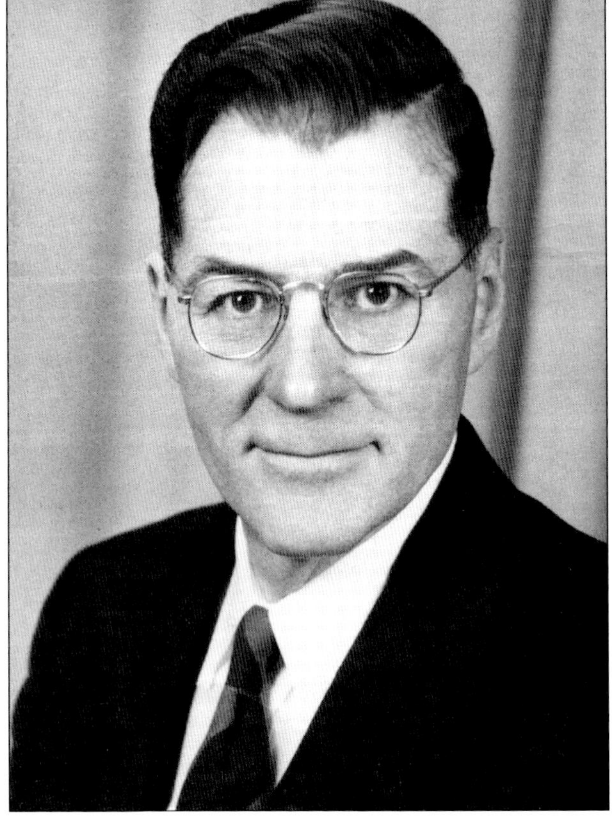

Frederic Melvin Wheelock (1902–1987) was a member of the faculty from 1937–1952. His *Wheelock's Latin*, first published in 1956, remains one of the most popular textbooks to the present day. Its approach, conceived during his time at Brooklyn and geared to veterans of World War II, provides a scaled and accessible approach to the language. Though different from the LGI method, it highlights the department's contributions to language pedagogy.

BROOKLYN COLLEGE

DEPARTMENT OF CLASSICAL LANGUAGES

January 22, 1953

WHEREAS Frederic Melvin Wheelock, sprung from the soil of New Hampshire and nurtured on the abundant store of classical learning in the schools and colleges of his native New England, brought to our city his knowledge and love of our classical tradition; and

WHEREAS he has shared these with absorbing dedication with his colleagues and students in the municipal colleges of the City of New York for almost two decades; and

WHEREAS he has been a devoted member of the Department of Classical Languages of Brooklyn College for fifteen years, with characteristic modesty giving unstintingly of his time and energy as teacher and colleague; and

WHEREAS his untiring efforts and sober judgment have been a source of strength to the Department of Classical Languages and to the continued vitality of the humanities at Brooklyn College; and

WHEREAS as a teacher of the youth he has ever sought to stir in them a love of the languages and cultures of the Greeks and Romans, and to guide them in their search for richer values and ethical standards;

THEREFORE BE IT RESOLVED that the Department of Classical Languages of Brooklyn College extend to Frederic Melvin Wheelock, colleague and friend, its warmest thanks for the many years of devoted service he rendered it, its deep regret at his decision to depart from this department and from the teaching profession, and its heartfelt best wishes for happiness and success for himself and his family in their return to the soil.

"Felix qui potuit rerum cognoscere causas....
Fortunatus et ille deos qui novit agrestis."

On Wheelock's departure, his colleagues issued a proclamation that, *inter alia*, noted how his "untiring efforts" had been a "source of strength to the Department of Classical Languages and to the continued vitality of the humanities at Brooklyn College." It concluded with a quote from Book II of Vergil's *Georgics*. Though Wheelock had intended to leave academia, he joined the faculty at Cazenovia College in 1954. A 1957 promotion to dean removed him from the classroom—his passion—and he subsequently returned to teaching. He eventually retired as a full professor from the University of Toledo in 1968. (Courtesy of Martha and Deborah Wheelock Taylor.)

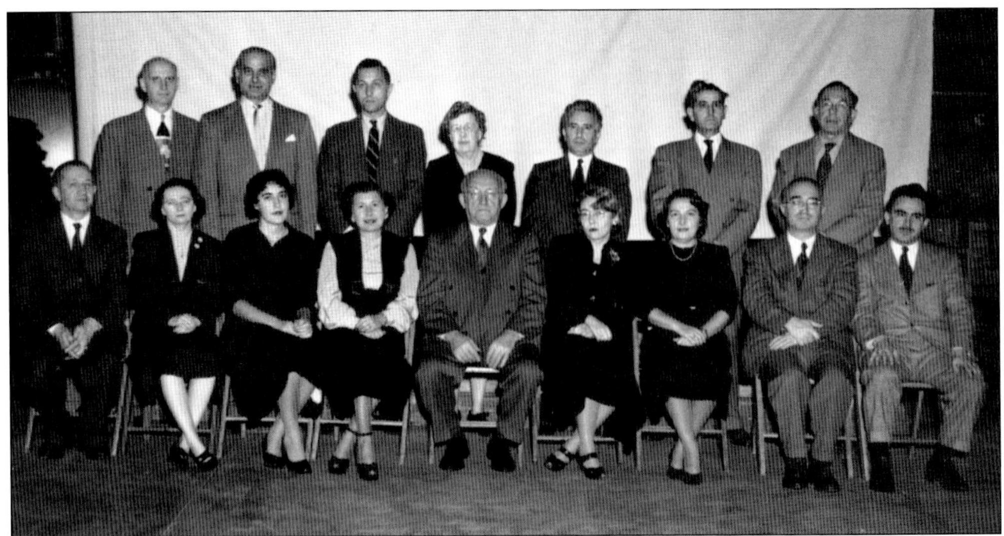

Meyer Reinhold (1909–2002) stands third from the right in this 1952 department photograph. An accomplished scholar of Roman civilization, he joined the faculty in 1939, achieving the rank of associate professor in 1952. In 1955, he resigned his position on account of the House Un-American Activities Committee. He was an advocate for popularizing the classics through literature in translation—a pioneer in broadening the appeal of the discipline.

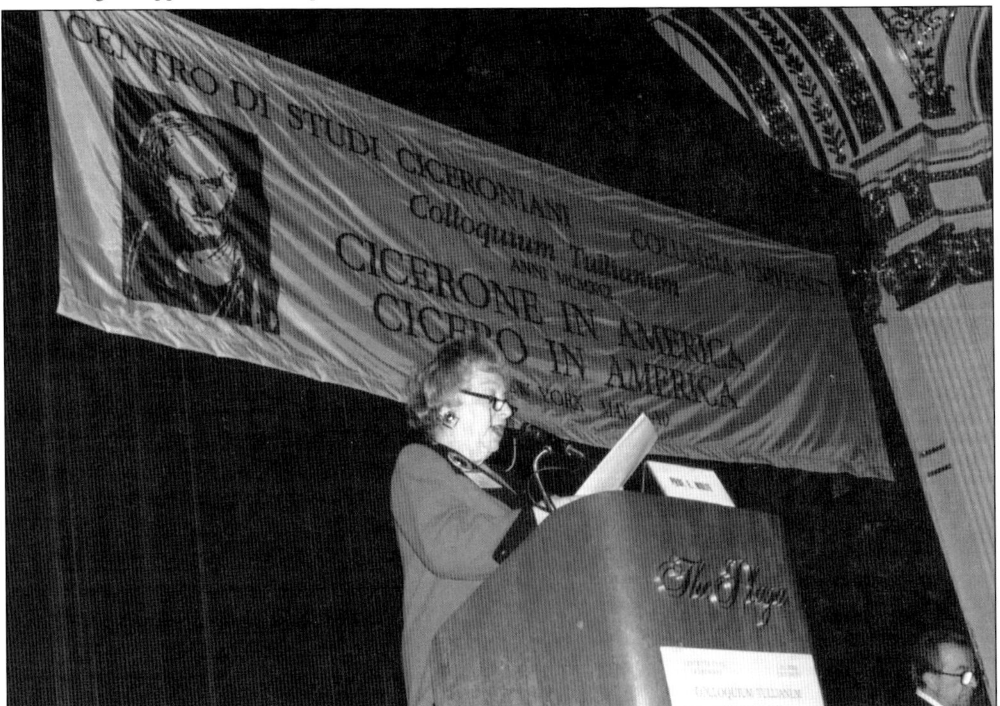

Ethyle Wolfe (1919–2010) joined the faculty as a lecturer in 1947 and was promoted to assistant professor upon completion of her PhD (New York University [NYU], 1950). Although an outstanding scholar, her true genius was as an administrator. She became department chair in 1967, then dean of humanities in 1971, and, in 1982, college provost—arguably the most impactful in the college's history. Here, she presents at the *Colloquium Tullianum Anni MCMXCI: Cicero in America*.

Vera Lachmann (1904–1985), a 1939 refugee from Germany, was a member of the department from 1948 to 1974. An accomplished Hellenist, she was one of two recipients of the College's first Excellence in Teaching awards (1962). In 1944, she and her life partner, American composer Tui St. George Tucker, established Camp Catawba in North Carolina. (Courtesy of Special Collections, Appalachian State University.)

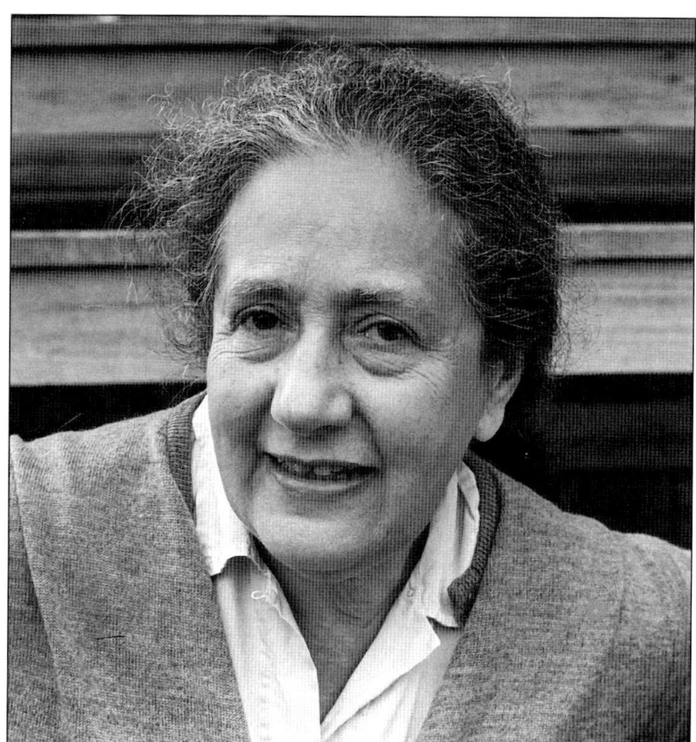

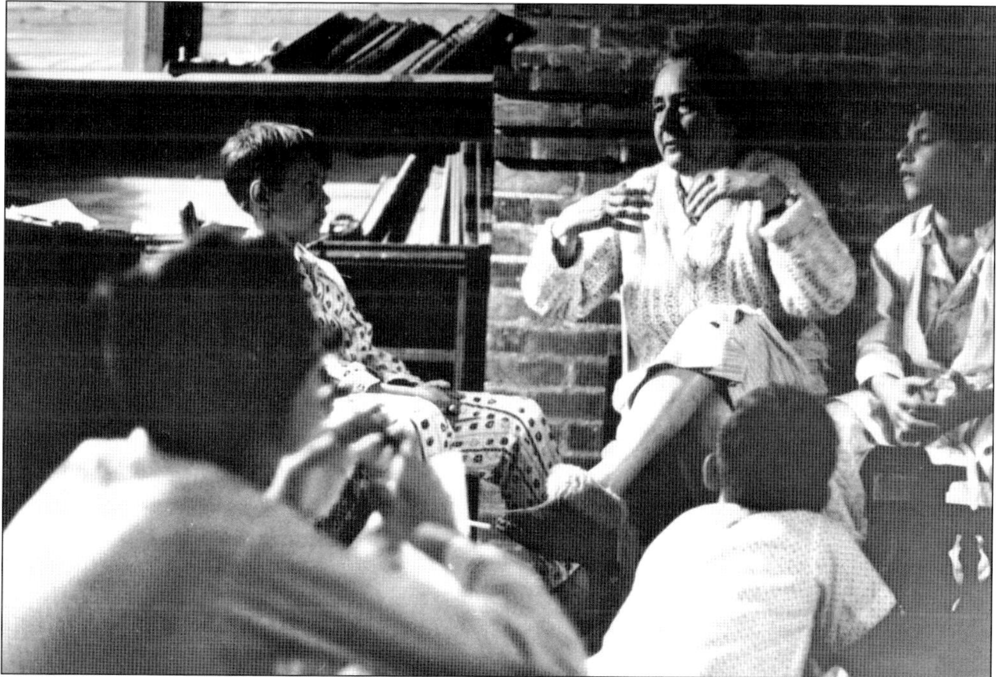

The camp, which Lachmann directed until its closure in 1970, was created to support and nurture the children of refugees. In addition to traditional camp activities, music and the classics played a central role. Tucker was the camp's music director, while each evening Lachmann narrated the *Iliad* and the *Odyssey* in alternating summers, as seen here in about 1967. (Courtesy of Special Collections, Appalachian State University.)

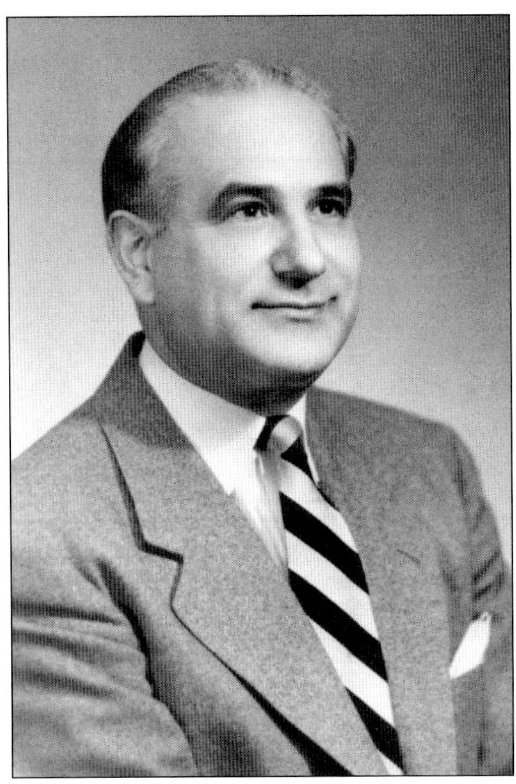

Procope S. Costas (1900–1974) was born in Sparta, Greece. He attended schools across Europe and, later, the United States, where he earned a PhD at the University of Chicago (1933). A polyglot (conversant in Greek, Italian, French, German, Russian, and English), he served as an intelligence officer during World War II.

Costas joined Brooklyn College as an assistant professor in 1950 and was promoted to associate professor in 1958. He retired as a full professor in 1973 and passed away the following year. Amiable, engaged, and charismatic, he was highly regarded by his students and colleagues. His scholarship, especially on the Greek language, offered significant contributions to the field.

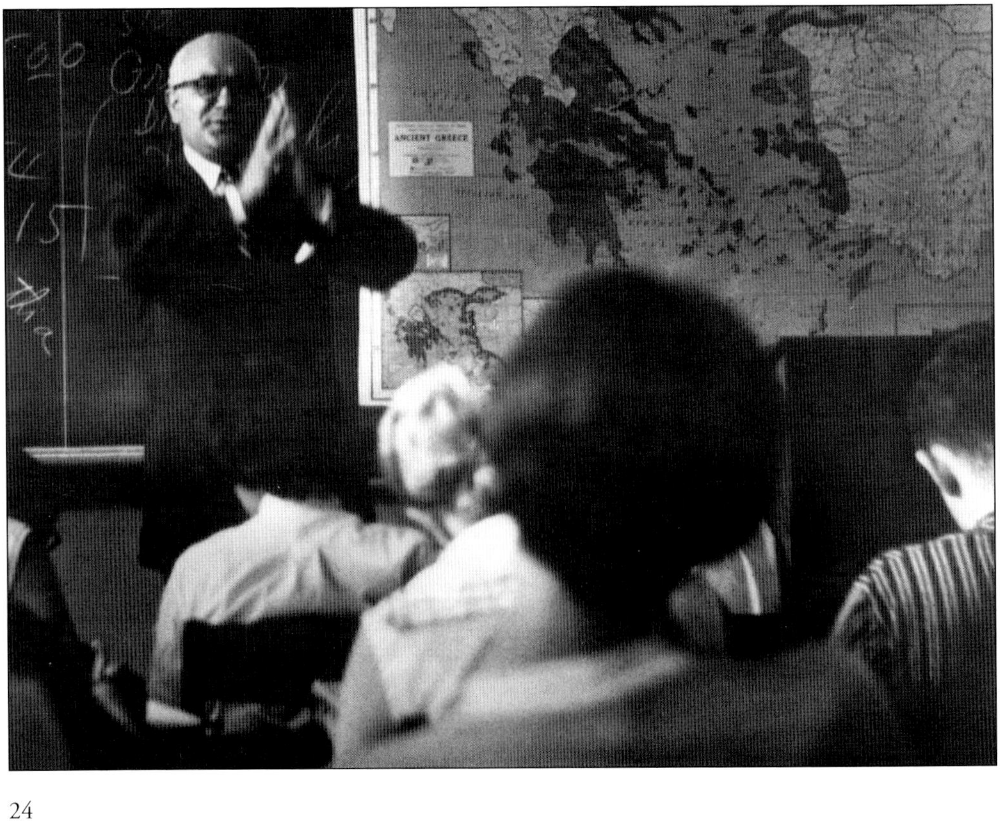

Naphtali Lewis (in the back, third from the right) was a member of the department from 1947 to 1976. A renowned papyrologist and author of several seminal books, he was later an associate dean at BC and classics executive officer at the GC. In this 1954 photograph, Wolfe is seated third from the right, adjacent to Joseph Pearl, the department's longstanding chair.

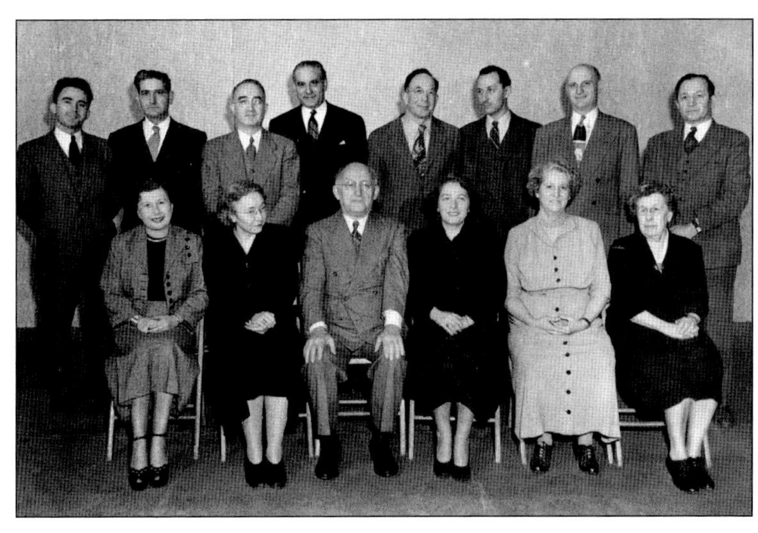

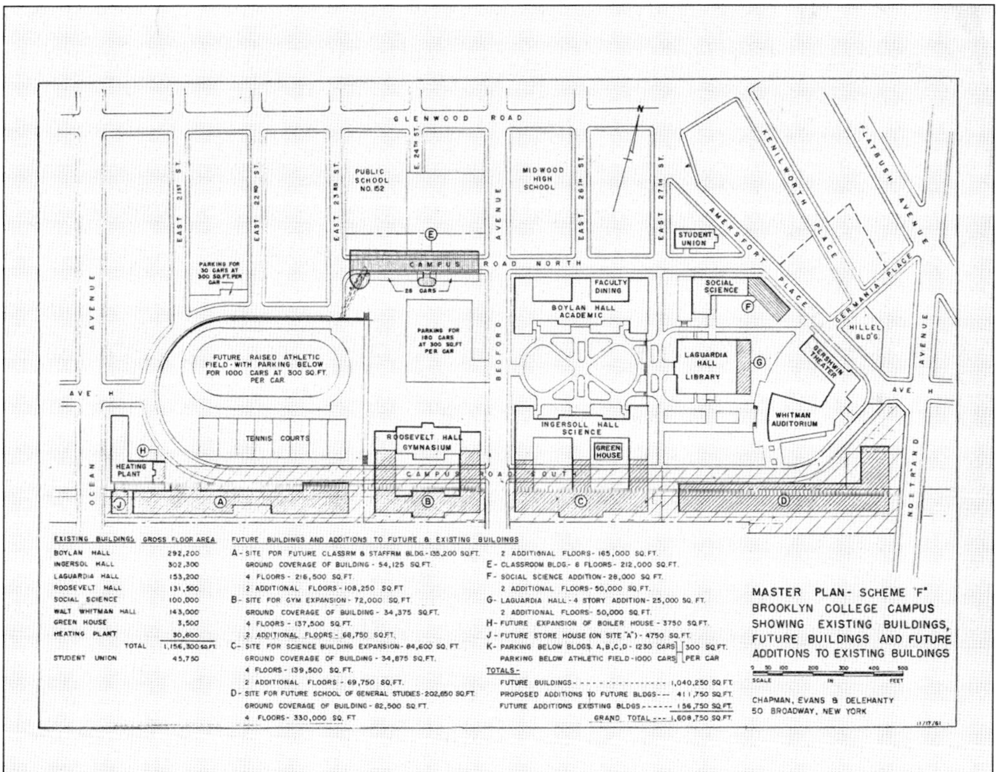

MASTER PLAN- SCHEME "F"
BROOKLYN COLLEGE CAMPUS
SHOWING EXISTING BUILDINGS, FUTURE BUILDINGS AND FUTURE ADDITIONS TO EXISTING BUILDINGS

EXISTING BUILDINGS	GROSS FLOOR AREA
BOYLAN HALL	292,200
INGERSOL HALL	302,300
LAGUARDIA HALL	153,200
ROOSEVELT HALL	131,500
SOCIAL SCIENCE	100,000
WALT WHITMAN HALL	143,000
GREEN HOUSE	3,500
HEATING PLANT	30,600
TOTAL	1,156,300 SQ.FT.
STUDENT UNION	45,750

FUTURE BUILDINGS AND ADDITIONS TO FUTURE & EXISTING BUILDINGS

A- SITE FOR FUTURE CLASSRM & STAFFRM BLDG.-135,200 SQ.FT.
GROUND COVERAGE OF BUILDING - 54,125 SQ.FT.
4 FLOORS - 216,500 SQ.FT.
2 ADDITIONAL FLOORS - 108,250 SQ.FT.
B- SITE FOR GYM EXPANSION - 72,000 SQ.FT.
GROUND COVERAGE OF BUILDING - 34,375 SQ.FT.
4 FLOORS - 137,500 SQ.FT.
2 ADDITIONAL FLOORS - 68,750 SQ.FT.
C- SITE FOR SCIENCE BUILDING EXPANSION - 84,600 SQ.FT.
GROUND COVERAGE OF BUILDING - 34,875 SQ.FT.
4 FLOORS - 139,500 SQ.FT.
2 ADDITIONAL FLOORS - 69,750 SQ.FT.
D- SITE FOR FUTURE SCHOOL OF GENERAL STUDIES - 202,650 SQ.FT.
GROUND COVERAGE OF BUILDING - 82,500 SQ.FT.
4 FLOORS - 330,000 SQ.FT.
2 ADDITIONAL FLOORS - 165,000 SQ.FT.
E- CLASSROOM BLDG.- 8 FLOORS - 212,000 SQ.FT.
F- SOCIAL SCIENCE ADDITION - 28,000 SQ.FT.
2 ADDITIONAL FLOORS - 50,000 SQ.FT.
G- LAGUARDIA HALL - 4 STORY ADDITION - 25,000 SQ.FT.
2 ADDITIONAL FLOORS - 50,000 SQ.FT.
H- FUTURE EXPANSION OF BOILER HOUSE - 3750 SQ.FT.
J- FUTURE STORE HOUSE (ON SITE "A") - 4750 SQ.FT.
K- PARKING BELOW BLDGS. A,B,C,D - 1230 CARS / PARKING BELOW ATHLETIC FIELD - 1000 CARS — 300 SQ.FT. PER CAR

TOTALS -
FUTURE BUILDINGS - 1,040,250 SQ.FT.
PROPOSED ADDITIONS TO FUTURE BLDGS - 411,750 SQ.FT.
FUTURE ADDITIONS EXISTING BLDGS - 156,750 SQ.FT.
GRAND TOTAL - 1,608,750 SQ.FT.

SCALE IN FEET: 0 50 100 200 300 400 500

CHAPMAN, EVANS & DELEHANTY
50 BROADWAY, NEW YORK

11/17/61

In its 1955 Middle States accreditation report, the visiting committee contrasted the college's "great vitality" with its "inadequate facilities." By 1962, several new buildings were added, including a new social science building and student center. Classroom space, however, remained in short supply. This 1964 plan for an expanded campus would be partially fulfilled, notably the additions to Roosevelt and Ingersoll halls.

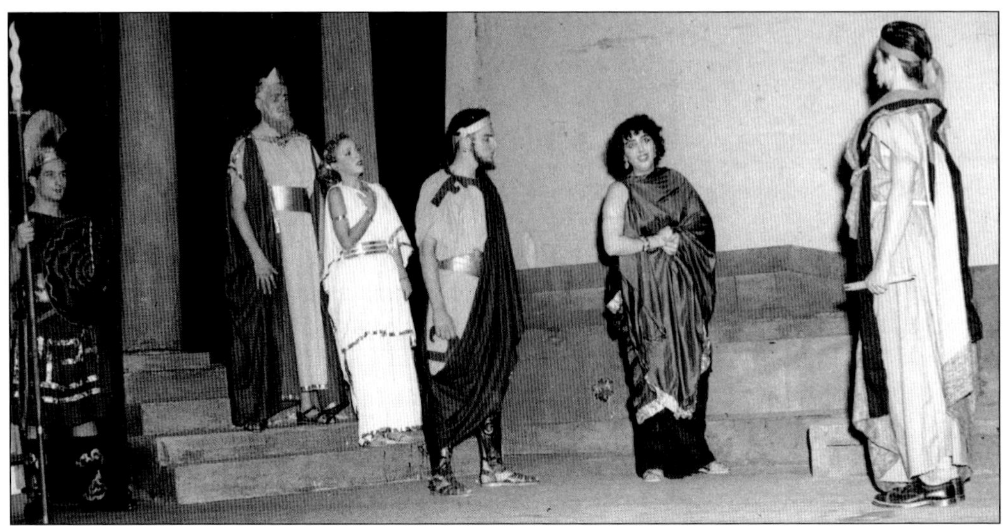

In the decades following World War II, the legacy of the classical world was manifest on campus in other contexts, an equipollent counterpart to the department's vibrancy and intellectual heft. On October 24, 1951, the Brooklyn College Varsity Players opened their first of a four-night run of *Medea*.

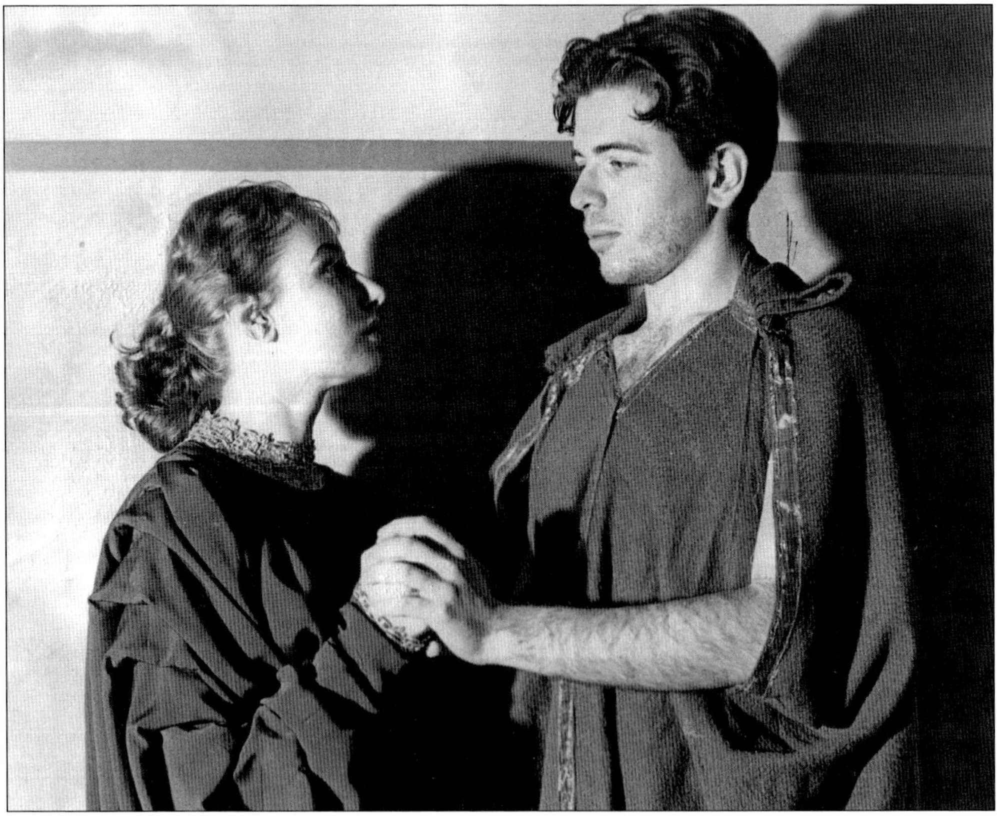

This publicity still is from the Varsity Players production of Sophocles's Οἰδίπους Τύραννος, which was performed in the George Gershwin Theater from November 20–22, 1958. The theater, which opened in 1954, sat 500. It was demolished in 2011 for the construction of the Leonard and Claire Tow Center for the Performing Arts.

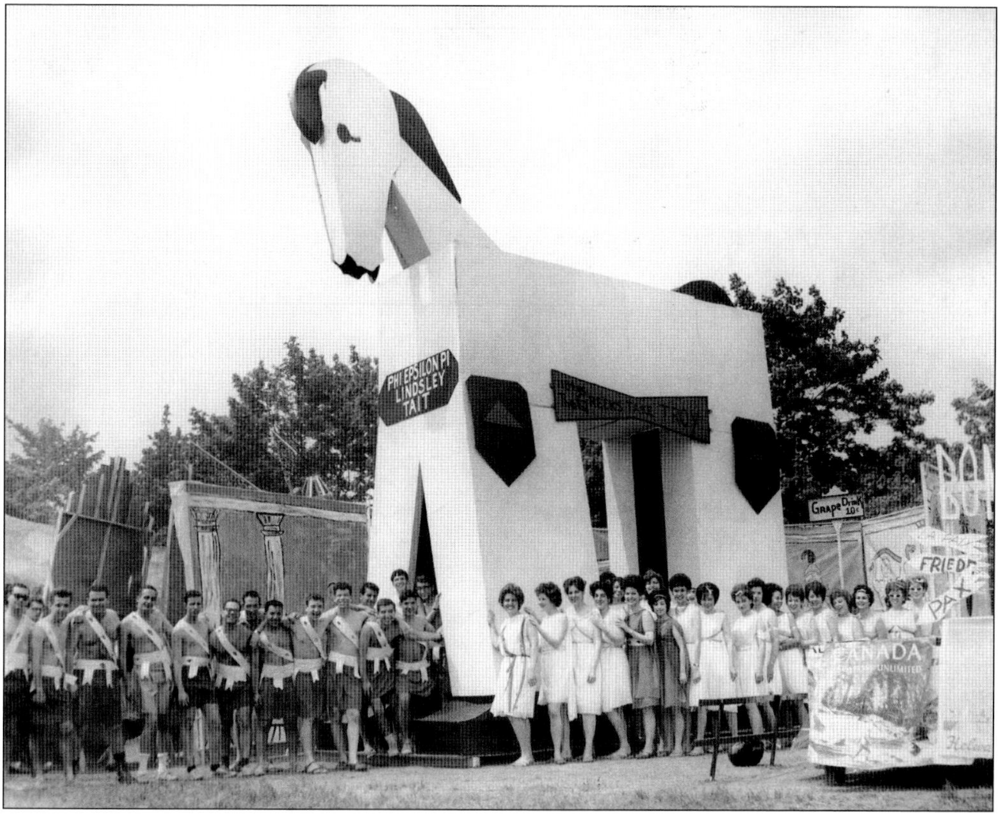

The annual Country Fair was a BC tradition from 1938 to 1994. A celebration of the college's birthday, its festivities included games, performances, and dances meant to evoke the original circus grounds. The 1966 celebration included a Trojan horse made by the students of the Phi Epsilon Pi, Lindsley, and Tait houses; from 1937 to the mid-1970s, communal organizations of the House Plan Association were central to the college's social life.

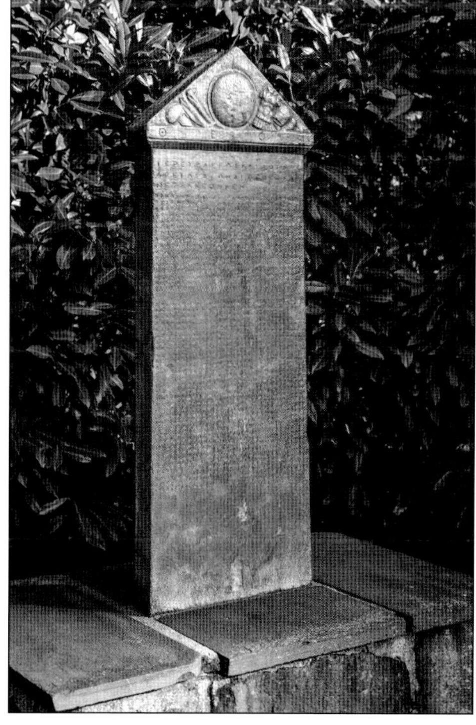

Beginning in 1932, graduates recited the Ephebic Oath, sworn by Athenian males on their entry to military service. A translated text was printed in the program, updated to affirm loyalty to the United States. The oath later fell out of favor and, despite a brief reintroduction by President Robert Hess (term, 1979–1992), ultimately discontinued. This replica of the oath, a copy of a fourth-century stela, stands before the library.

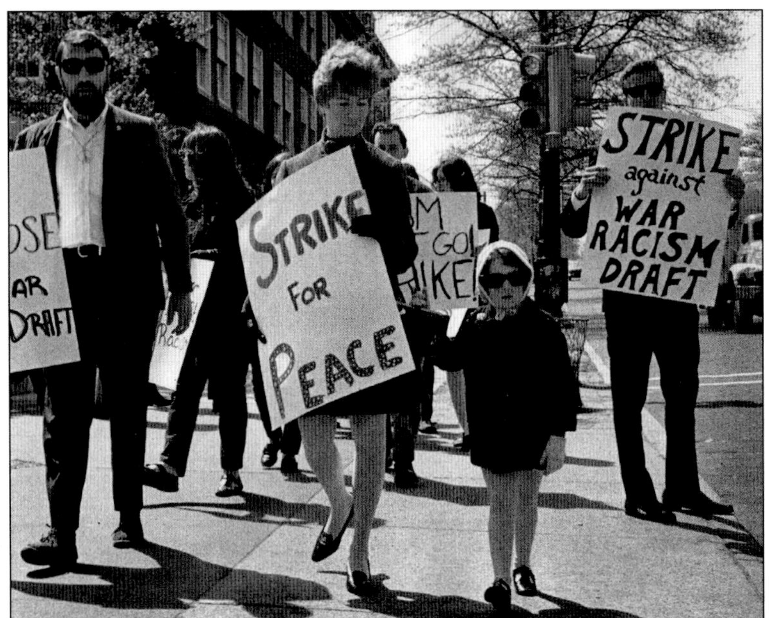

From its inception, Brooklyn College has had a countercultural, rebellious streak, often manifest through student activism. Initially focused on such issues as academic freedom, both civil rights and the antiwar movement became increasing concerns. Here, members of the college community participate in the National Strike Day on April 26, 1968, in protest of the Vietnam War.

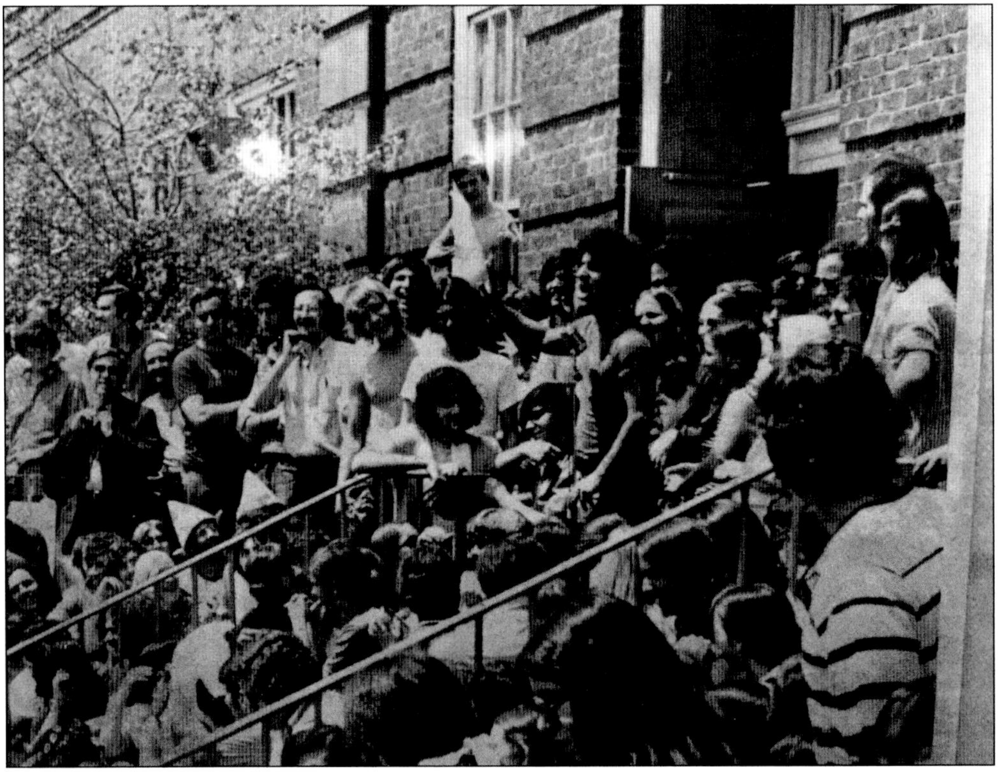

By 1970, antiwar activities had become frequent and often disruptive affairs. On May 11, famed Yippie Abbie Hoffman delivered a fiery speech on the steps of Boylan Hall. The Youth International Party (YIP) was an anarchical, anti-authoritarian group that engaged in highly theatrical protests in support of various radical causes.

During the turbulent 1960s and 1970s, the classics evolved with the zeitgeist and helped inform and inspire many of the era's rapid changes. Dr. Frederica Wachsberger, professor of art and an historian of ancient Greek art, was one of the cofounders of the Women's Studies Program. This striking poster, which she likely designed, masterfully utilizes the goddess Athena to promote a 1975 conference.

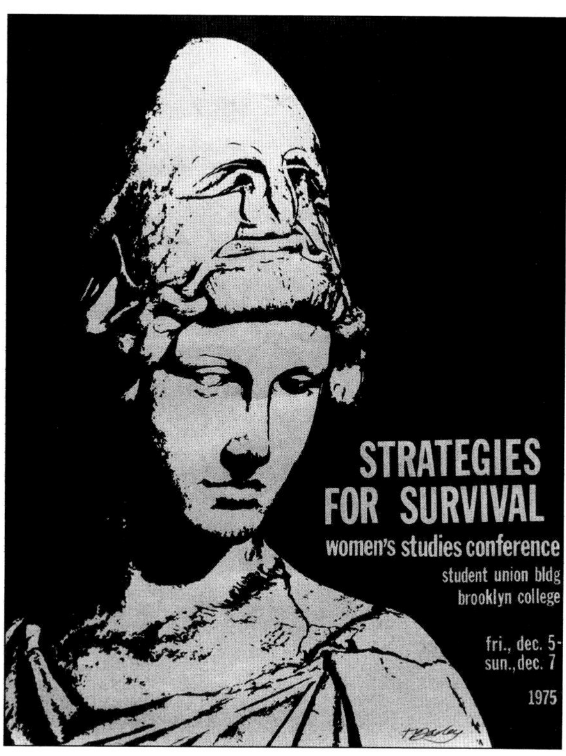

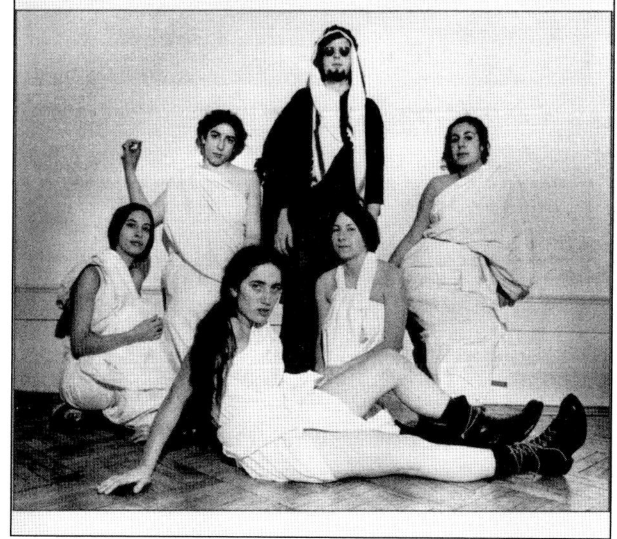

Classics students were part of the spirit and energy of the times, as reflected in this 1970 yearbook entry for its student club. In the same year, CUNY instituted an open admissions policy that would vastly increase the number of students at the college: by mid-decade, enrollment neared 30,000, far exceeding its capacity. Open admissions continued until 1976, when a fiscal crisis resulted in the college charging tuition.

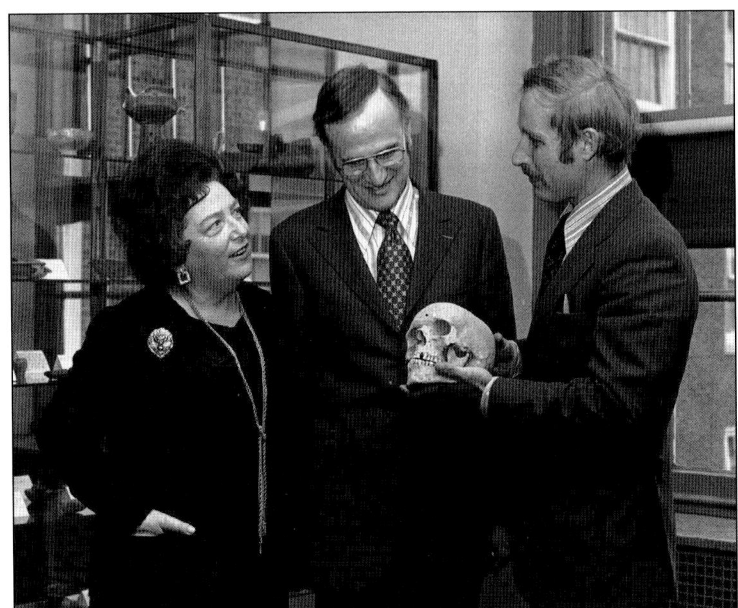

Ethyle Wolfe stands with John Kneller, BC president (1969–1979) and professor of anthropology and archaeology, and classical archaeologist Edward Ochsenschlager (holding skull). An advocate for the humanities, Wolfe promoted establishing a humanities institute and a program in intensive classical languages. This latter aspiration would ultimately bring the LGI into existence, and her advocacy and support would be critical to its ultimate success.

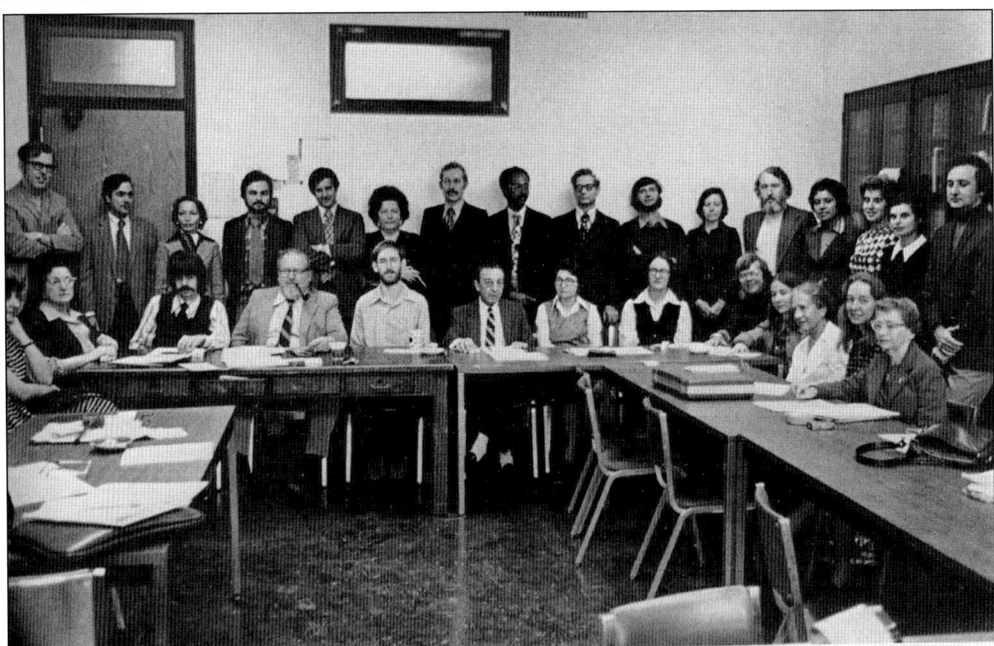

(L TO R) LOWER ROW: G. Shoemaker, F. Raanes, E. Winter, J. Mantinband, S. Becroft, R. Marcellino, E. Constantinider, J. Gaisser, W. Owen, A. Fromchuck, V. Lachmann, M. Whitfield, A. Griffiths. (L TO R) UPPER ROW: R. Dunkle, H. Hansen, J. Plotnick, F. Moreland, H. Wolman, E. Wolfe, E. Ochsenschlager, S. Edwards, P. Zaneteas, V. Christides, W. Hull, K. Whitfield, G. Smith, R. Passweg, D. Clayman, R. Hash, Ochsenschlager — Chairman.

To complement her academic and administrative acumen, Wolfe also had an eye for talent. By the early 1970s, she had added depth to the classics department, which would prove essential to her vision of a classical language enterprise. This photograph of the classics department from the 1974 *Broeklundian* includes four members of the Institute: Hardy Hansen, Floyd Moreland, Joan Plotnick, and Gail Smith.

Two

In Principio
The CUNY Latin Institute 1973–1977

Floyd Moreland joined Brooklyn College's classics department in the fall of 1971. In addition to acclimating to the obligations and expectations of the professoriate, he was further tasked with establishing an intensive program in Latin.

As the Berkeley Latin Workshop had demonstrated, the right faculty were essential to success, and Moreland immediately set about recruiting. One Friday afternoon, Moreland overheard a part-time instructor drilling her students on Latin forms. The class had been struggling, and she had asked them to come in on their off day to review and practice. Moreland, impressed by her commitment to their success, had found his first instructor and future administrative director: Rita Fleischer. If Moreland was the Institute's paterfamilias, it now had its materfamilias.

In advance of the inaugural summer, Moreland trained Fleischer and the other faculty he recruited on his methods, establishing a uniform vocabulary for grammar and syntax. Delivery of instruction was to be as consistent as possible, with an avoidance of contradictions or variance in terminology. As at Berkeley, handouts and materials were prepared, many of which would form the nucleus of an eventual textbook, then still several years away.

Another consideration was the location. Although the Brooklyn College campus was bucolic and welcoming, both Wolfe and Moreland were concerned about its accessibility for visiting students: as a commuter school, it lacked student housing and transportation options were limited. Accordingly, it was decided to offer the Institute at the CUNY Graduate Center, located in midtown Manhattan. Consequently, though most alumni associate the Institute with the GC, the relationship is, in fact, almost entirely informal: the LGI remains the responsibility of Brooklyn College's Department of Classics.

With a faculty assembled and location determined, recruiting students was the next order of business. Though marketing opportunities were limited, word of mouth, newspaper advertisements, and direct mail proved effective and, on Monday, June 11, 1973, the Latin Institute welcomed 40 students to its inaugural summer.

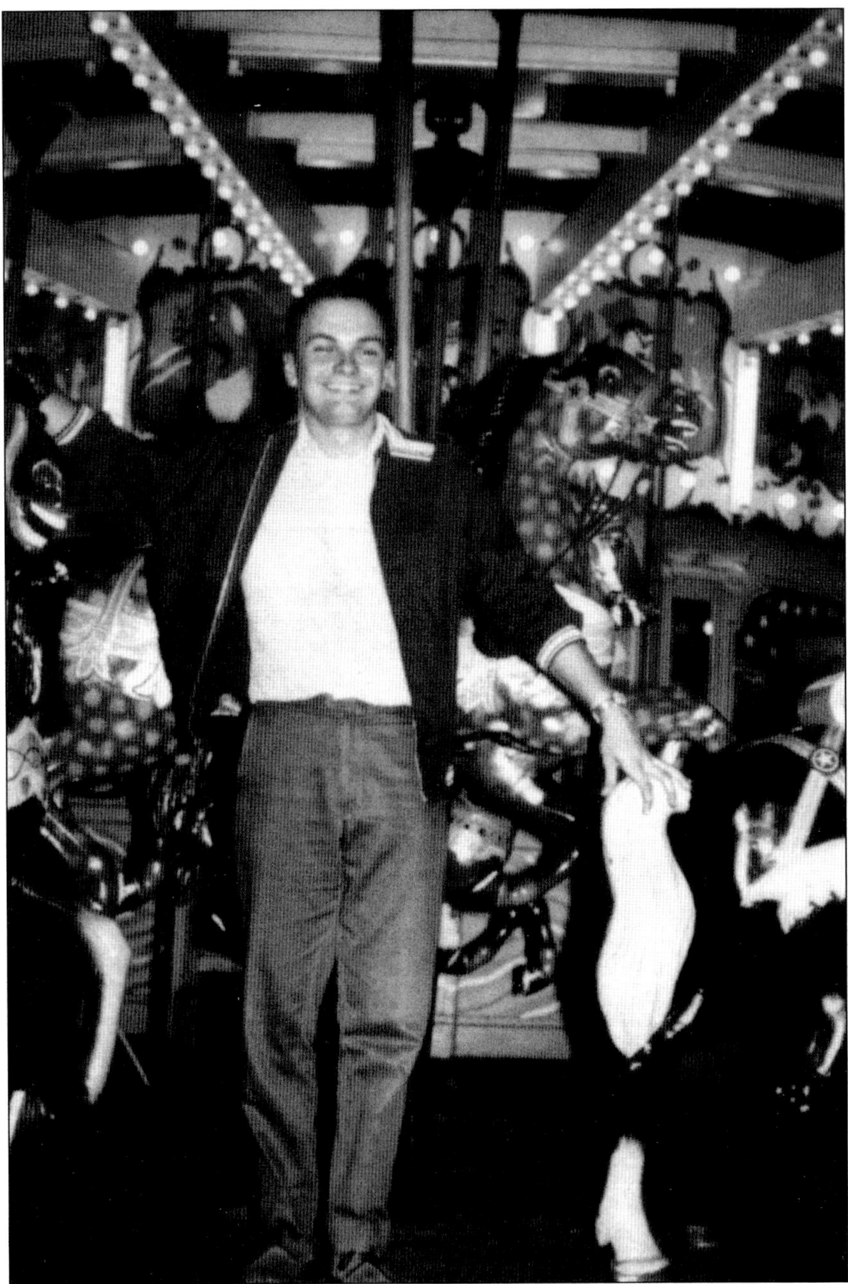

Floyd L. Moreland was born and raised in Passaic, New Jersey. As a youth, his Latin teacher, Barbara Flores, often took him to the opera and on trips to various museums across New York City. In addition to a love of Latin, she instilled in him a passion for teaching, learning, and inquiry. Most significantly, her commitment to nurturing his intellectual development stimulated his interest in student mentoring and the holistic nature of teaching. Years later, Moreland took satisfaction in her occasional visits to the Institute. In addition to his weekends in Flores's care, Moreland also spent two weeks every summer with his family in Seaside Heights, New Jersey. He later worked as an operator of its famed carousel (as seen here in 1961), which he first rode at the age of two. The carousel would play an ongoing and important role in his life—perhaps equal to that of the Institute. (Courtesy of Floyd L. Moreland.)

January 25, 1971

Mr. Floyd L. Moreland
25 Park Avenue
Passaic, New Jersey 07055

Dear Mr. Moreland:

It gives me great pleasure to inform you that the Appointments Committee of the Department of Classics and Comparative Literature has authorized me to offer you an appointment for the academic year 1971-1972 at the rank of Assistant Professor with initial salary of $15,430, as of October 1, 1971. This position is a tenure-bearing line with the requirement of a Ph.D. at the time of appointment, September 1, 1971.

As I indicated to you orally, the appointment is renewable subject to annual review and the normal tenure probationary period is five years with tenure contingent on evaluation of performance. Of course, all appointments, promotions, and tenure are subject to ultimate approval by the Board of Higher Education.

On a more personal note, let me say that I enjoyed our meeting on Sunday. Please notice that I cleared with the Dean of the Faculties at 10 a.m. on Monday morning! I appreciate the decision you are facing and sincerely want you to do what will be best for you.

Please let me know in writing whether you wish to accept the position.

Cordially,

Ethyle R. Wolfe
Chairman
Department of Classics
and Comparative Literature

ERW:AR

25 Park Avenue
Passaic, New Jersey 07055

27 January 1971

Professor Ethyle R. Wolfe
Department of Classics
and Comparative Literature
Brooklyn College
Brooklyn, New York 11210

Dear Professor Wolfe:

Thank you for your letter of 25 January. Since our meeting on Sunday, I have been weighing the advantages and disadvantages of each offer in terms of my own personal goals and my potential contribution to each institution. After very careful consideration, I have definitely decided on Brooklyn. I gratefully accept your offer.

I wish to thank the Appointments Committee for the interest and consideration they have shown me, and I look forward to joining you in the fall.

Yours sincerely,

Floyd L. Moreland

Ethyle Wolfe interviewed Moreland in January 1971, and an offer of employment followed soon thereafter; it was the only interview at which Moreland was extensively queried about the Berkeley Latin Workshop. A rapport is evident in their earliest correspondence, and their friendship would prove durable and longstanding. As Wolfe rose through the ranks of institutional leadership, she remained actively engaged with the Institute and, in its earliest years, an essential *patrona*.

Rita Fleischer attended Flushing High School, where her Latin teacher, Viola Chester, inspired her love of the language and mastery of its grammar. Fleischer subsequently received BA and MA degrees in Classics at NYU and later joined Brooklyn College as a part-time instructor (seated to the left in this 1973 yearbook entry). In addition to her teaching skills, her administrative and operational abilities would prove essential to the Institute.

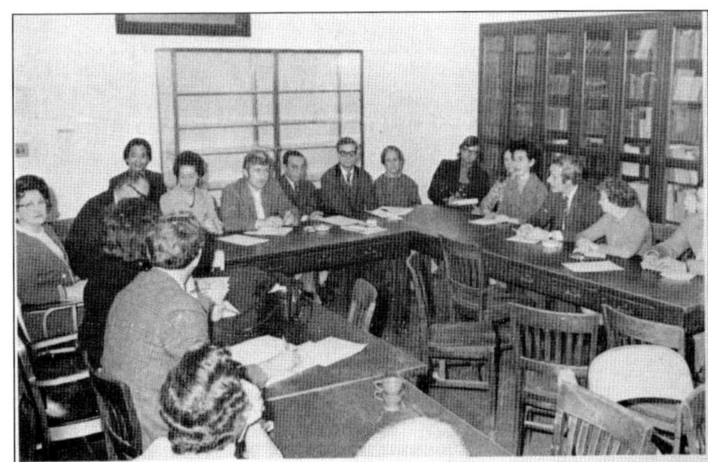

Left to Right: (Facing Camera) **Florence Raanes, Haskell Block, Won Ko, Rita Fleischer, Dennis Spininger, Ralph Marcellino, Peter Zaneteas, Vera Lachmann, William Owen, Marie Giuriceo, Edward Ochsenschlager, Anne Griffiths, Floyd Moreland.** *(Back to Camera)* **Dean. Ethyle R. Wolfe.**

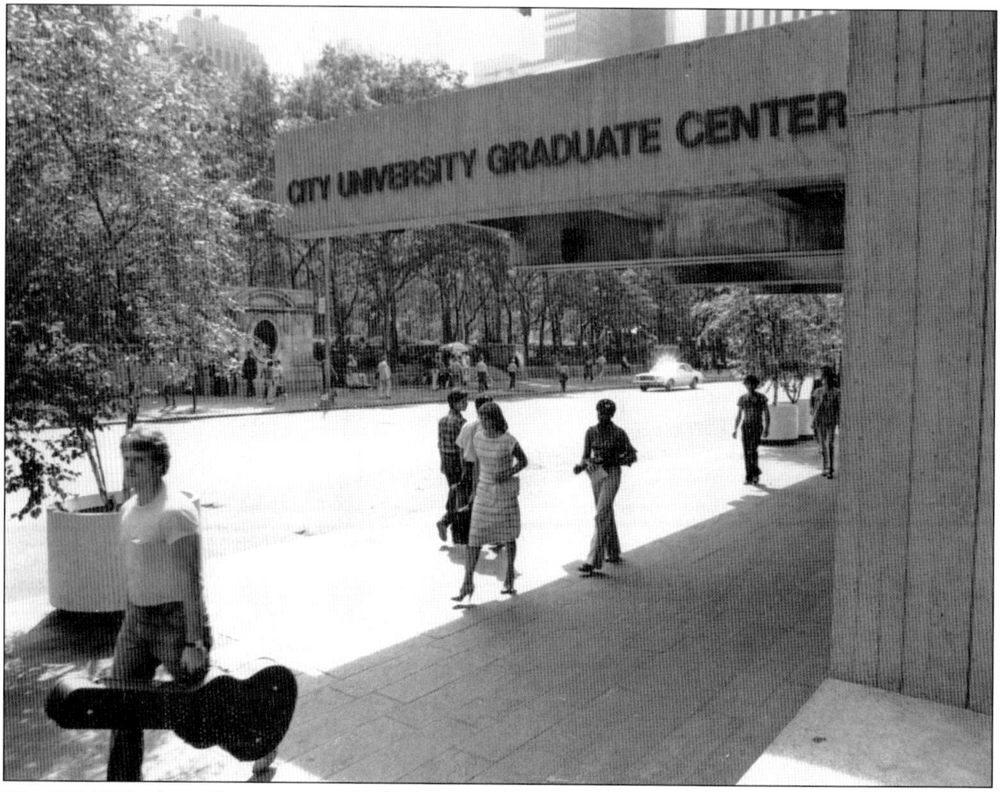

The CUNY Graduate Center was established in 1961, staffed, and supported as a CUNY-wide consortium. It initially offered only four PhD programs; by 2023, this had grown to thirty (in addition to a number of certificate, MA, and standalone research units). In 1966, the GC took up residence at 29-33 West Forty-Second Street, centrally located across from Bryant Park. (Courtesy of the Office of Building Design and Exhibitions [OBDE], CUNY Graduate Center.)

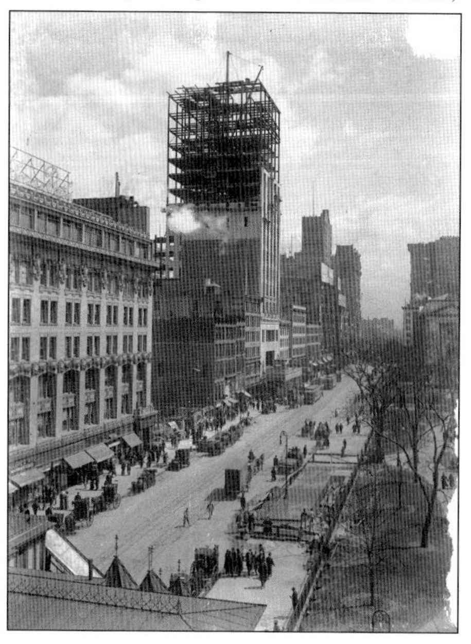

Known as the Aeolian Building, it was designed by Whitney Warren and Charles D. Wetmore, two prominent and prolific architects of the early 20th century (their best-known work is New York City's Grand Central Terminal). The structure was completed in 1912 as the headquarters of the Aeolian Company which was founded in 1887 and manufactured musical instruments and accessories. The company ceased operations in 1985. (Courtesy of the William D. Hassler Photograph Collection, PR83_1118, New-York Historical Society.)

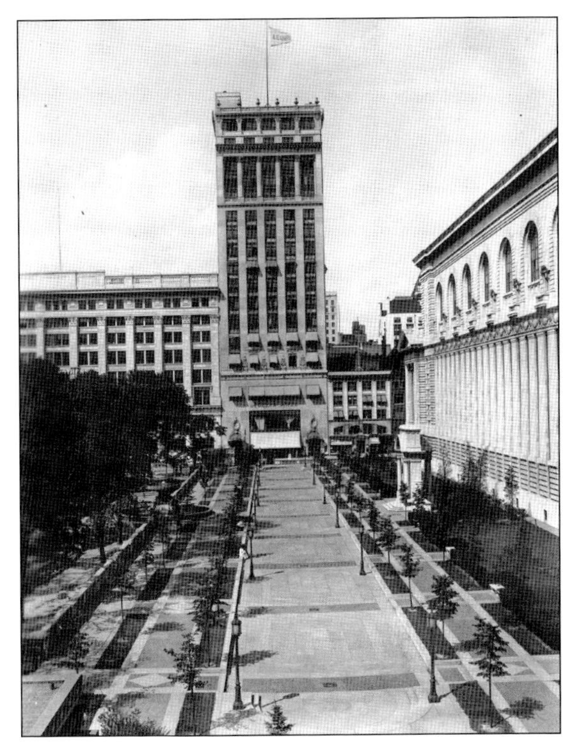

The building stands 260 feet tall and contains 18 floors, the first two of which originally housed a 1,100-seat theater, Aeolian Hall, which was one of the most popular avant-garde venues of the day. On February 12, 1924, George Gershwin's *Rhapsody in Blue* premiered here as part of the landmark concert, "An Experiment in Modern Music." By the time of the GC's residence, all traces of the theater, which closed in 1927, were gone, although Institute check-in was sometimes within its former footprint. In 2000, the building became home to the State University of New York's College of Optometry. (Right, courtesy of the George P. Hall & Son Photograph Collection, PR024_b-14_f-123_012-01, New-York Historical Society; below, courtesy of Subway Construction Photograph Collection, 1900-1950, nyhs_pr-069_b-073_014, New-York Historical Society [by permission of the New York Transit Museum].)

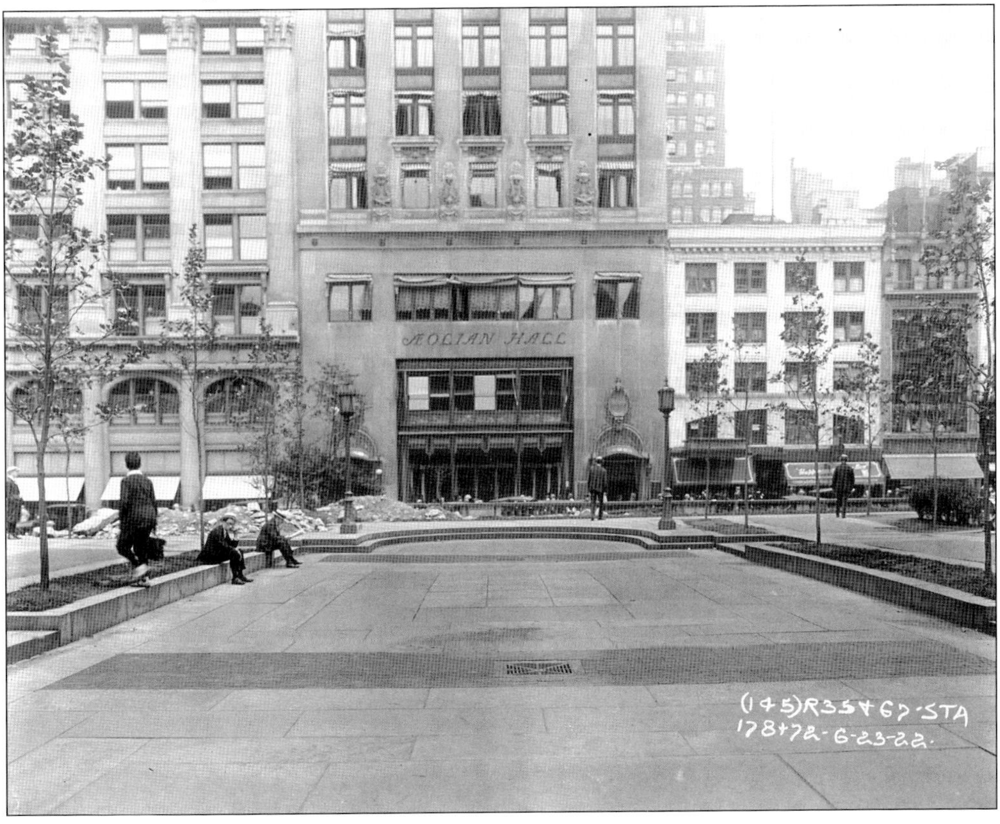

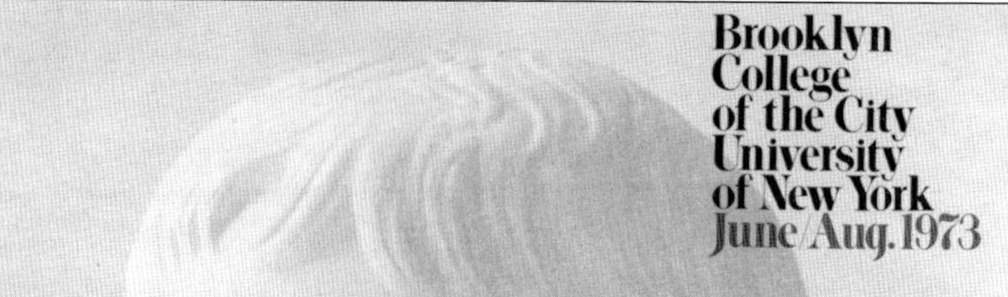

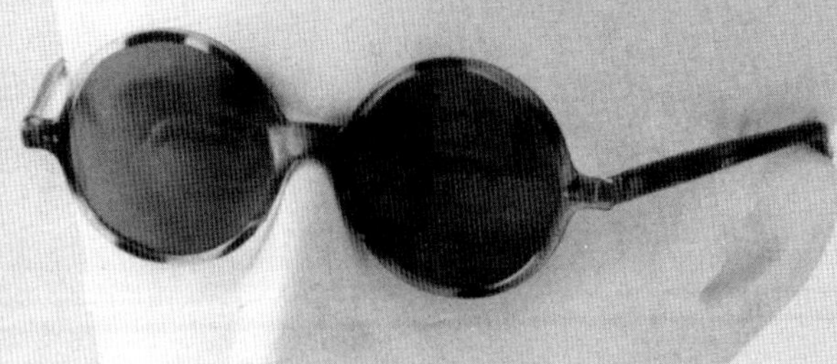

Brooklyn College of the City University of New York
June/Aug. 1973

THE SUMMER LATIN INSTITUTE

The Summer Latin Institute, sponsored by the Department of Classics and Comparative Literature, will provide qualified students a thorough introduction to Latin and extensive practice in the reading of ancient authors equivalent to a minimum of two years of conventional college-level course instruction or four years of high school instruction in a period of ten weeks.

It is modeled on the Berkeley Latin Workshop, which is now in its seventh year.

The intensive and specially designed course requires no previous knowledge of Latin, provides 12 semester units of credit, and aims to enable graduate students in other fields and undergraduates of proven language ability to read, interpret, and use original material after 50 days of instruction.

The Institute will be held at the Graduate Center of the City University of New York, 33 West 42nd St., New York City. There are four regularly scheduled hours of class each day, with extra tutorials and discussion groups arranged to fill individual needs. Four weeks will be devoted to explanatory lectures, drills, and exercises in Latin forms and grammar, while the remaining six weeks will be spent treating selected classical and medieval texts.

Features of the program are:

- **Intensive language drills**
- **Lectures on the structure and history of the language**
- **Techniques in literary criticism**
- **Guest lectures by distinguished scholars on literary and philological problems**
- **Tutorials in grammar and sight reading**
- **Readings: Vergil (*Aeneid* IV); Horace (10 odes); Catullus (15 poems); Cicero (*First Catilinarian*); Elective courses in four other major authors and genres**
- **Small Student/Faculty ratio (approximately 7/1) (a continual rotation of faculty will insure that each student has extensive direct contact with each of the five faculty members)**

Applications must be submitted no later than May 15, 1973. In addition to filing an application for the Institute, prospective students must make

Moreland and Fleischer promoted the inaugural Latin Institute in multiple ways, including sending posters to relevant humanities departments. These remain ubiquitous across the United States and Canada; in 2023, the LGI mailed out over 1,000. The poster for the Institute's inaugural summer was a simple affair, with a limited mailing and reach. This basic design was used in various colors through 1977.

Moreland also took out advertisements in various publications and Fleischer created a simple, eye-catching button with the telephone number for the program office prominently highlighted. One surviving example remains on display in the ninth-floor LGI office (see photograph on page 113).

THE SUMMER LATIN INSTITUTE

Brooklyn College and the Graduate School
The City University of New York
June 18/ August 31

The Summer Latin Institute, modeled on the Latin Workshop at the University of California at Berkeley, will provide qualified students a thorough introduction to Latin and extensive practice in the reading of ancient authors equivalent to a minimum of two years of conventional college-level instruction or four years of high school instruction in a period of ten weeks.

The specially designed program aims to enable graduate students in other fields and undergraduates of proven language ability to read, interpret, and use original material after fifty days of instruction.

- **Four hours of class per day**
- **Intensive language drills**
- **Guest lectures on literary and philosophical problems**
- **Readings: Vergil (*Aeneid* IV); Horace (10 *Odes*); Catullus (15 poems); Cicero (*First Catilinarian*) Elective courses in four other major authors and genres**
- **Small student/faculty ratio (7/1)**

Applications and information on fees and housing may be obtained from
Prof. Floyd L. Moreland
Summer Latin Institute
Department of Classics and Comparative Literature
Brooklyn College of CUNY
Brooklyn, New York 11210

Applications should be submitted by May 15.

The Institute will be held at the Graduate School of CUNY—33 W. 42nd St., New York

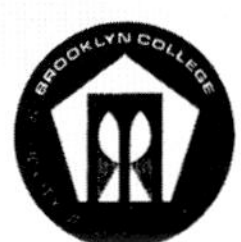

SUMMER LATIN INSTITUTE
OFFICE OF THE DIRECTOR

Department of Classics and Comparative Literature
Brooklyn College
of The City University
of New York
Brooklyn, New York 11210
Telephone: (212) 780-5191, 2
(staffroom, 780-5193)

December 1972

Dear Colleague:

In the summer of 1973, Brooklyn College of the City University of New York will launch a Summer Latin Institute, modeled on the Berkeley Latin Workshop (University of California), which I structured and which has just completed its sixth successful year. The Institute, which assumes no previous knowledge of Latin, has very ambitious goals, and we hope to attract some exceptionally qualified and motivated students, both graduates and undergraduates. I append the course description and a statement of justification for bringing the program to New York City.

Early in the Spring semester posters advertising the Institute will be sent to departments of Classics and related fields throughout the eastern United States along with specific information about fees and application procedures. I am sending this communication in advance to apprise you of the innovative program which will be held in New York next summer. I hope that you will pass on the information to students who may be interested in an intensive introduction to language, literature, and philology and who want a quick and efficient way to prepare in a brief space of time for serious advanced work in Latin and/or for M.A. or Ph.D. Latin exams for other disciplines.

I shall be delighted to answer any questions you may have about the Institute or to send you additional literature about the structure and results of the Workshop at Berkeley. Meanwhile, I am grateful for your cooperation.

Sincerely,

Floyd L. Moreland
Assistant Professor of Classics
Director, Summer Latin Institute

FLM:cs
Enclosure

Finally, letters were sent to various departments and individuals with more detailed information. Moreland and Fleischer also wrote colleagues at other institutions to help spread the word. Many, of these, in turn, shared with their own contacts and connections.

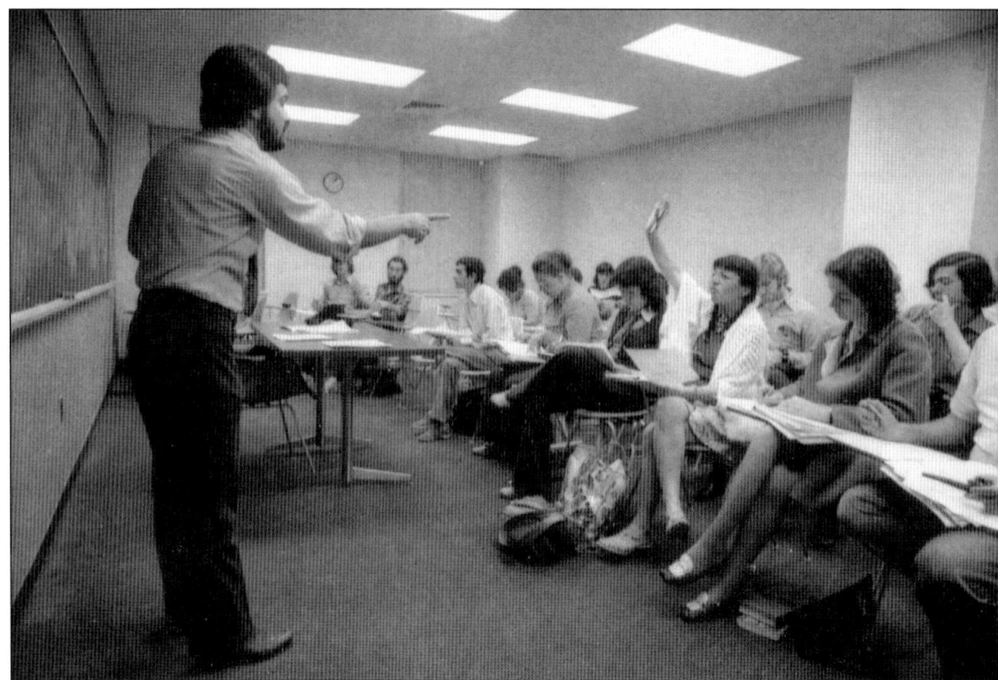

Forty students entered the 1973 Latin Institute, ranging in age from 20 to 47 and with academic experience spanning the undergraduate to postdoctoral. Twenty-five ultimately went on to complete—about 62.5 percent. Over the last half century, the completion rate for both basic programs has hovered around 80–85 percent, though persistence to completion has increased in the last two decades. Although Moreland had experience with the Berkeley Workshop, the first year of the Latin Institute was capped at 40 students to ensure faculty sufficiency and effective delivery of the program. Over the next few years, the numbers would steadily increase.

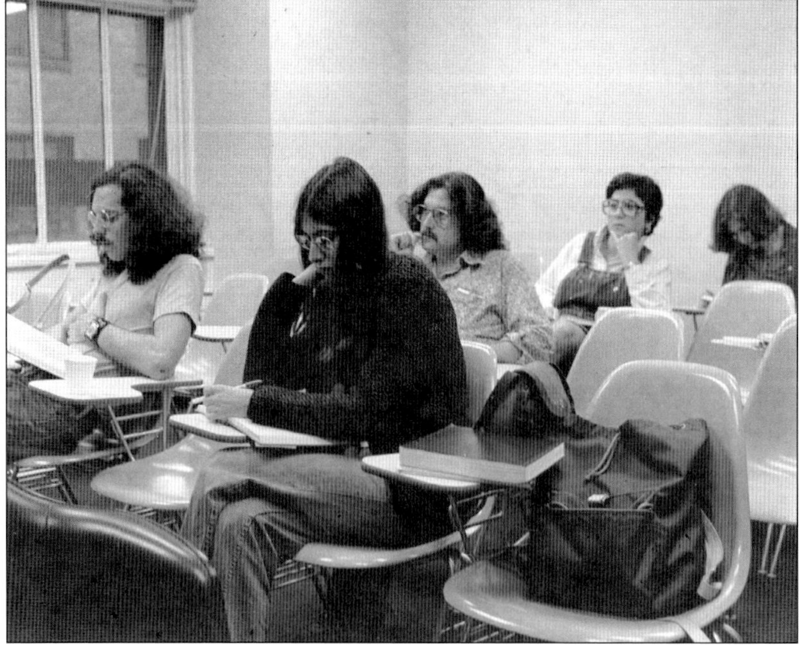

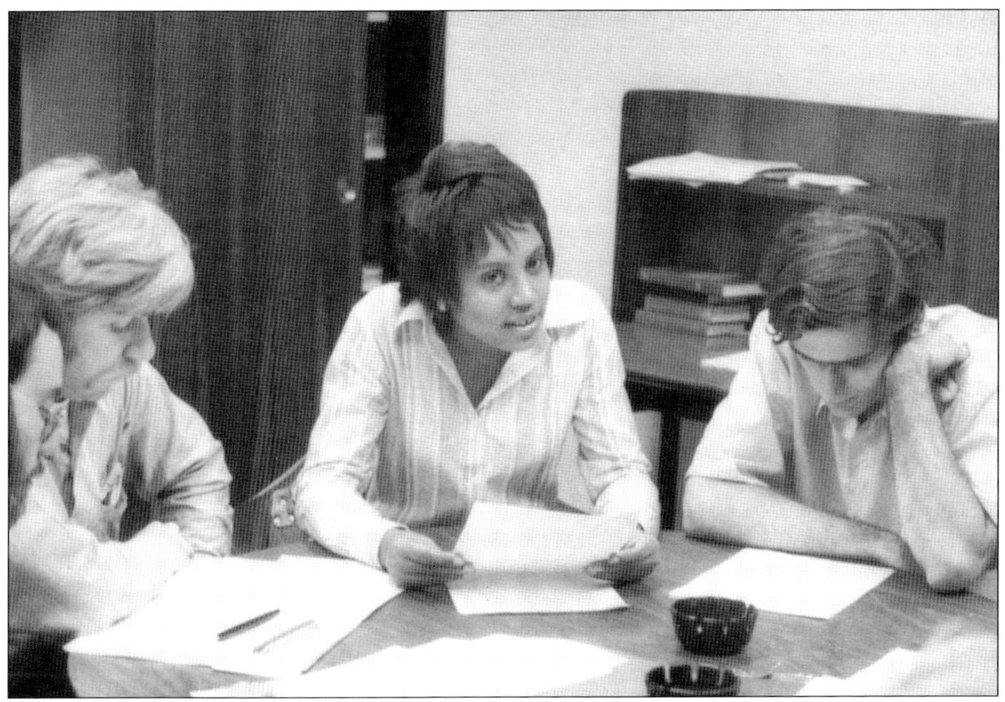

Dennis Spininger (second from left) completed the Institute in its inaugural year, while simultaneously serving as chair of classics and comparative literature (and as such, colleague—and supervisor—of the Institute faculty). A disciplinary marriage of convenience, Spininger's expertise was in American literature. He, along with Wolfe, is thanked in the preface of the Institute's eventual textbook (see Chapter 4). He passed away in 1995.

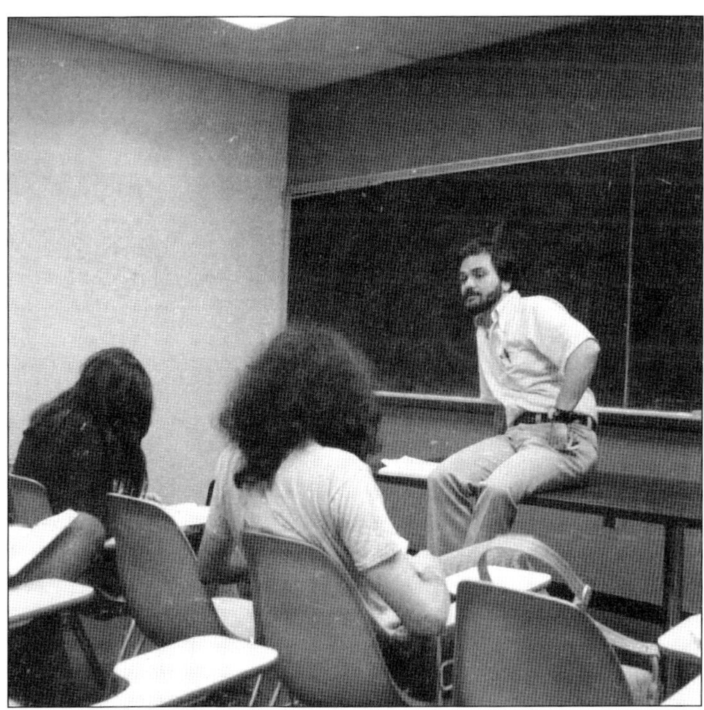

Along with his gift for curriculum design, Moreland was a dynamic, engaging, and quick-witted instructor who moved energetically around the classroom. He held himself and the Institute's instructors to the highest standards, as evident in the faculty whom he recruited and trained for the launch of the Latin Institute.

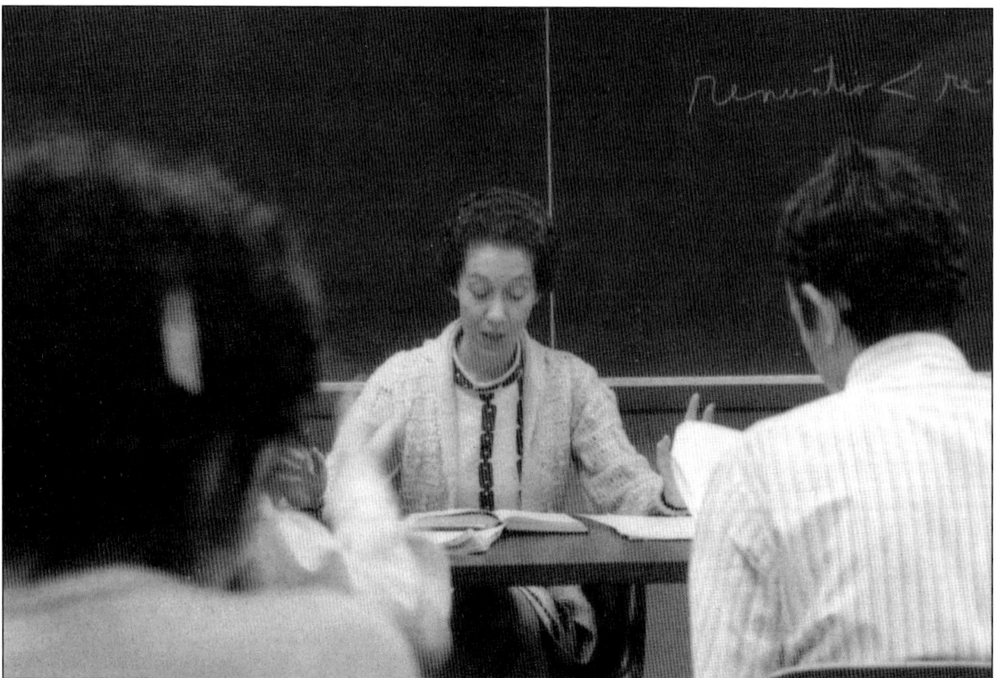

Fleischer was one of Moreland's first recruits from Brooklyn College, and her lifelong dedication to the Institute has been essential to its success. She has been involved as faculty and/or administrator almost every summer since its inception. In later decades, as the ranks of graduates grew, she also became indispensable to maintaining alumni relations. Here, with any significant number of alumni still years away, she conducts morning drill in the first SLI. Although her last full summer of teaching was in 1991, she has continued to deliver the occasional vocabulary lecture and sight-reading optional, as well as sit in on pre-program work with the Latin faculty.

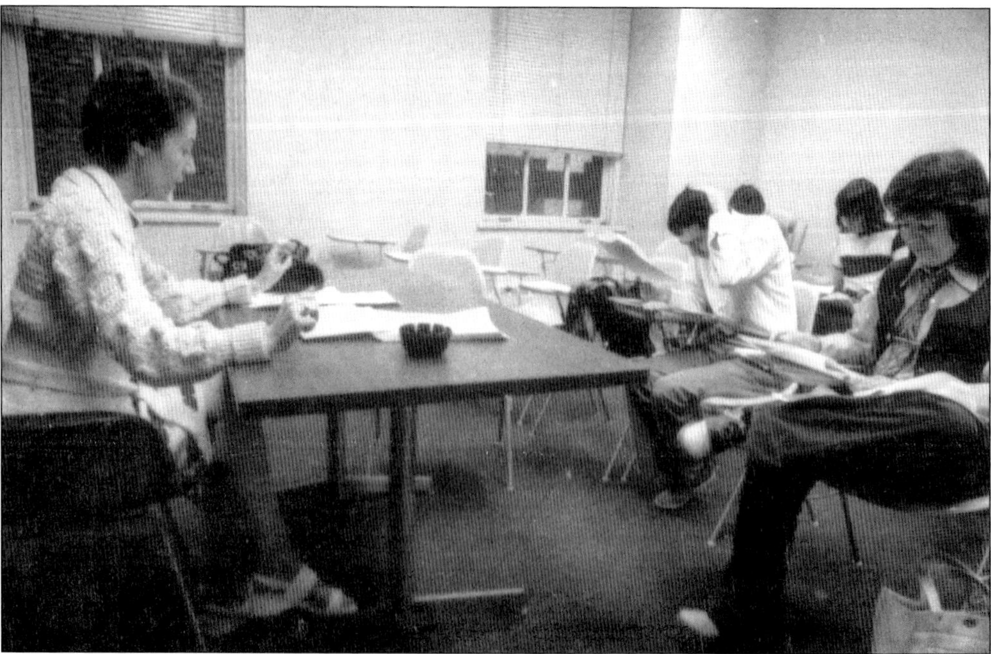

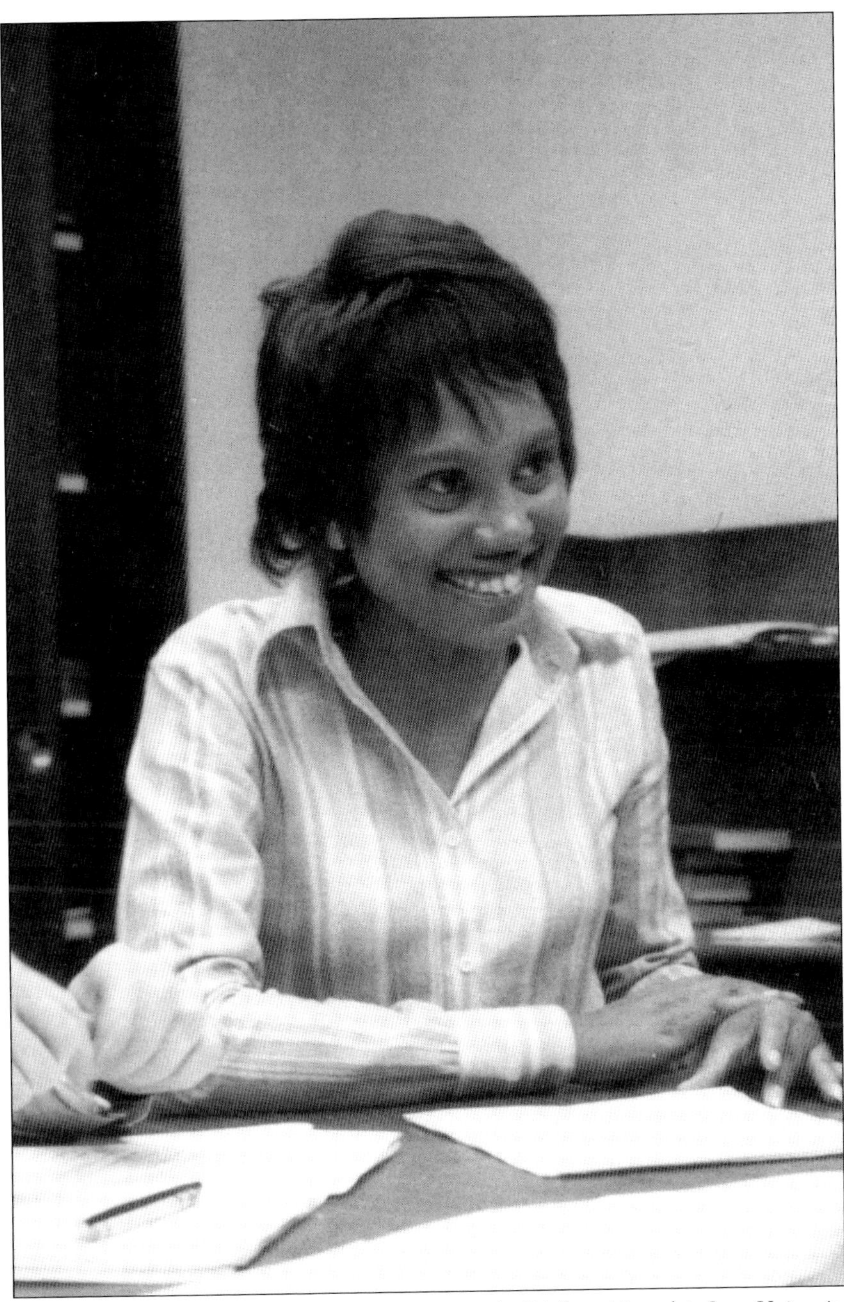

Gail Smith (1938–2023) was another Wolfe hire. She received a BA from Montclair State University, an MA in Latin and Greek from Columbia University, and a PhD in classics from NYU. In the Institute's first decade, she would teach in the Basic Latin and, later, Basic Greek, and Advanced Latin programs. She played an important role in the Institute's first decade, where her outstanding teaching helped ensure the high standards for instruction and student engagement that Moreland had established. Outside the Institute, much of her research focused on connections between people of African descent and the classics, from both ancient and modern perspectives. In 1974, she was appointed to the editorial board of the *Classical Outlook* and served as its editor in 1977. In subsequent decades, she often taught courses in the Department of Africana Studies.

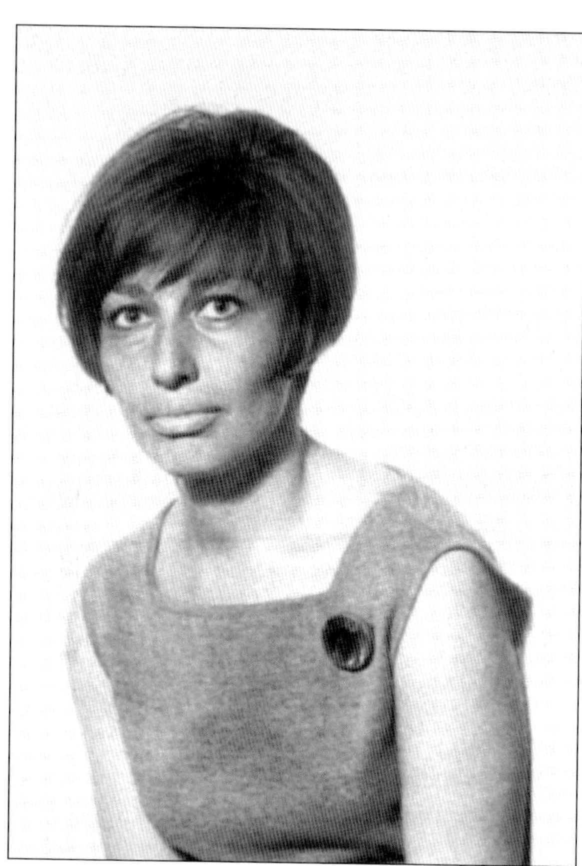

Joan Plotnick was a Brooklyn College alumna and faculty member who taught in the Latin Institute's first two years. She received a BA in classics from Brooklyn College and an MA from the CUNY Graduate Center. She was hired by Procope Costas as a lecturer in classics in 1965, and she remained on faculty until her 1998 retirement.

John Wyatt (1937–2008) had been a fellow graduate student with Moreland and, at the time, was an assistant professor of comparative literature and classics at Beloit College. A medievalist, here, he teaches a selection from the *Decem Libri Historiarum* of Gregory of Tours. Like Moreland, Wyatt had a reputation as a dynamic lecturer.

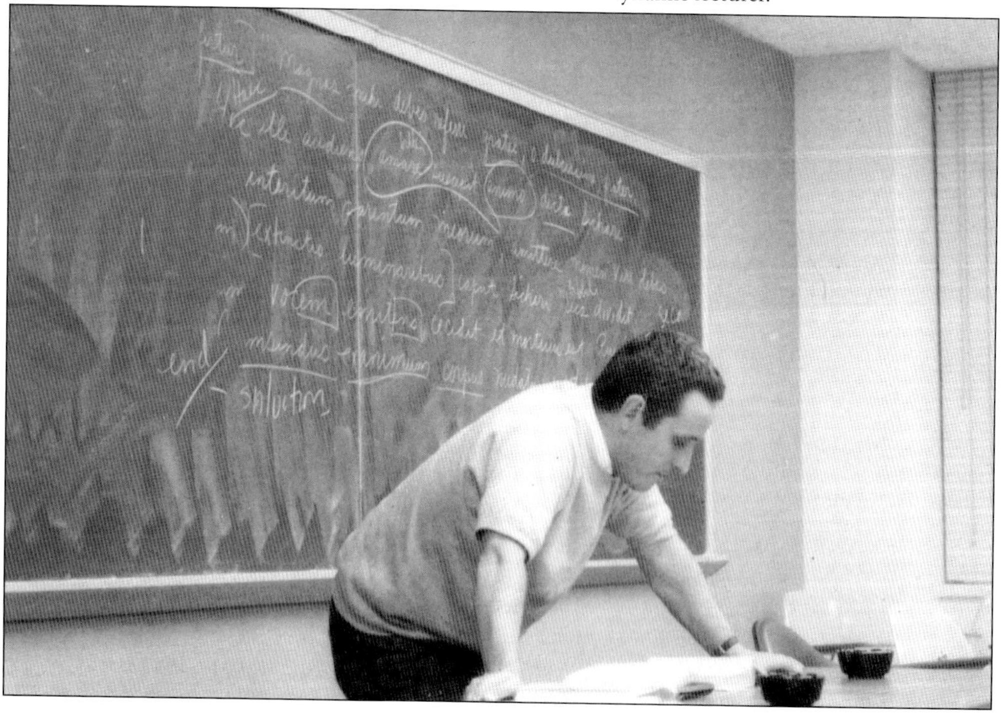

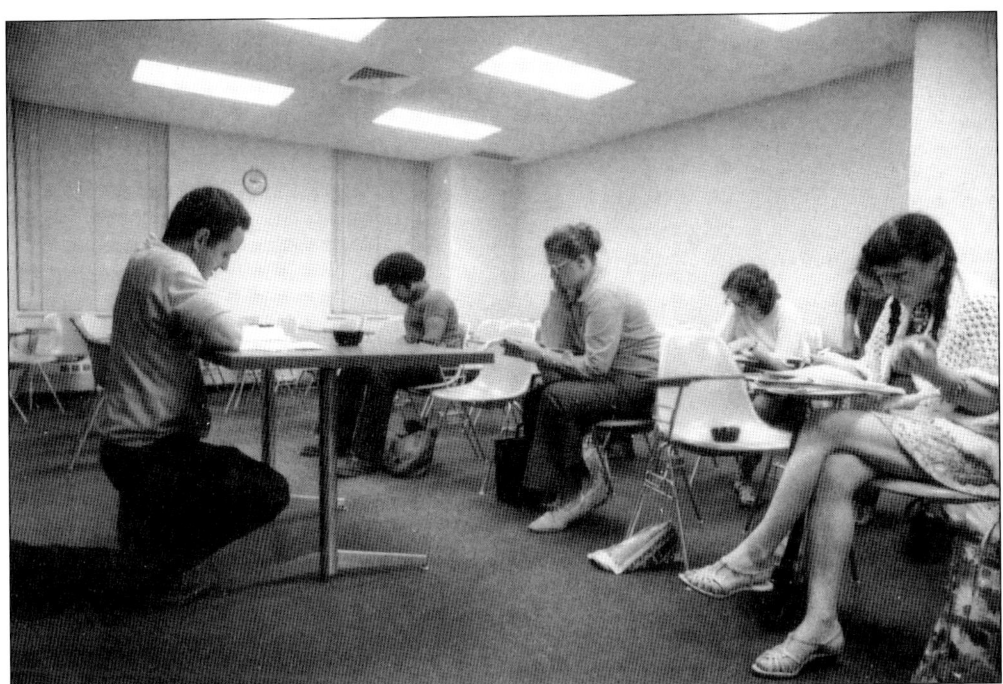

Wyatt also had a distinct—and frequently remarked upon—style of teaching. When not in motion, he often conducted class on his knees, adjacent to the table at the front. Though he taught only one summer, it befitted an extraordinarily diverse career: *Inter alia*, he founded the Center for Language Studies at Beloit (1982), translated Chekhov for the American Players Theater, and was dean of the Frank Lloyd Wright School of Architecture.

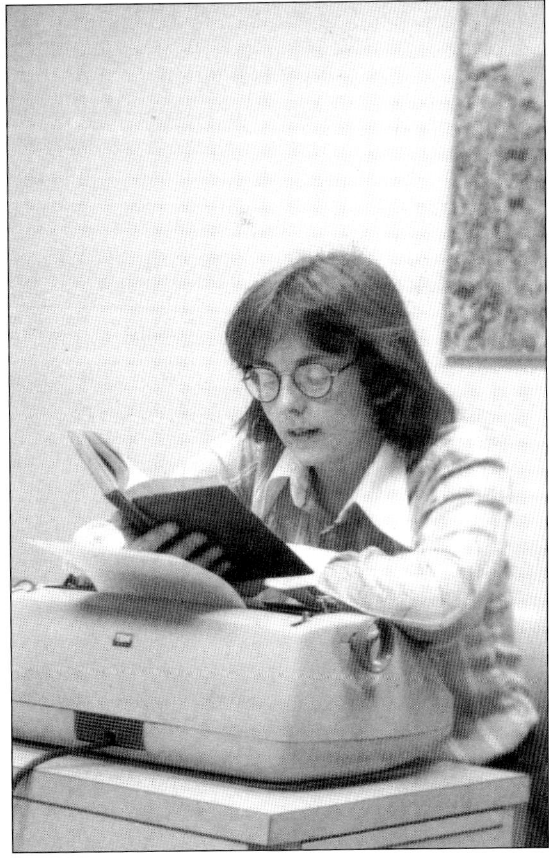

Stephanie Russell was one of the Institute's longest-serving and most recognized faculty members, teaching in the Basic Latin, Greek, and Advanced Latin programs. In the Institute's first two years, however, she was its administrative assistant. The title is somewhat misleading, however, as it involved significant engagement with the Institute's curriculum and pedagogy.

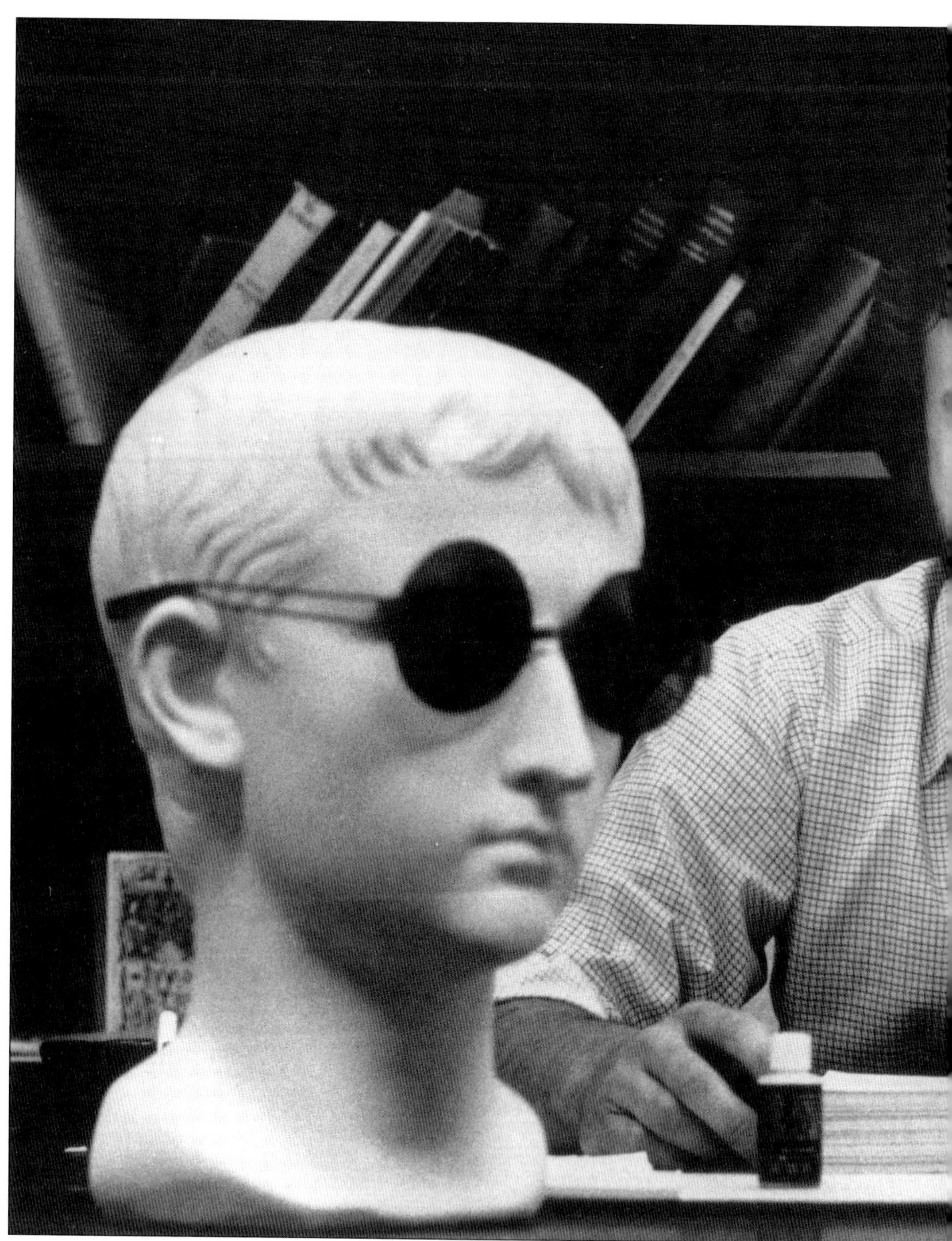

In its inaugural summer, the Latin Institute was profiled in the August 6 edition of the *New York Times*. Amid the tumult of higher education in the early 1970s, it was certainly something of an anomaly. Over the next half century, the LGI would be profiled in a range of publications, including the *New Yorker* (twice), *National Review* (twice), the *International Herald Tribune*, as well as an array of local newspapers and CUNY publications. In its October 13, 2018, edition, the *New York Post* included the LGI in its list of "Hottest

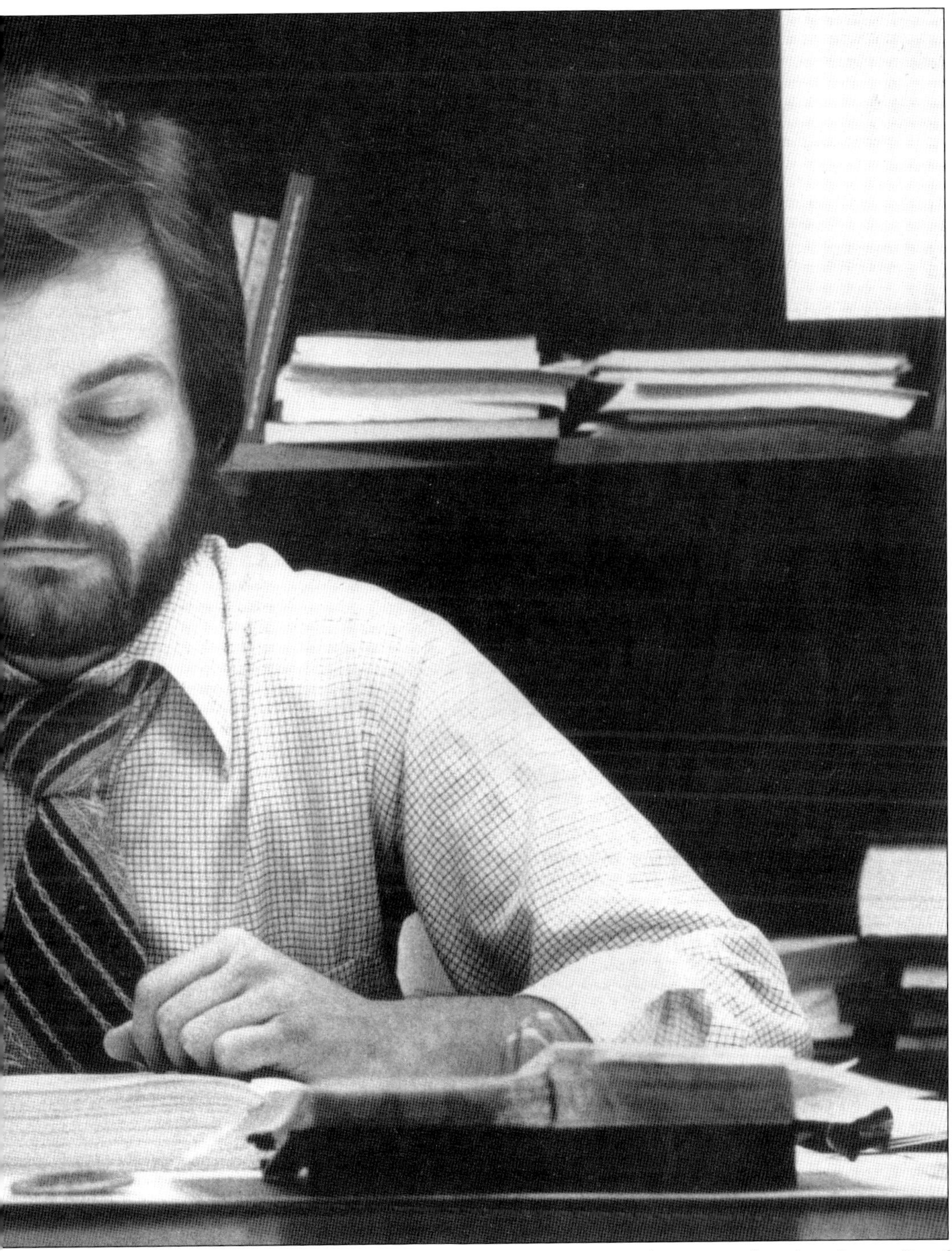

College Classes in NYC." The Institute has also been discussed in academic journals and cited in studies of language learning. This picture of Moreland, used in the 1973 *New York Times* article, is probably the best-known and most widely disseminated photograph of the LGI's founder. (Courtesy of Don Hogan Charles, the *New York Times*, and Redux.)

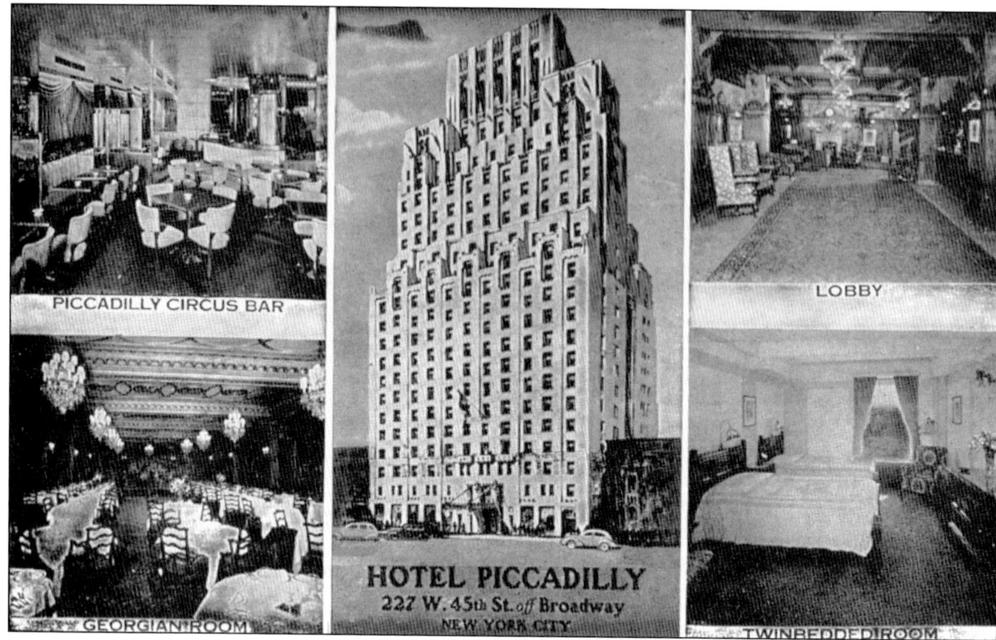

At the close of the inaugural summer, program participants gathered at the Piccadilly Hotel (227 West Forty-Fifth Street, since demolished) for an informal celebration. It was a simple affair and included a student parody of *Aeneid* IV, culminating in a singing of "Light My Pyre" led by a student dressed as the god Mercury. Over the next few years, this impromptu celebration evolved into a more formal event (Chapter 6).

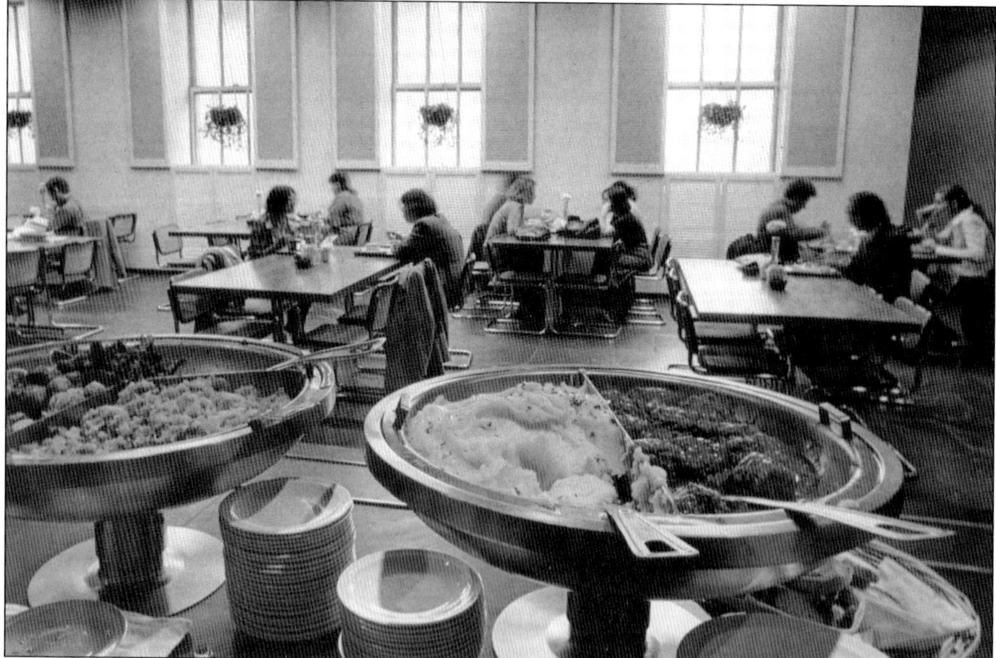

The GC Dining Commons, located on the 18th floor, was comfortably outfitted with cozy seating, a cash bar, and a menu that changed daily. Although never popular with Institute students, the faculty occasionally enjoyed its Friday afternoon happy hour. It was here that Moreland and Fleischer met almost every night to review the day and finalize the next day's material. (Courtesy of the OBDE, CUNY GC.)

By 1976, Russell had become a core member of the faculty. In 2003, she and Andrew Keller (AL 1980, and later SLI and UL faculty), published the well-regarded *Learn to Read Latin*, which references their time at the Institute. A Greek textbook came soon thereafter.

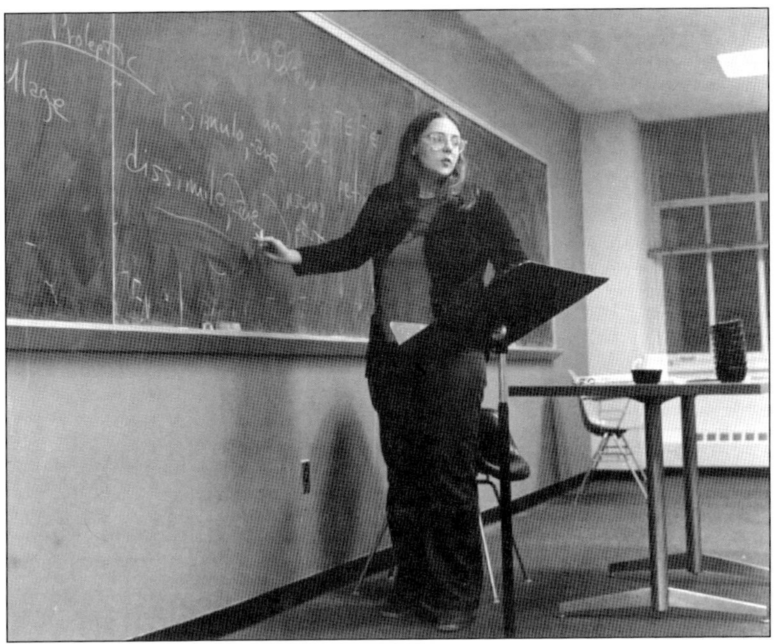

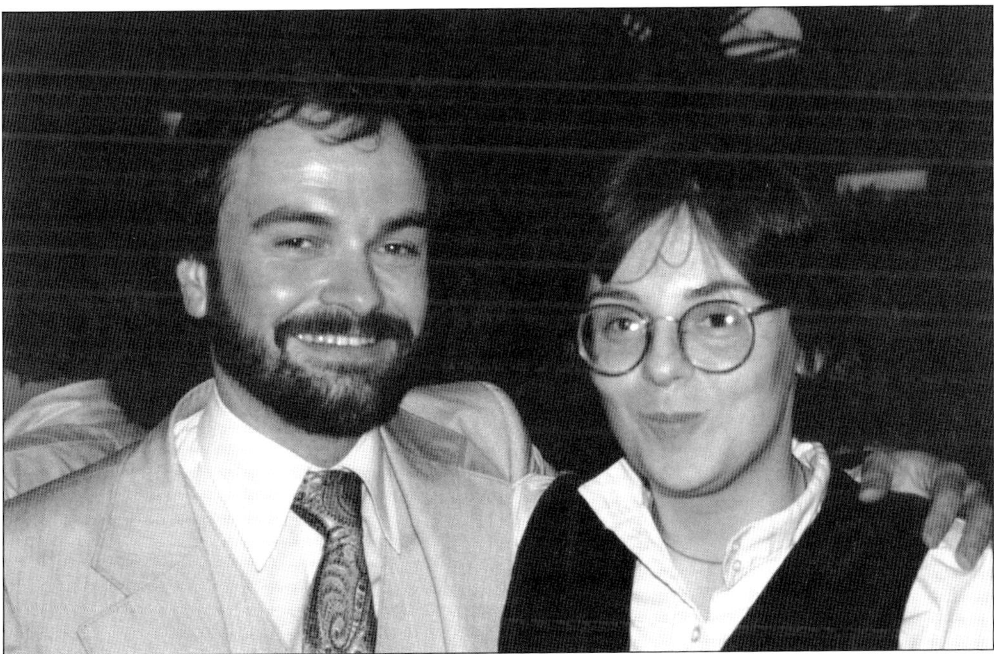

This 1977 photograph of Moreland and Russell, likely taken at the end of the summer celebration, reflects the strong camaraderie and esprit de corps among the faculty in the Institute's first decade. Moreland, at the time, still an untenured junior faculty member, led the Institute through an array of challenges facing CUNY and Brooklyn College. In subsequent decades, his managerial acumen and inspiring leadership would draw the attention of the wider university.

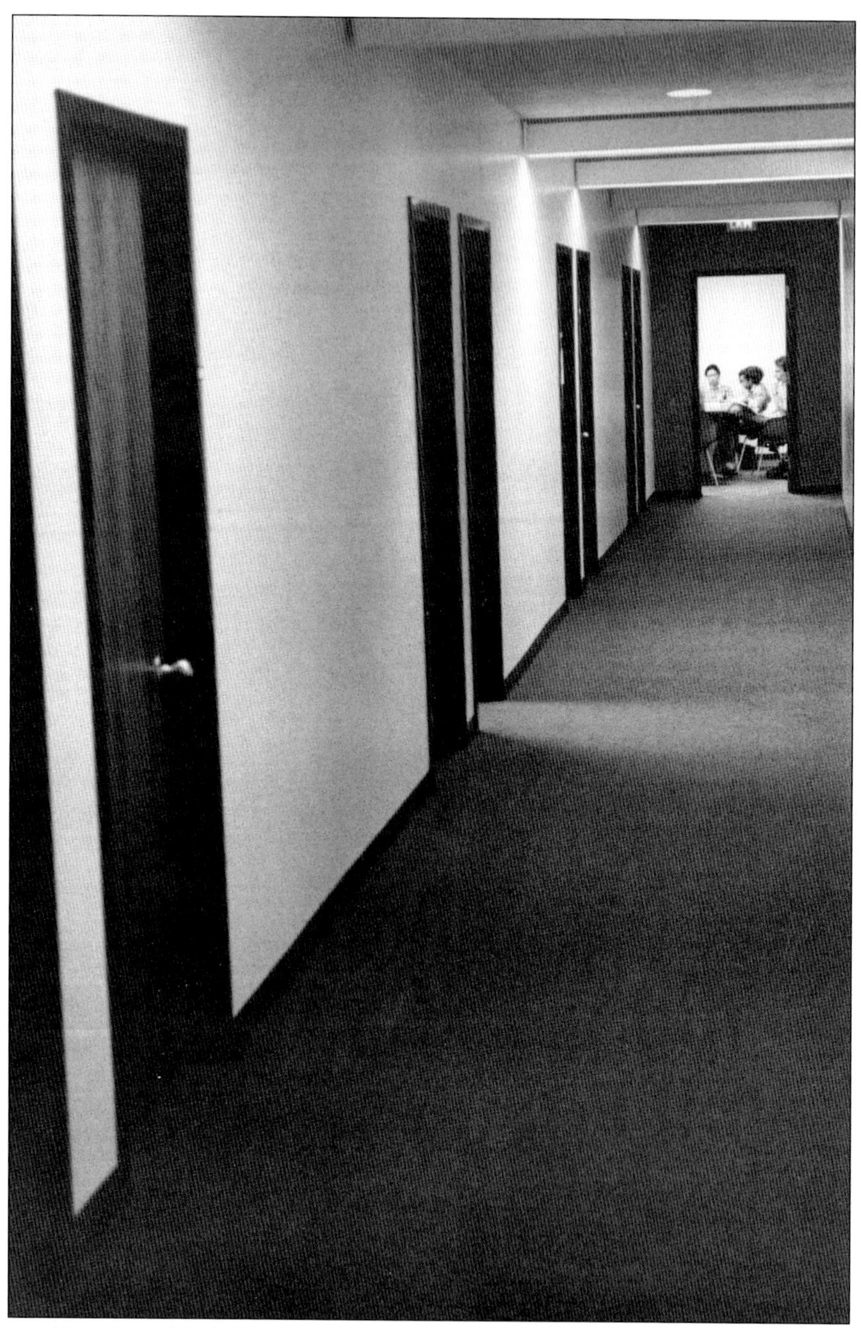

Institute students are visible down a hall in the confines of the Graduate Center, sometime in the mid-1970s. Then, as now, Institute students comprised the largest program population at the GC during the summer months. In its earliest years, the Institute used the unoccupied office of the classics department (room 1012) as its base of operations. When not in class, students often spread out across the floor, which had small areas for congregation. It was also a decade of contrasts. Some students attended in suits, others in more relaxed summer wear. Smoking was also an ongoing issue. Although permitted indoors, after some students complained, Moreland bifurcated the main lecture room (1025) into smoking and nonsmoking halves. (Courtesy of the OBDE, CUNY GC.)

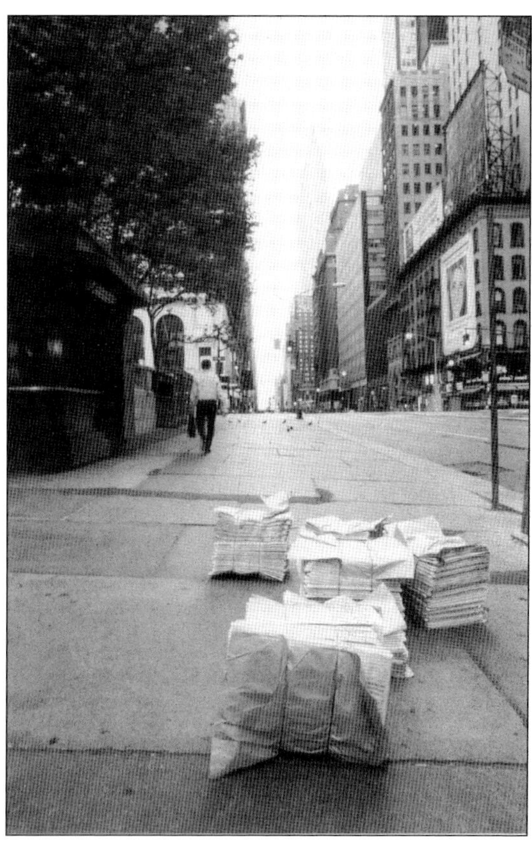

Although the GC was more conveniently located than Brooklyn College, the surrounding area was dismal in the 1970s and 1980s. The stretch of Forty-Second Street adjacent the GC, especially after hours, could be desolate. Ten-acre Bryant Park, opposite, provided no refuge either. Originally known as Reservoir Square (after the adjacent reservoir, now the site of the New York Public Library), it was rebuilt and renamed in 1884 in honor of the poet, newspaper editor, and civic reformer William Cullen Bryant (1794–1878). By the 1970s, however, it had acquired the sobriquet of "Needle Park" and was generally avoided. In 1992, after a $10 million dollar renovation, the public began returning and soon thereafter the park became a welcoming locale for Institute students. (Right, courtesy of Brian Merlis; below, courtesy of Browning Photograph Collection, PR 009, New-York Historical Society, 93599d.)

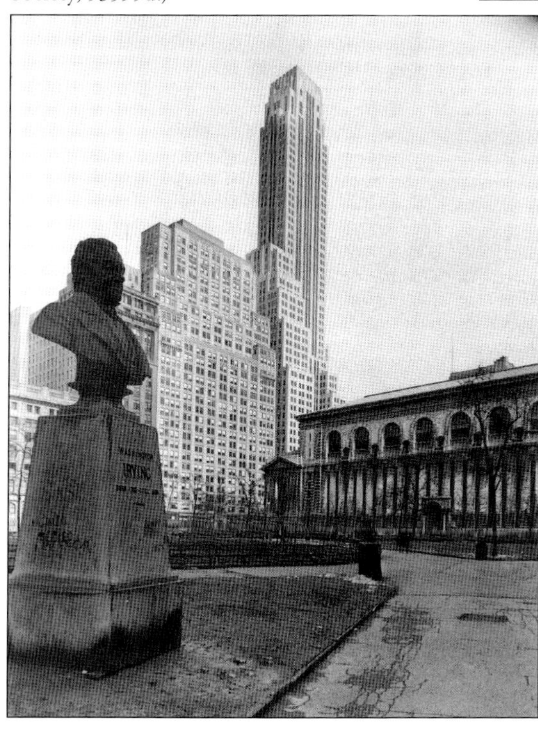

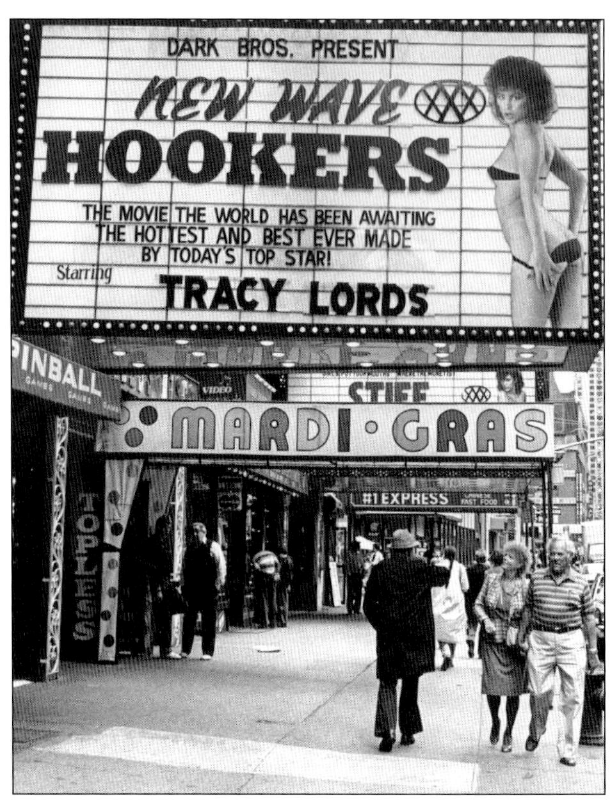

One block west was the crossroads of Times Square. Its surrounding neighborhood contained New York City's famed theater district and a mix of cheap restaurants, discount stores, peep shows, penny arcades, and massage parlors. By the 1970s, many of the grand old theaters had become grindhouses and/or showcases for explicit films. In addition to the commercialized sex readily available in brick-and-mortar establishments, Forty-Second Street was infamous for its street prostitution. As with Bryant Park, a significant—if somewhat more controversial—effort was made to improve the area in the 1990s. (Left, courtesy of the Eugene Gordon photograph collection, 1970–1990, nyhs_PR248_b-2_f-15_42, New-York Historical Society; below, courtesy of Eugene Gordon photograph collection, 1970–1990, 1985. PR248_b-2_f-15_10, New-York Historical Society.)

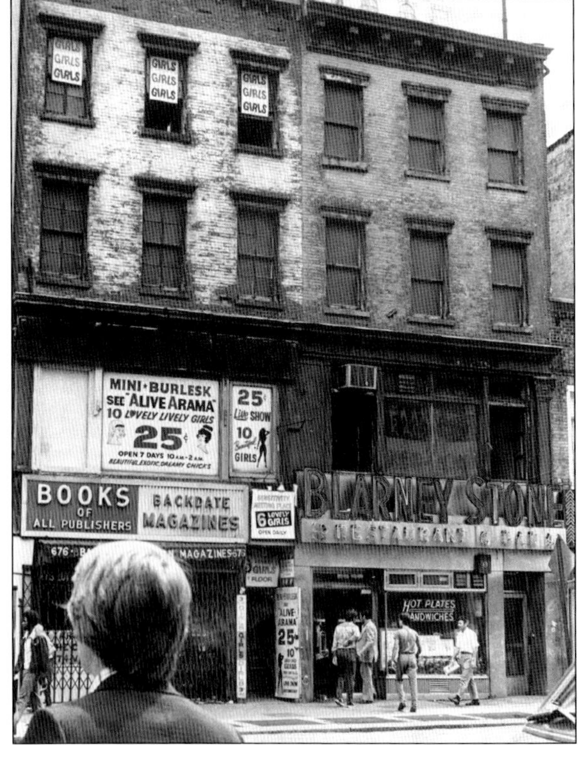

Three

The Latin/Greek Institute

1978–1999

In its first three decades, the Institute expanded in every regard: enrollments grew, new programs were introduced, and various customs and traditions came into being. This growth and maturation remained rooted, however, in the centrality of the curriculum: Floyd Moreland's pioneering work on pedagogical detail, precision, and accuracy coalesced and evolved into a broader Institute methodology, which continues to guide and inform every aspect of the Institute's programs and their delivery.

The introduction of additional programs was all but inevitable. From the inception of the Latin Institute—indeed, as early as the Berkeley workshops—Moreland had wanted to establish a parallel program in Greek. Once the Latin Institute proved a success, this addition became inevitable. Unlike the essentially theoretical, de novo construction of an immersive Latin program, Greek was benefited by the lessons learned with Latin, as well as the presence of a talented and energetic colleague at Brooklyn College, Hardy Hansen. As Moreland has often remarked, Hansen's involvement all but ensured the program's success.

Hansen in turn had an ideal partner in Gerald M. Quinn, a member of the Latin Institute faculty in 1976 and 1977. The two began work on the program in the fall of 1977, and its emerging curriculum was intensively practiced and workshopped in the months that followed. In the summer of 1978, the new Greek program was launched with 23 students enrolled. As with its Latin predecessor, the program achieved its stated objectives in its inaugural year, a confirmation of the meticulous planning and attention to detail that are the essential hallmarks of the Institute.

From 1980 to 1988, the Institute also offered advanced programs in Latin and Greek. Administered through the Graduate Center's classics department, these were ultimately discontinued after a fiscal crisis forced CUNY to impose austerity measures and limit program offerings; at the same time, the number of SLI and SGI faculty was reduced from 4 to 3, and the annual newsletter mailing suspended for five years. Upper-level programs were reintroduced in 1995, though not consistently offered until 2010.

Through 1999, the LGI would also experience its share of triumphs, tragedies, and transitions—and the millennium would close with one very big change.

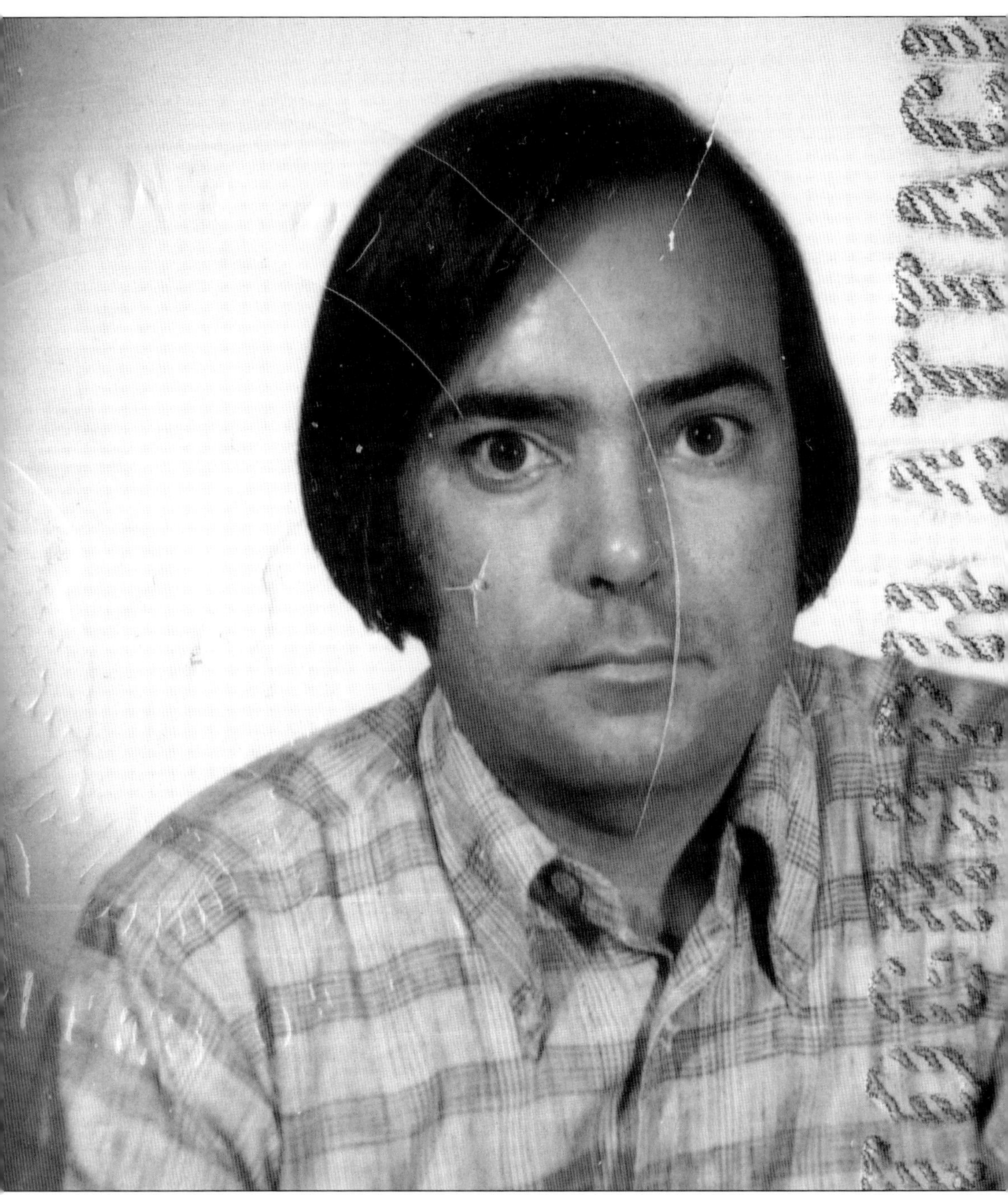

Hardy Hansen, born in 1941, grew up in Bethesda, Maryland. As with Moreland and Fleischer, his love of the classics was also fostered by a high school teacher, Jim Downton, at Bethesda-Chevy Chase High School. He received a PhD in classics from Harvard and was, like Moreland, recruited by Wolfe in 1971. He had met Fleischer in 1968 when both were teaching at NYU's Bronx campus (now Bronx Community College). In addition to his later directorship of the Institute, he has taught every summer since 1978: the entirety of basic Greek through 2017 and subsequently in three- or four-week stints (as of this publication). (Courtesy of Hardy Hansen.)

the summer latin institute

of the School of Humanities of Brooklyn College and the CUNY Graduate Center

is proud to announce

the inception of a parallel intensive program in Greek, and its new name,

the summer latin/greek institute

19 June – 31 August, 1978

address inquiries to: Prof. Floyd L. Moreland
33 West 42nd St., N.Y., N.Y. 10036

Recalling the introduction of the Latin Institute, Moreland and Fleischer—now joined by Hansen and Quinn—began notifying colleagues and institutions about the impending launch of the new Greek program in various ways, including sending these hand-calligraphed postcards.

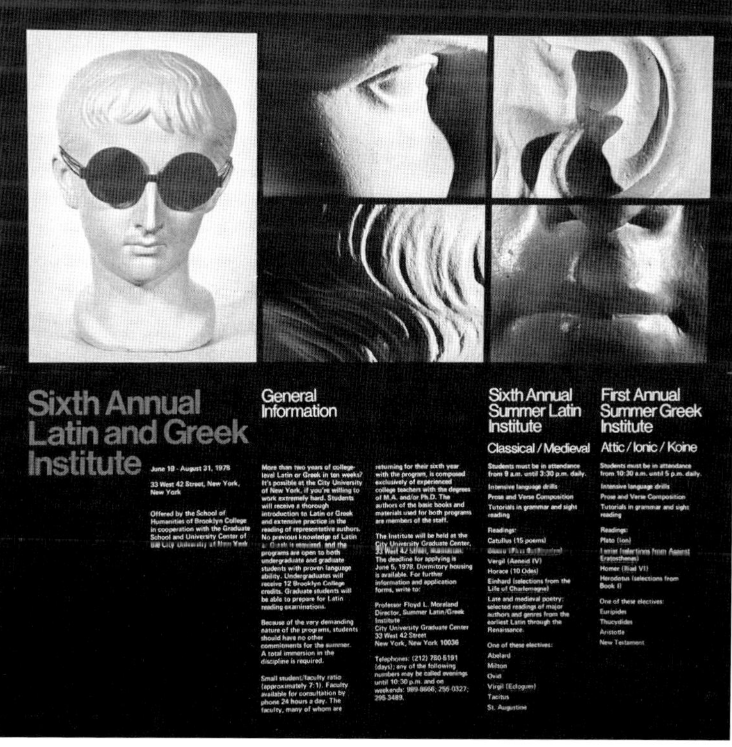

The official 1978 poster celebrated the launch of the parallel Greek program at the newly renamed CUNY Latin and Greek Institute. The "and" was dropped soon thereafter and the LGI became the Latin/Greek Institute. In its inaugural year, there were three faculty members and one administrative assistant for Greek, compared to five instructors and one administrative assistant for Latin.

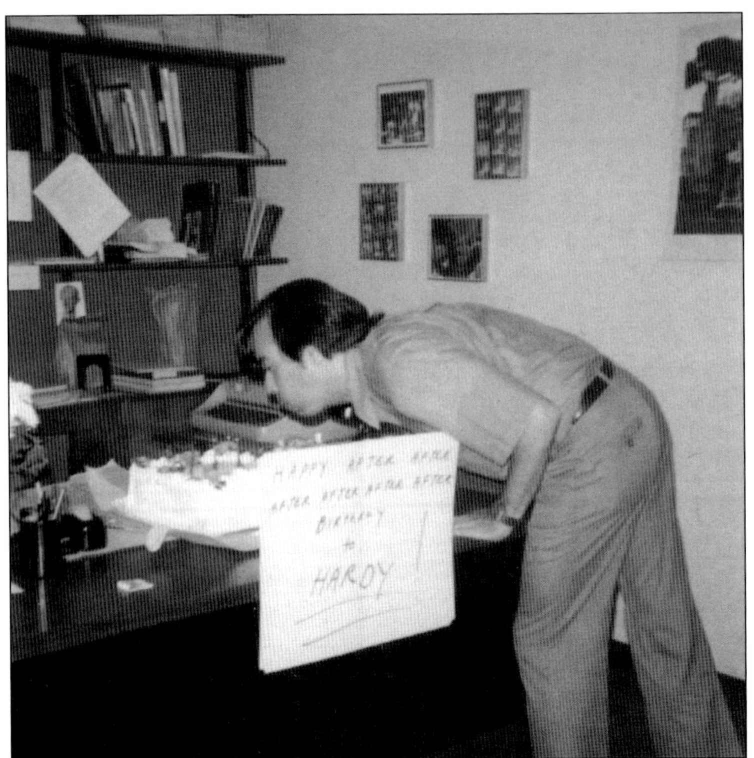

Hansen's birthday comes mid-summer. As 1978 also marked the nascence of the new program in Greek, both occasions were celebrated with an "afterhours" (or, as noted here, with an "after, after, after, after, after, after birthday") cake. Days at the Institute are long, so such festive moments among the faculty and staff are especially cherished.

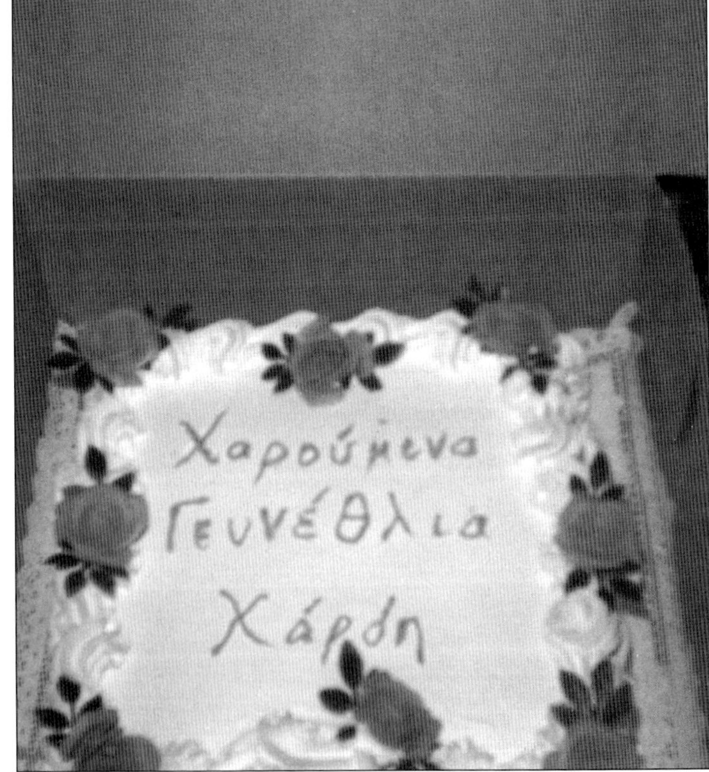

In addition to "Happy Birthday" in Greek, Hansen's first name is rendered phonetically: χάρδη. A clever idea, as his name traditionally used at graduation, μόλις εὐώψ, had yet to be devised. (Chapter 6 discusses LGI naming conventions.)

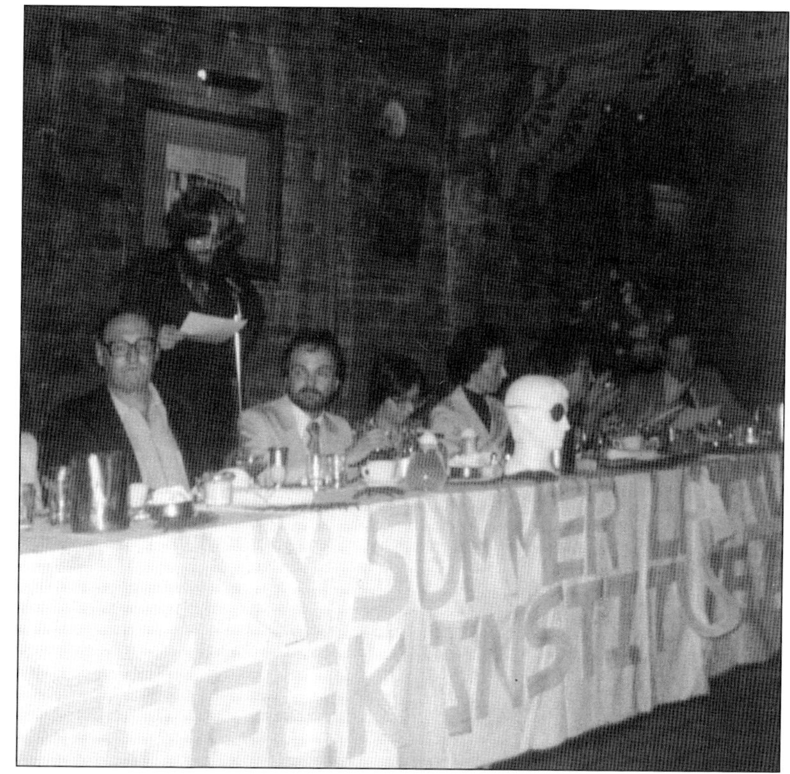

A handmade table skirt adorned the faculty/VIP table at the 1978 end-of-summer party, celebrating the Institute's new name. Faculty member Jack Collins is at the microphone; Moreland and Fleischer (among others) are seated.

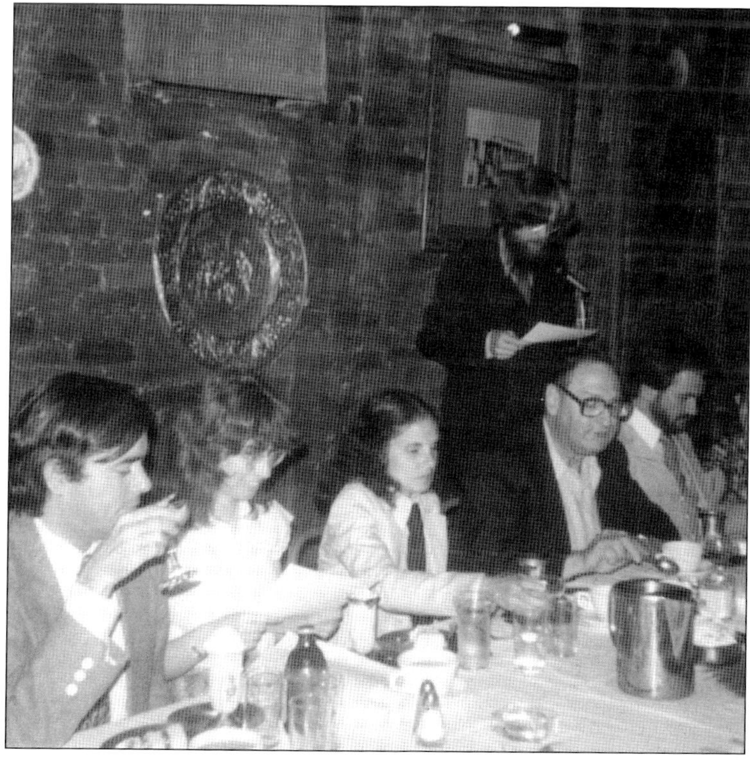

In this closeup of the table, Hansen's wife, Christina, is seated to his left and, to her left, Dee Clayman. Clayman, another Wolfe hire, joined the BC faculty in 1972 after completing her PhD at the University of Pennsylvania. She became a full professor in 1982 and was executive officer of GC classics from 1995 to 2023. She was a pioneer in the use of digital technology in the classics.

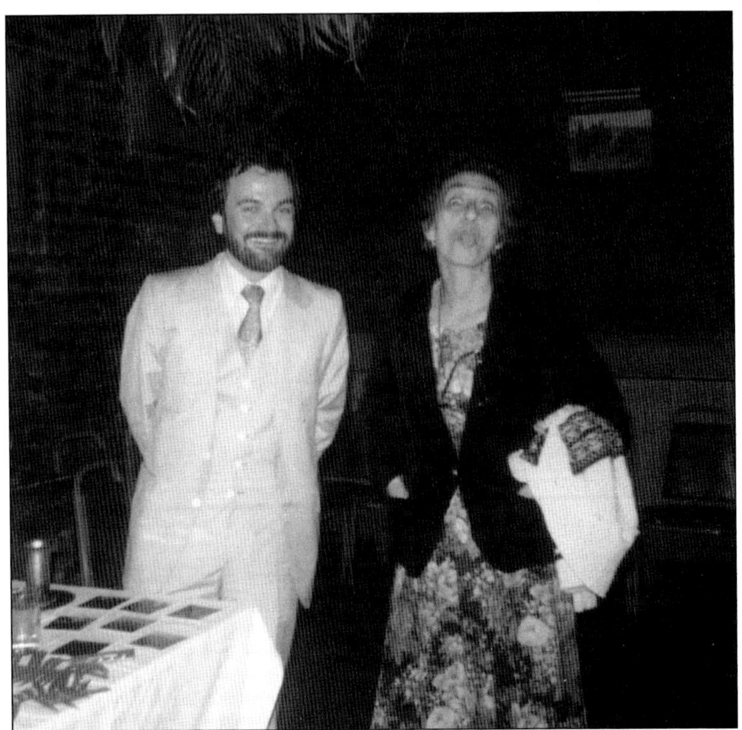

This photograph, one of the author's favorites, captures a festive moment at the 1978 graduation. The relationship between Moreland and Fleischer was critical to the Institute's success: their skills were complementary, and both were committed to the highest standards in every dimension of academics and operations.

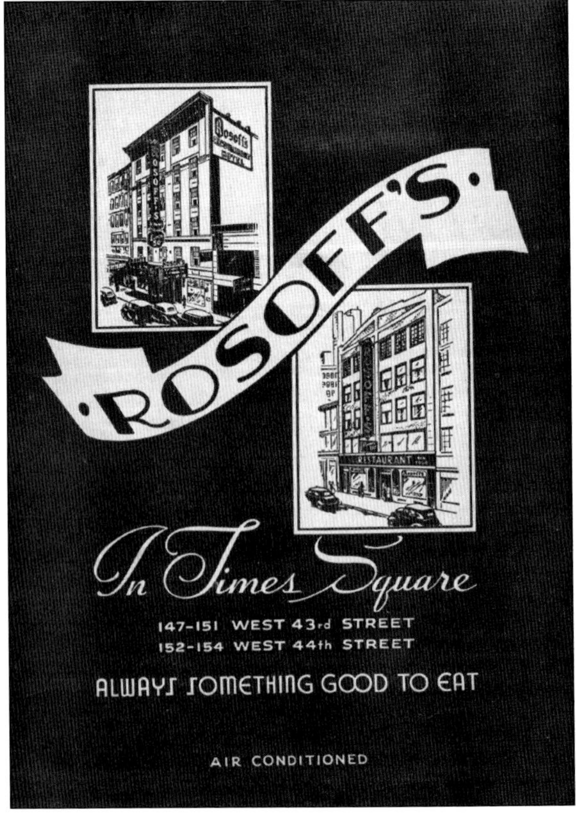

The 1978 end-of-the-summer celebration was held at Rosoff's Restaurant, which was located right behind the Aeolian Building. Opened in 1918, the restaurant closed in 1981, though the building remains standing as of this writing. The party, though not a true graduation, was becoming increasingly more elaborate and incorporating its own traditions and distinct features. (Courtesy of the Rare Book Division, The New York Public Library. (1940). Rosoff's. Retrieved from https://digitalcollections.nypl.org/items/b917eb3b-ddb8-ad32-e040-e00a18060e3e.)

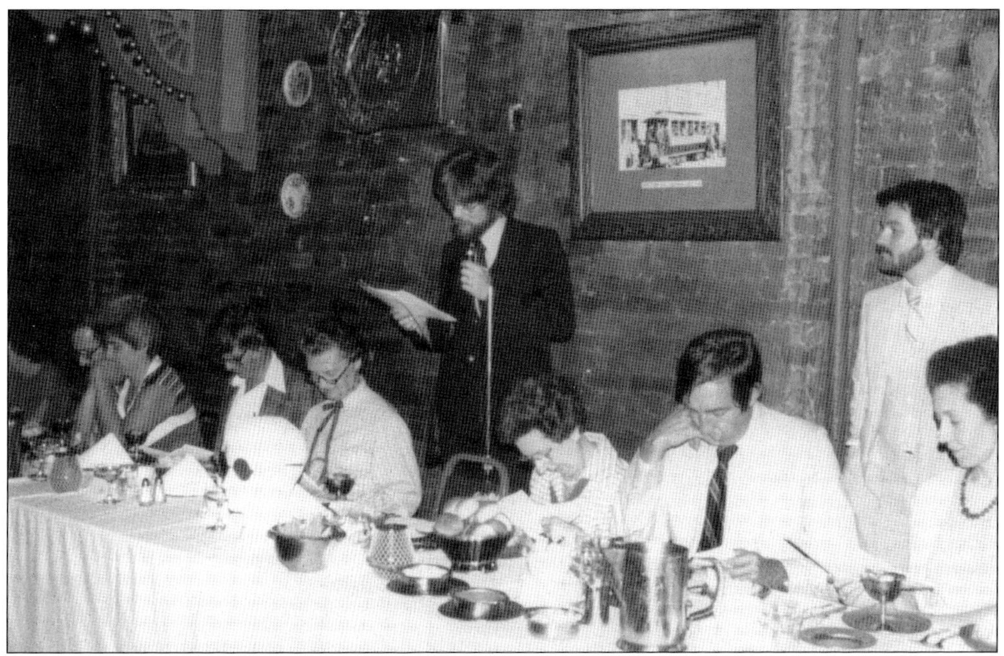

One year later, this image of the summer end party looks almost the same: the venue is again Rosoff's, and Jack Collins is once more at the microphone. There was one change, however: the number of Greek students had doubled in the second year, almost on par with Latin.

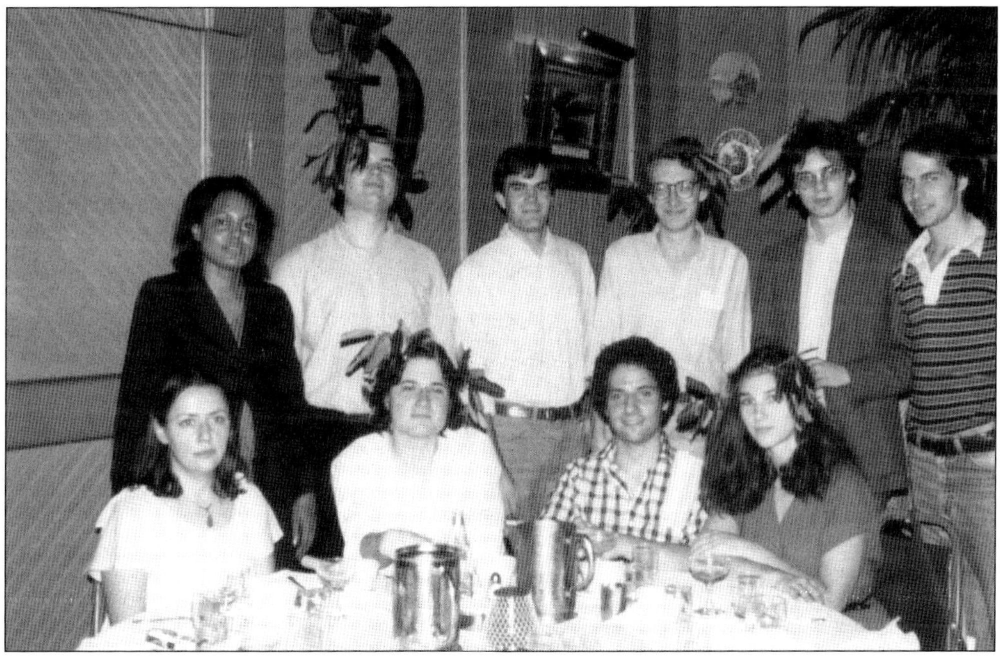

Gail Smith's scholarship increasingly focused on the reception of the classics by 19th- and 20th-century African American thinkers. Her academic interests would later transcend the discipline: in 1991, she was appointed founding director of the CUNY Pipeline Program and, as assistant provost at the GC (1995-2013), served as the principal investigator for several high-profile National Science Foundation and National Institutes of Health bridge programs. Here, she (standing on the left) poses with 1979 graduates.

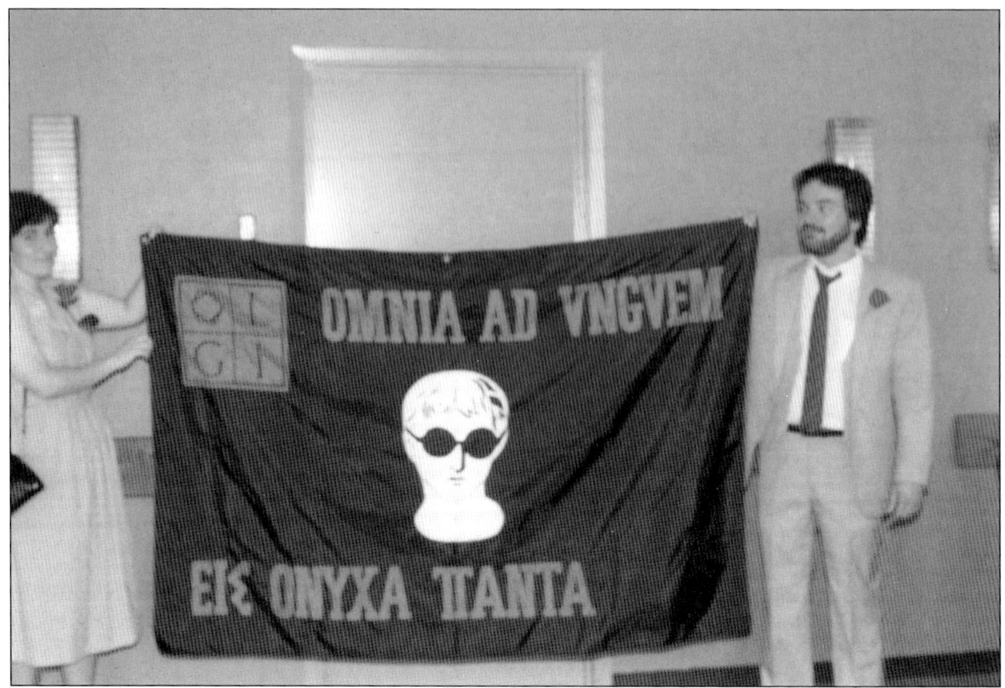

The Institute's official flag, displayed here in 1981, was created soon after the introduction of the Greek program. Along with an embroidered Augustus, it includes the original logo of the GC (upper left), interlocked pentagons meant to represent the five boroughs. Although later dropped by the GC, the icon remains in use by the LGI. The flag's colors, orange and blue, are those of New York City.

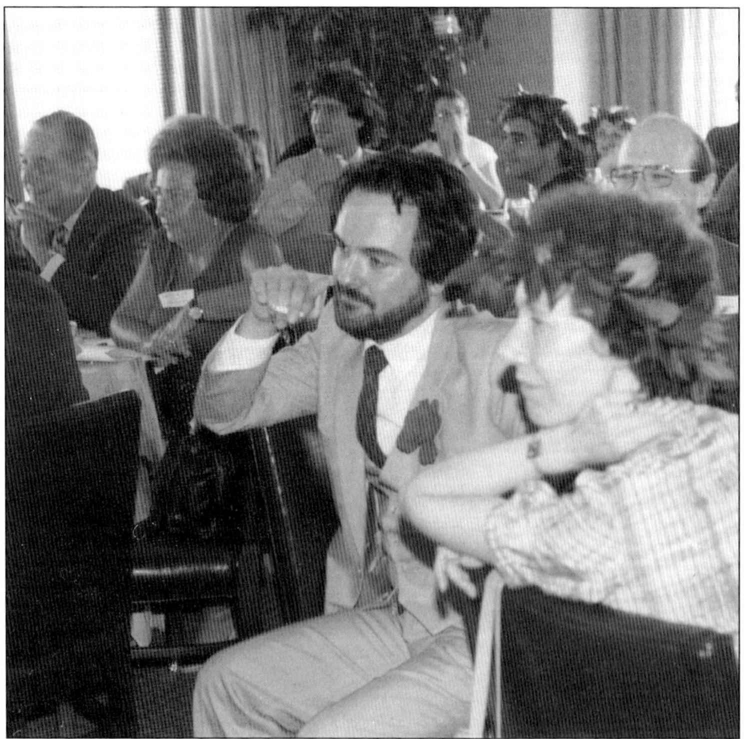

Ethyle Wolfe and her husband, Columbia classics professor Coleman Benedict (to her right), sit with Moreland and Fleischer at the 1981 LGI graduation. The 1980s would prove very favorable to the Institute: CUNY was in reasonably sound financial shape, Wolfe's star was nearing its apogee, and Moreland was appointed associate dean of research and university programs at the GC in 1984. As such, there was strong advocacy and support within CUNY.

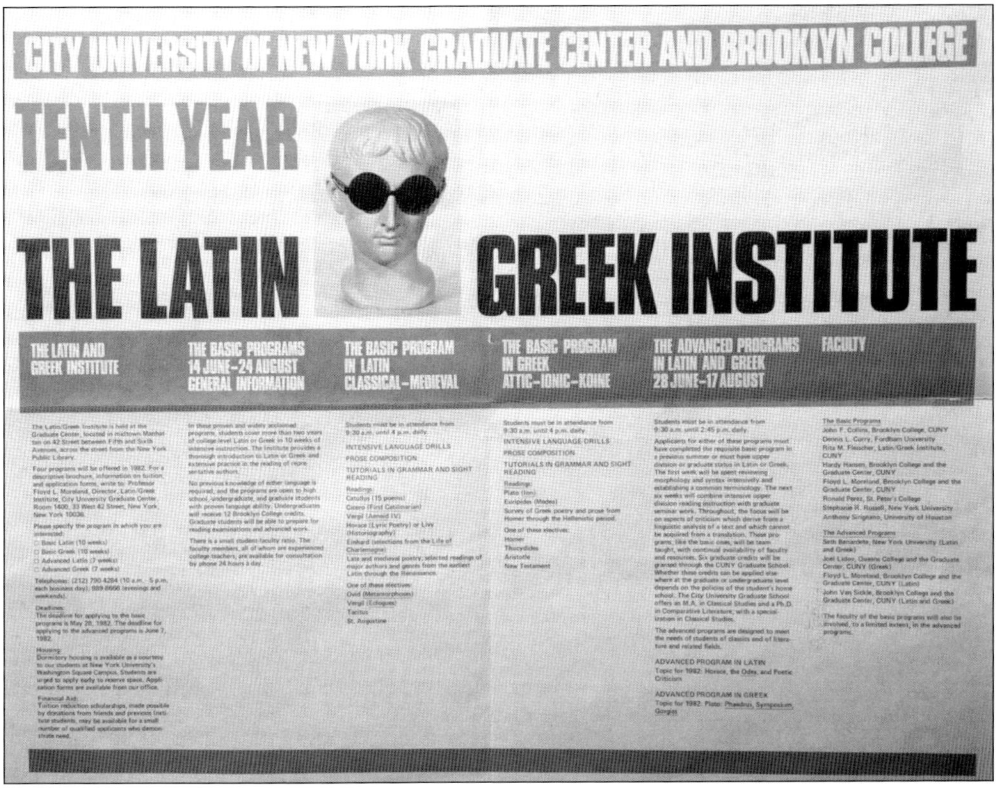

CITY UNIVERSITY OF NEW YORK GRADUATE CENTER AND BROOKLYN COLLEGE

TENTH YEAR

THE LATIN GREEK INSTITUTE

THE LATIN AND GREEK INSTITUTE

THE BASIC PROGRAMS 14 JUNE–24 AUGUST GENERAL INFORMATION

The Latin/Greek Institute is held at the Graduate Center, located in midtown Manhattan on 42 Street between Fifth and Sixth Avenues, across the street from the New York Public Library.

Four programs will be offered in 1982. For a descriptive brochure, information on tuition, and application forms, write to: Professor Floyd L. Moreland, Director, Latin/Greek Institute, City University Graduate Center, Room 1400, 33 West 42 Street, New York, New York 10036.

Please specify the program in which you are interested:

- Basic Latin (10 weeks)
- Basic Greek (10 weeks)
- Advanced Latin (7 weeks)
- Advanced Greek (7 weeks)

Telephone: (212) 790-4284 (10 a.m.–5 p.m. each business day); 889-6666 (evenings and weekends).

Deadlines:
The deadline for applying to the basic programs is May 28, 1982. The deadline for applying to the advanced programs is June 7, 1982.

Housing:
Dormitory housing is available as a courtesy to our students at New York University's Washington Square Campus. Students are urged to apply early to reserve space. Application forms are available from our office.

Financial Aid:
Tuition reduction scholarships, made possible by donations from friends and previous Institute students, may be available for a small number of qualified applicants who demonstrate need.

In these proven and widely acclaimed programs, students cover more than two years of college-level Latin or Greek in 10 weeks of intensive instruction. The Institute provides a thorough introduction to Latin or Greek and extensive practice in the reading of representative authors.

No previous knowledge of either language is required, and the programs are open to high school, undergraduate, and graduate students with proven language ability. Undergraduates will receive 12 Brooklyn College credits. Graduate students will be able to prepare for reading examinations and advanced work.

There is a small student-faculty ratio. The faculty members, all of whom are experienced college teachers, are available for consultation by phone 24 hours a day.

THE BASIC PROGRAM IN LATIN CLASSICAL–MEDIEVAL

Students must be in attendance from 9:30 a.m. until 4 p.m. daily.

INTENSIVE LANGUAGE DRILLS

PROSE COMPOSITION

TUTORIALS IN GRAMMAR AND SIGHT READING

Readings:
Catullus (15 poems)
Cicero (First Catilinarian)
Vergil (Aeneid IV)
Horace (Lyric Poetry) or Livy (Historiography)
Einhard (selections from the Life of Charlemagne)
Late and medieval poetry, selected readings of major authors and genres from the earliest Latin through the Renaissance.

One of these electives:
Ovid (Metamorphoses)
Vergil (Eclogues)
Tacitus
St. Augustine

THE BASIC PROGRAM IN GREEK ATTIC–IONIC–KOINE

Students must be in attendance from 9:30 a.m. until 4 p.m. daily.

INTENSIVE LANGUAGE DRILLS

PROSE COMPOSITION

TUTORIALS IN GRAMMAR AND SIGHT READING

Readings:
Plato (Ion)
Euripides (Medea)
Survey of Greek poetry and prose from Homer through the Hellenistic period.

One of these electives:
Homer
Thucydides
Aristotle
New Testament

THE ADVANCED PROGRAMS IN LATIN AND GREEK 28 JUNE–17 AUGUST

Students must be in attendance from 9:30 a.m. until 2:45 p.m. daily.

Applicants for either of these programs must have completed the requisite basic program in a previous summer or must have upper division or graduate status in Latin or Greek. The first week will be spent reviewing morphology and syntax intensively and establishing a common terminology. The next six weeks will combine intensive upper division reading instruction with graduate seminar work. Throughout, the focus will be on aspects of criticism which derive from a linguistic analysis of a text and which cannot be acquired from a translation. These programs, like the basic ones, will be team taught, with continual availability of faculty and resources. Six graduate credits will be granted through the CUNY Graduate School. Whether these credits can be applied elsewhere at the graduate or undergraduate level depends on the policies of the student's home school. The City University Graduate School offers an M.A. in Classical Studies and a Ph.D. in Comparative Literature, with a specialization in Classical Studies.

The advanced programs are designed to meet the needs of students of classics and of literature and related fields.

ADVANCED PROGRAM IN LATIN
Topic for 1982: Horace, the Odes, and Poetic Criticism

ADVANCED PROGRAM IN GREEK
Topic for 1982: Plato: Phaedrus, Symposium, Gorgias

FACULTY

The Basic Programs
John F. Collins, Brooklyn College, CUNY
Dennis L. Curry, Fordham University
Rita M. Fleischer, Latin/Greek Institute, CUNY
Hardy Hansen, Brooklyn College and the Graduate Center, CUNY
Floyd L. Moreland, Brooklyn College and the Graduate Center, CUNY
Ronald Perez, St. Peter's College
Stephanie R. Russell, New York University
Anthony Sirignano, University of Houston

The Advanced Programs
Seth Benardete, New York University (Latin and Greek)
Joel Lidov, Queens College and the Graduate Center, CUNY (Greek)
Floyd L. Moreland, Brooklyn College and the Graduate Center, CUNY (Latin)
John Van Sickle, Brooklyn College and the Graduate Center, CUNY (Latin and Greek)

The faculty of the basic programs will also be involved, to a limited extent, in the advanced programs.

The year 1982 is one of the best-documented years in the Institute's history, a reflection, in part, of promotional efforts connected to its 10th anniversary. The first decade had been an unqualified success: enrollments were strong, Greek was an immediate draw, and the Institute had received repeated national recognition. The GC dispatched photographers on various occasions, including the LGI's graduation at the famed Rainbow Room.

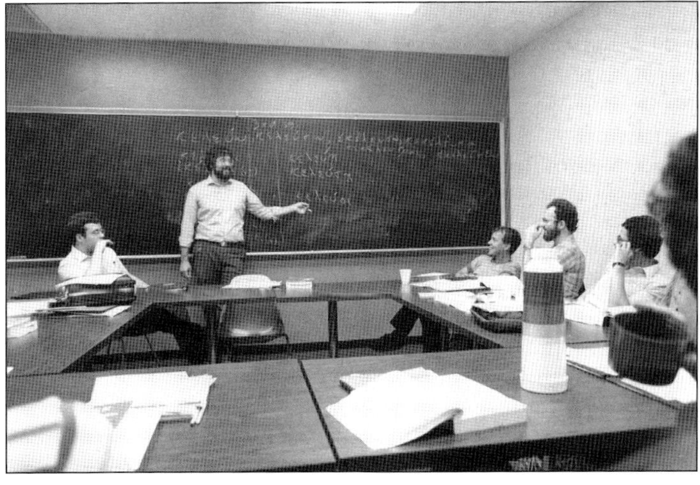

A Graduate Center photographer captured this in-class moment, which, based on the board materials, can be identified as Day 5 of the SGI, either the second hour of morning drill or afternoon review. In the SGI's first few years, a verb synopsis was a feature of the second drill hour. The instructor, Dennis Curry, taught in the SGI from 1981 to 1985 before pursuing a career in the Foreign Service.

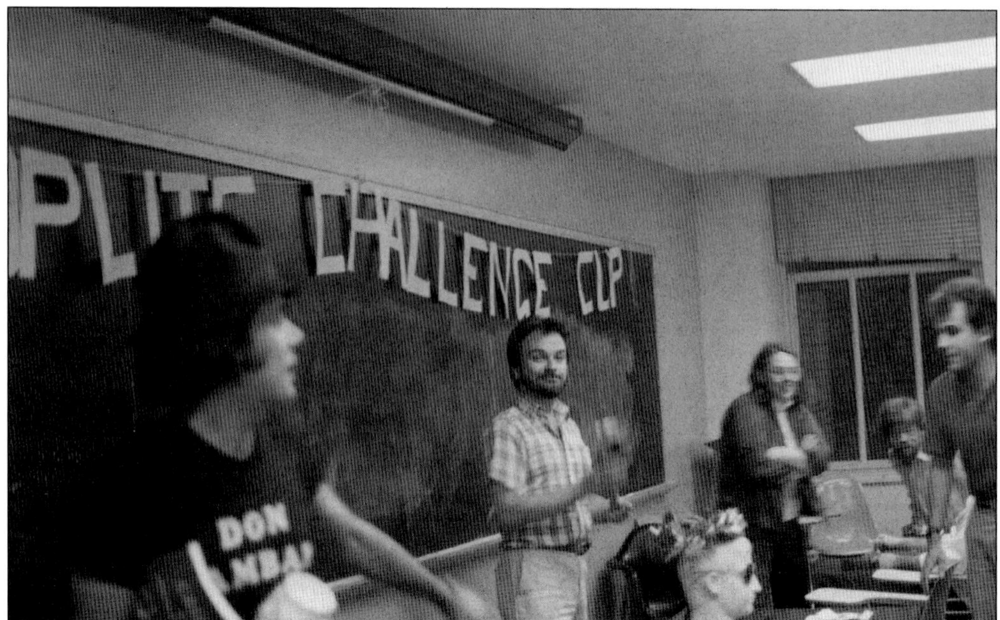

The 1982 Hoplite Challenge Cup was the first to be documented in photographs. This annual and eagerly anticipated contest is held at the end of the grammar portion of the SGI. Though the specifics have evolved over the decades, the basic competition consists of a duel of verb morphology between the students and faculty. Its rules and distinct features are detailed in Chapter 6.

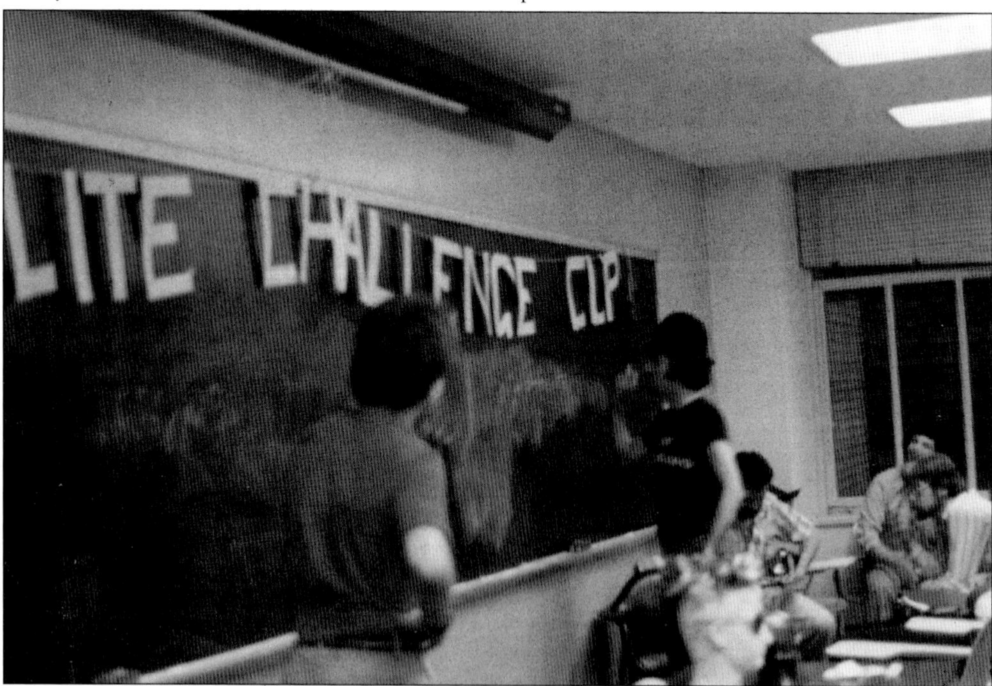

For years, Hansen competed in the guise of "Don Lambano"—the game's unrivaled boss (and a clever play on the verbs δίδωμι [aorist participle: δόν] and λαμβάνω, which are "give" and "take"). Here, "the Don" prepares to write the verb form requested by his opponent. Whenever the Don erred—a rare occurrence—he would begin the next drill hour with a paper bag over his head, inscribed with the correct form.

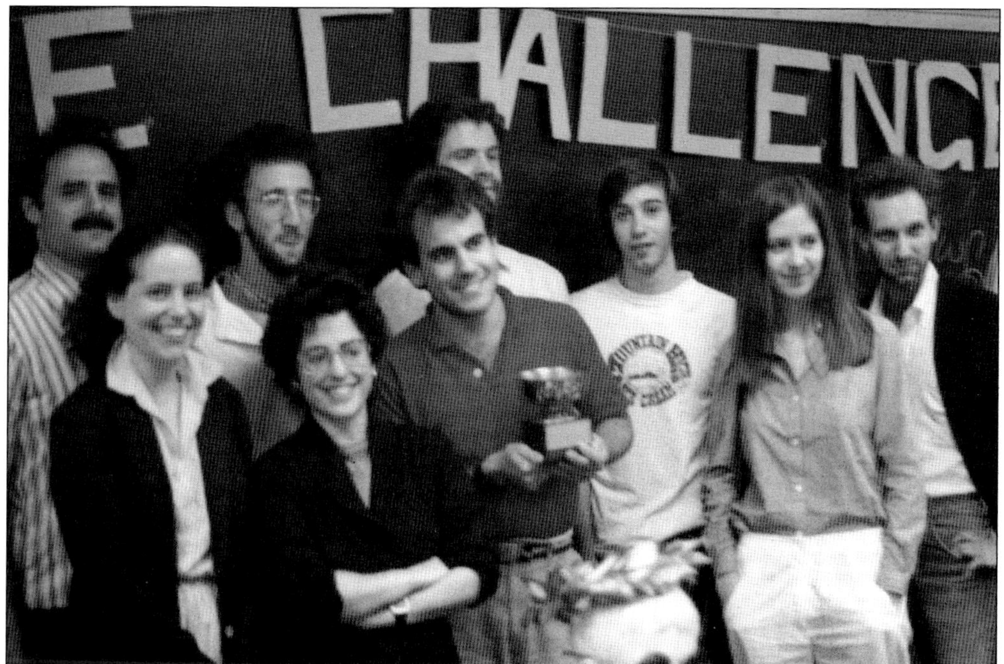

Though it was a hard-fought contest, the 1982 students ultimately emerged victorious. In commemoration of their triumph, the winning team posed with the Hoplite Challenge Cup in hand. Moreland had the trophy, inscribed with "LGI," made soon after the contest became a regular feature of the SGI.

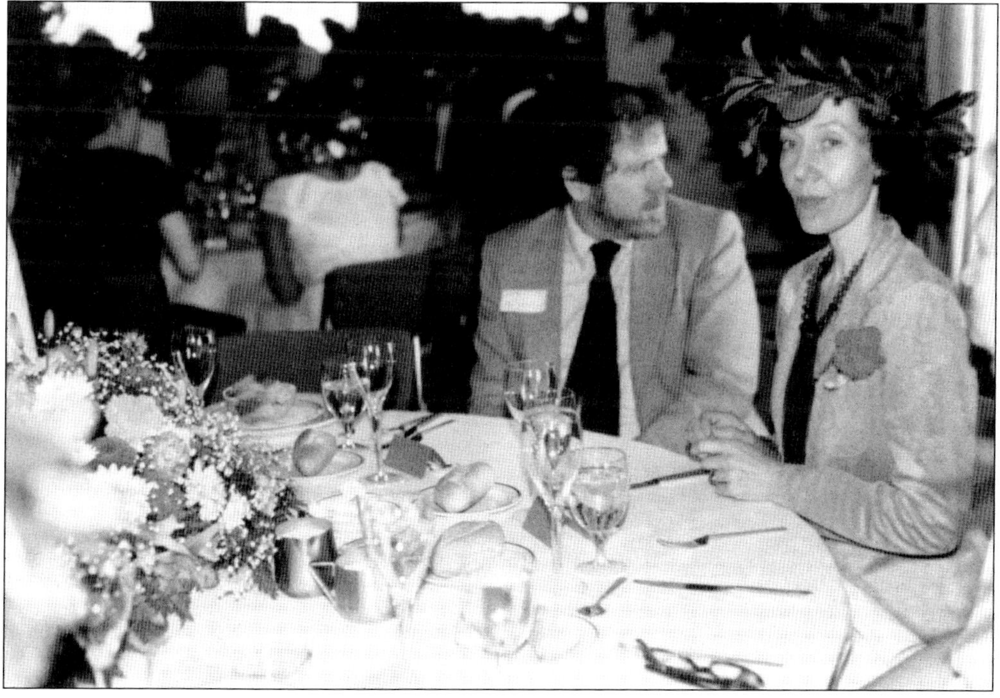

The 1982 end-of-summer celebration was held at the Rainbow Room in Rockefeller Center. It was a lavish, sit-down affair attended by almost 150 celebrants: 106 students, 15 faculty, and dozens of guests and VIPs. Here, Fleischer, looking regal in her wreath, observes the proceedings. (Courtesy of the OBDE, CUNY GC.)

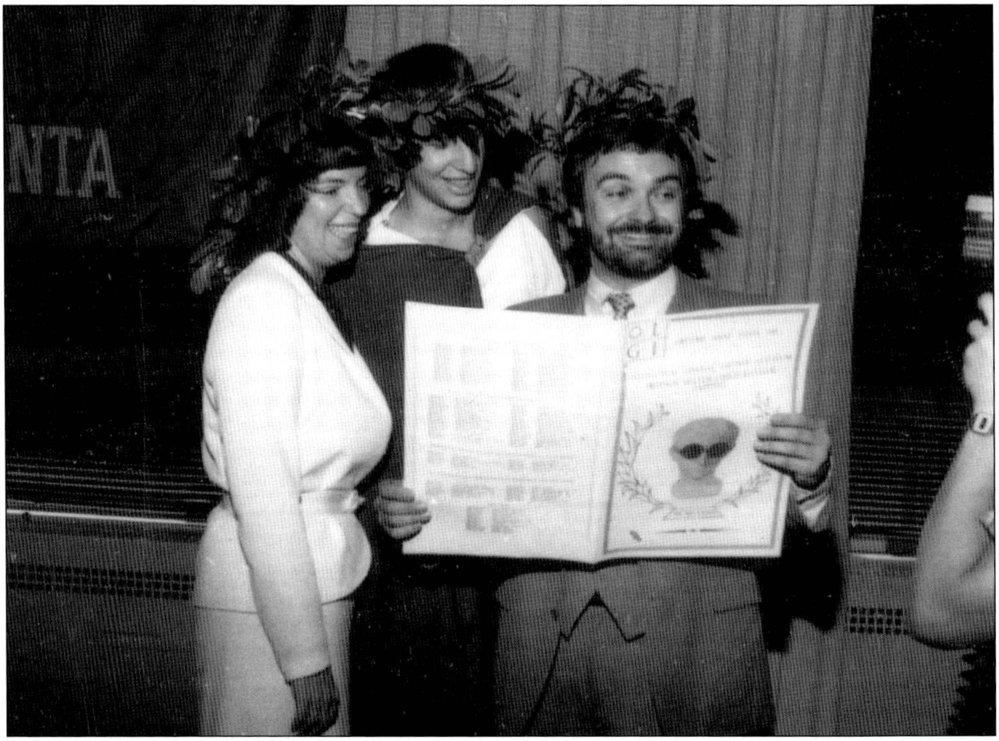

Moreland reads from the 1982 party program flanked by Barbara Mickus (L 1975) and an appropriately attired Gideon Rose (G 1982). Rose, following receipt of a BA in classics (Yale) and a PhD in government (Harvard), went on to a distinguished career in foreign policy. In a contribution to *Foreign Affairs* (March/April 2021), he likened the January 6 occupation of the Capitol to a "mass live production of Euripides' *Bacchae*." (Courtesy of the OBDE, CUNY GC.)

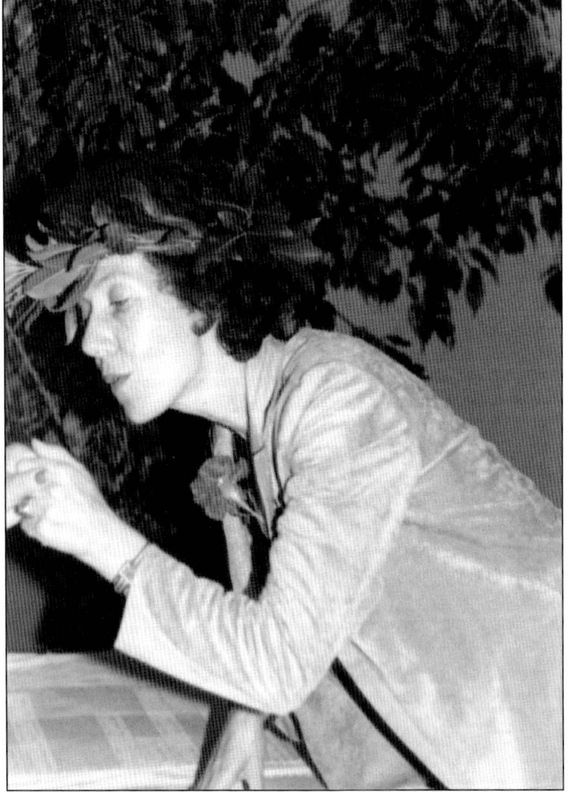

Rita Fleischer greets arriving students, guests, and VIPs. Through its first 50 years of existence, Fleischer has participated in every summer (with the exception of the Covid pandemic, 2020–2021). Over this timeframe, her role has evolved; significantly, she has been the one constant shared by almost every single alumnus/a, regardless of program.

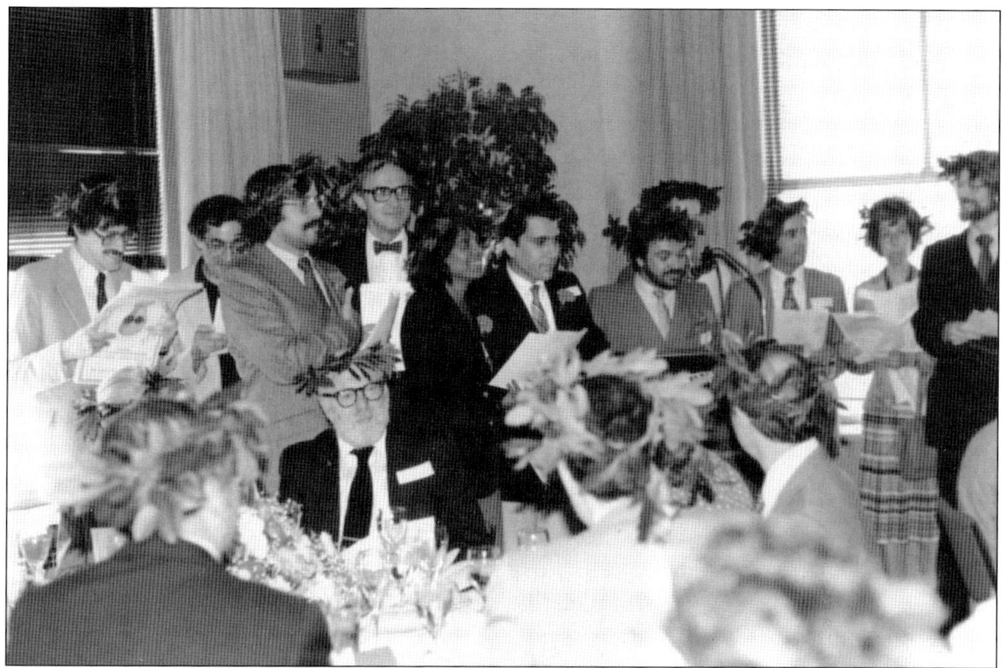

The majority of the faculty assembled adjacent to the podium to lead the traditional singing of *Gaudeamus Igitur*. From left to right Joel Lidov, Seth Benardete, Dennis Curry, John Van Sickle, Smith, Ron Perez, Moreland, Ken Rothwell (behind), Hansen, Fleischer, and Collins. (Courtesy of the OBDE, CUNY GC.)

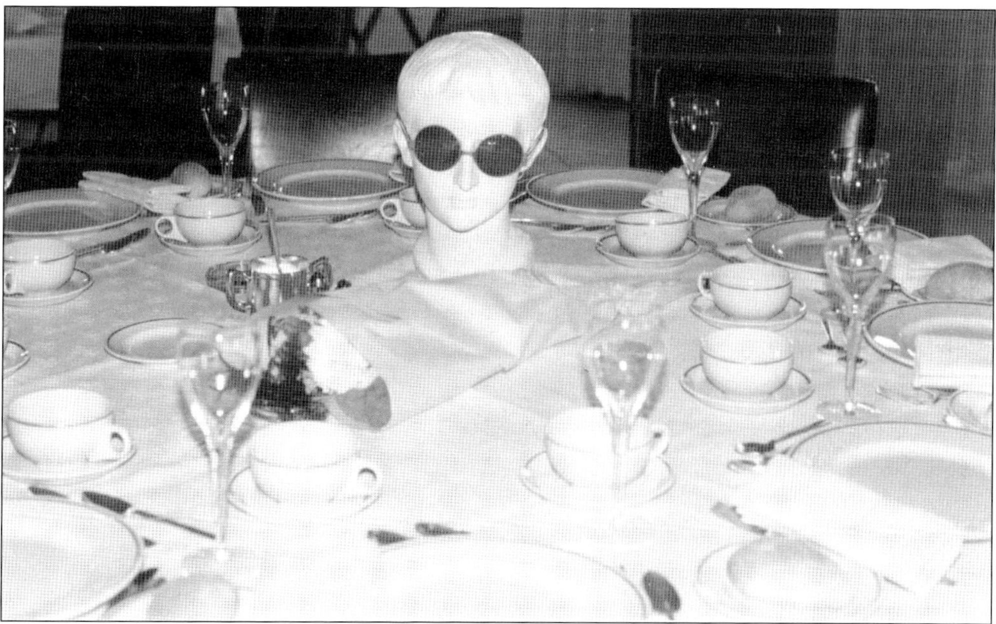

This photograph of the Institute's mascot amid the table setting captures the refinement of the event. Located on the 65th floor of the RCA (now Comcast) building, the Rainbow Room opened in 1934. Its windowed space offers fantastic views of the city. (Courtesy of the OBDE, CUNY GC.)

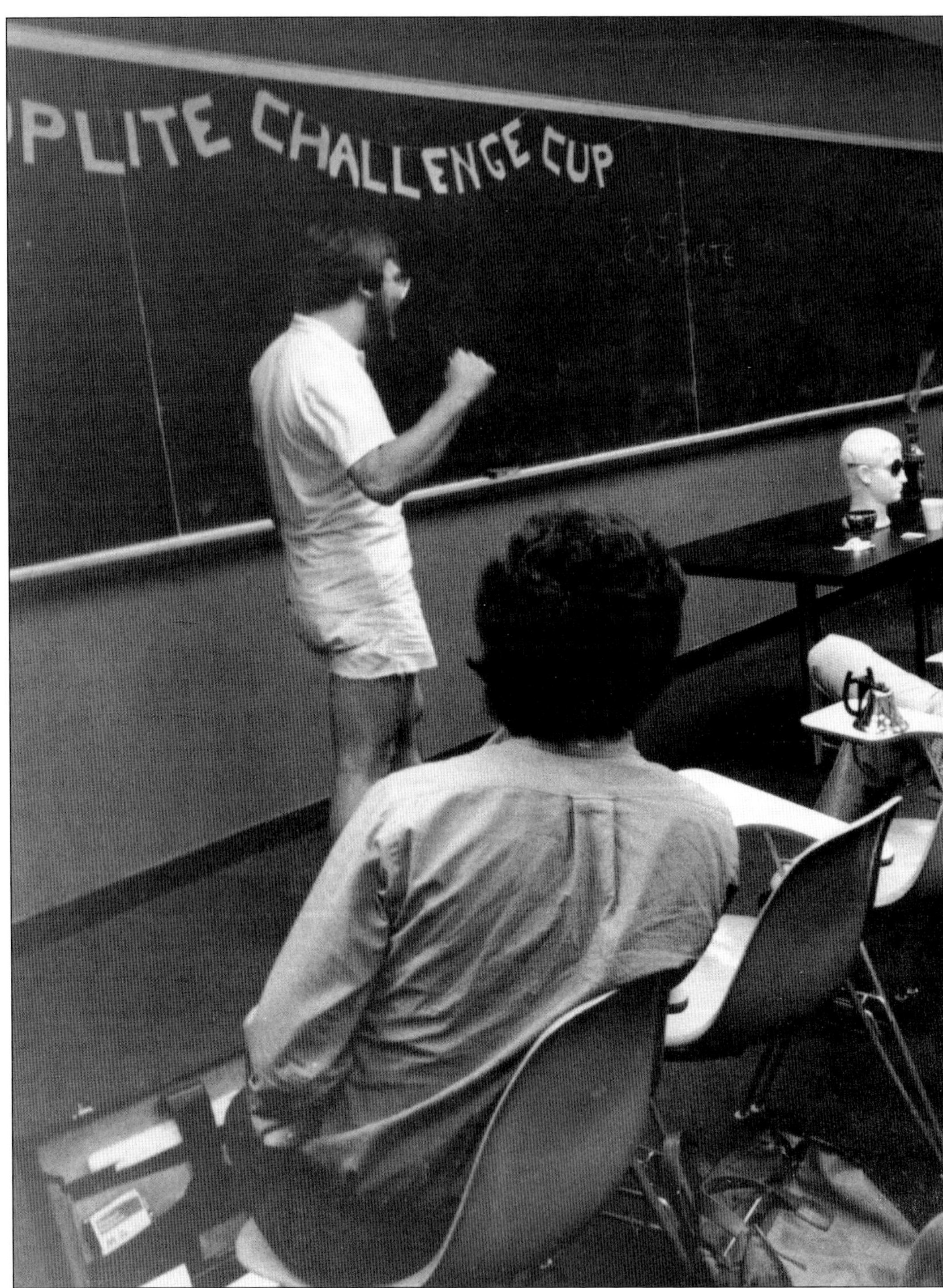

A photographer from the Graduate Center captured this moment from a mid-1980s Hoplite Challenge Cup. Given the reaction of the students, it appears that a student challenger has just scored against the Don. Among student competitors, Hansen has always been considered the ultimate opponent and besting him a well-earned source of pride. Though the contest is now a highlight of the summer, it began as something of

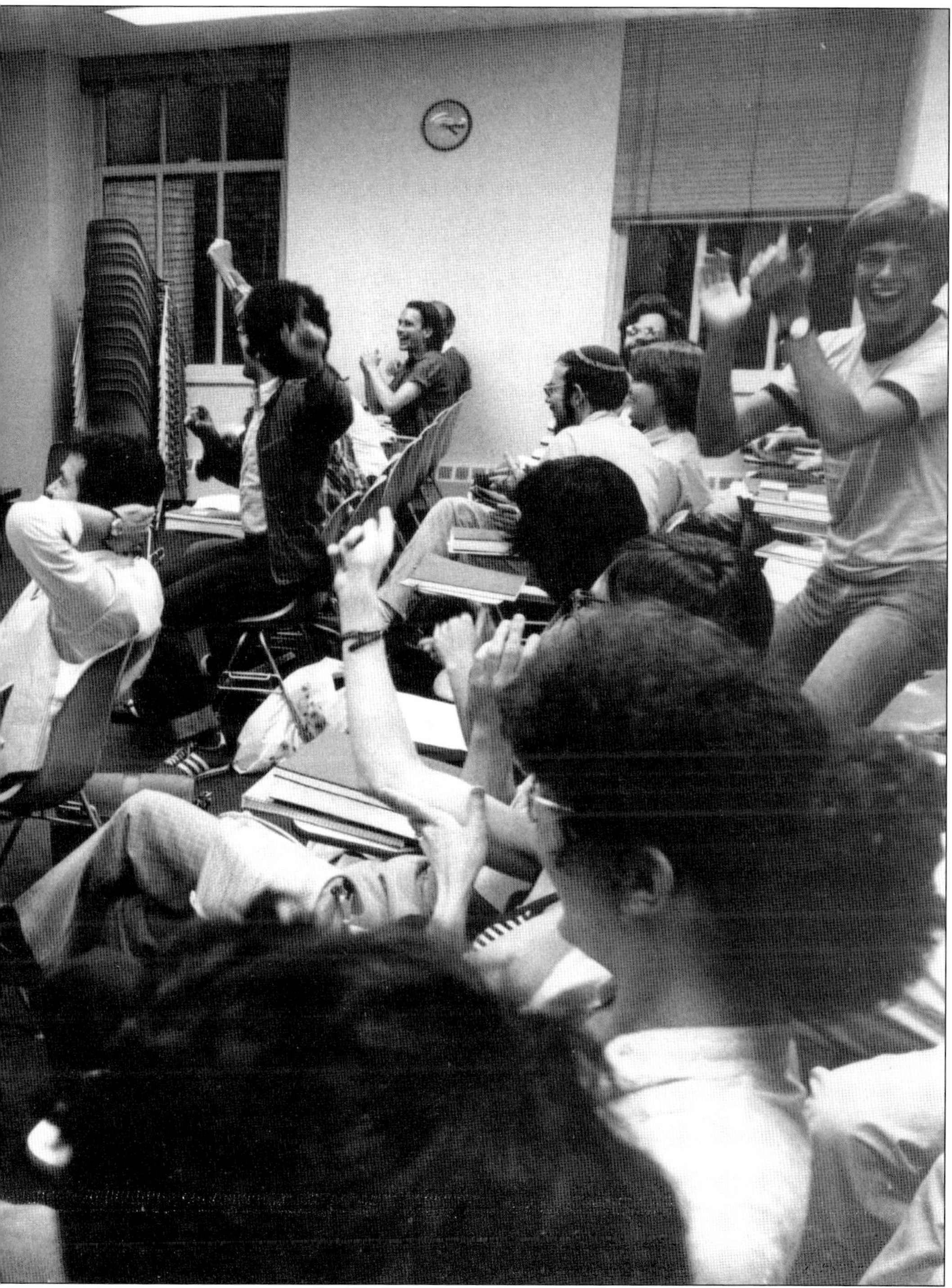

an artifice: students in the inaugural summer of the SGI asked the faculty to drill them on verb forms, to which Quinn would respond that this was good practice for the (then nonexistent) Hoplite Challenge Cup. After students inquired as to when this would take place, Hansen and Quinn devised one. (Courtesy of the OBDE, CUNY GC.)

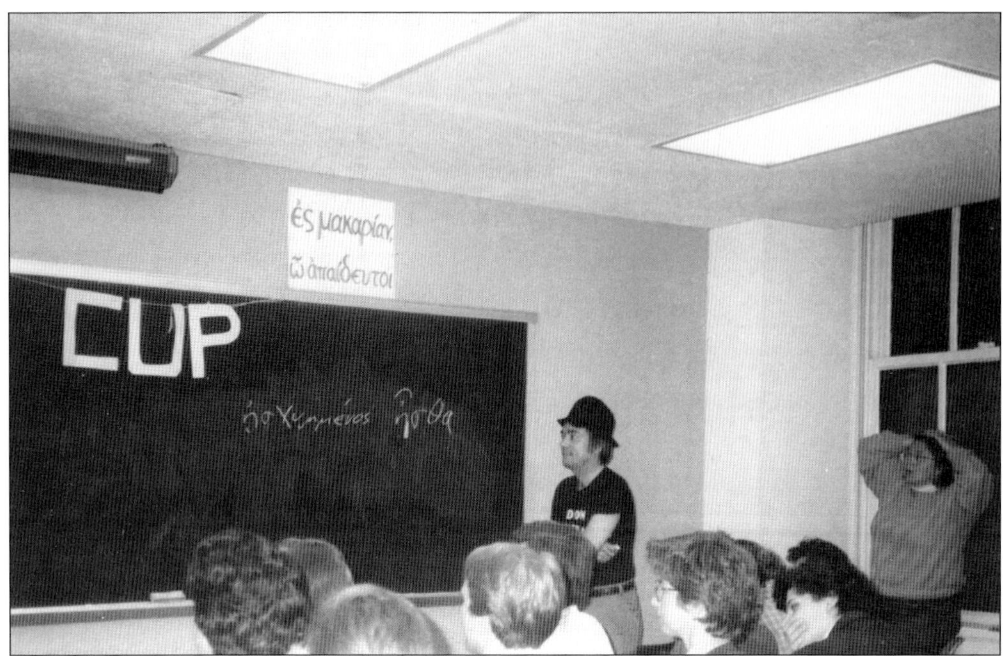

At the 1986 Hoplite Challenge Cup, Hansen awaits completion of his opponent's verb form as Russell looks on intently. With more than 15,800 possible forms of the 114 verbs mastered by Day 29, the ability of students to compete is itself a testament to the LGI's effectiveness: the students had learned the Greek alphabet a mere six weeks before.

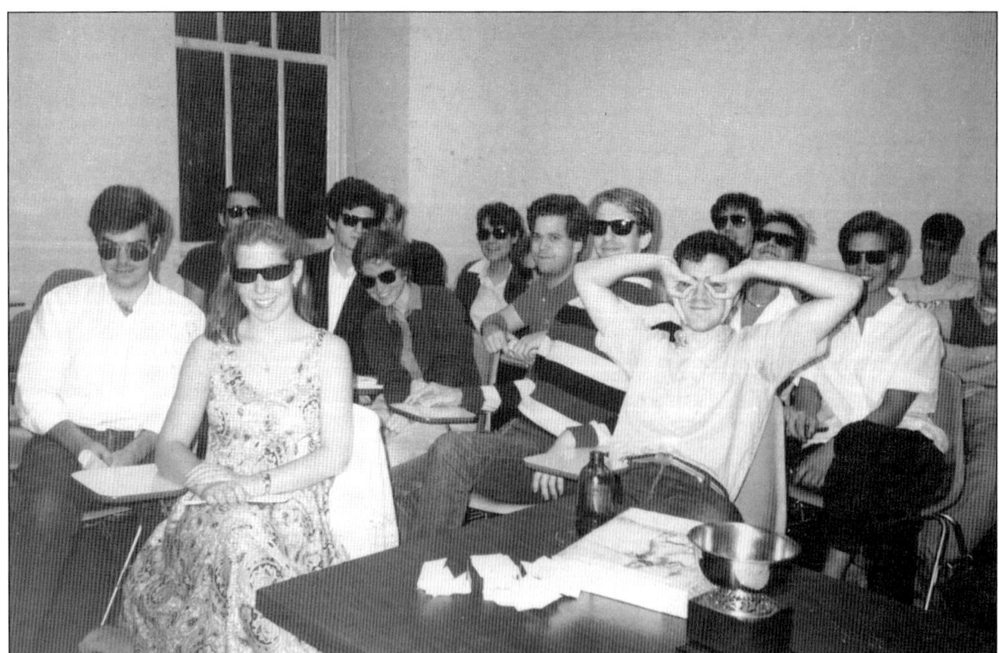

Spectators at the 1986 Hoplite Challenge Cup honor the Don. The character was inspired by the iconic *Godfather* movies, which, though already more than a decade old (Part I was released in 1972, and Part II followed in 1974), remained incredibly popular in the public imagination. As students became less familiar with the films, the Don was eventually retired.

Jason Schwalb, appropriately attired in a tunic, celebrates his victory over Hansen in the 1987 Hoplite Challenge Cup. Schwalb later received an MD from Yale and entered practice as a neurosurgeon. As noted earlier, a number of doctors and other medical professionals are counted among LGI alumni/ae.

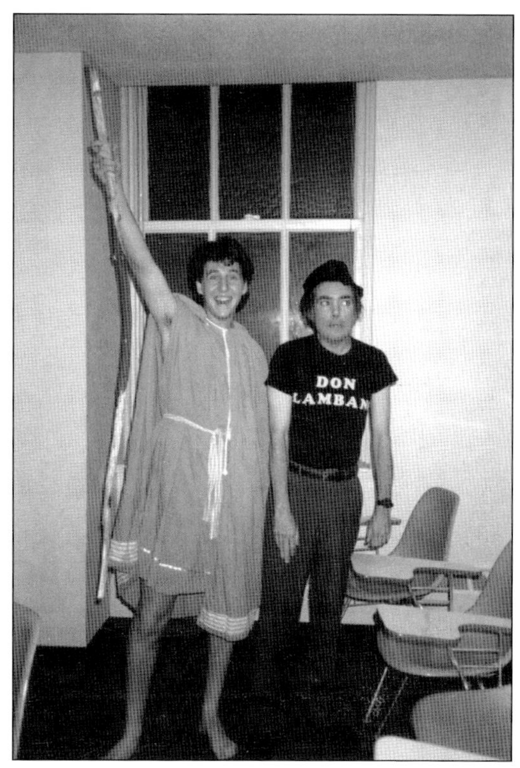

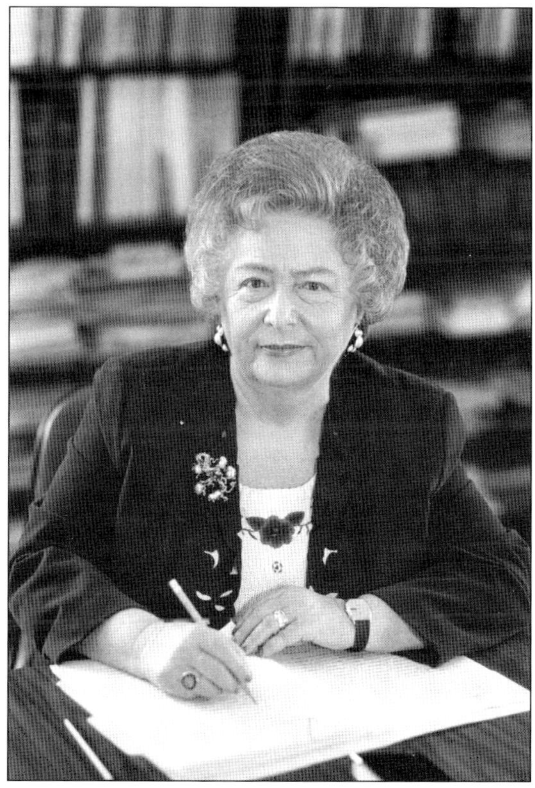

In 1989, Ethyle Wolfe retired from Brooklyn College. In recognition, the college renamed its Humanities Institute, which she had founded, in her honor. Her last day, memorialized in this photograph, meant that the LGI lost its initial patron and most ardent champion. Fortunately, the Institute was by then well established.

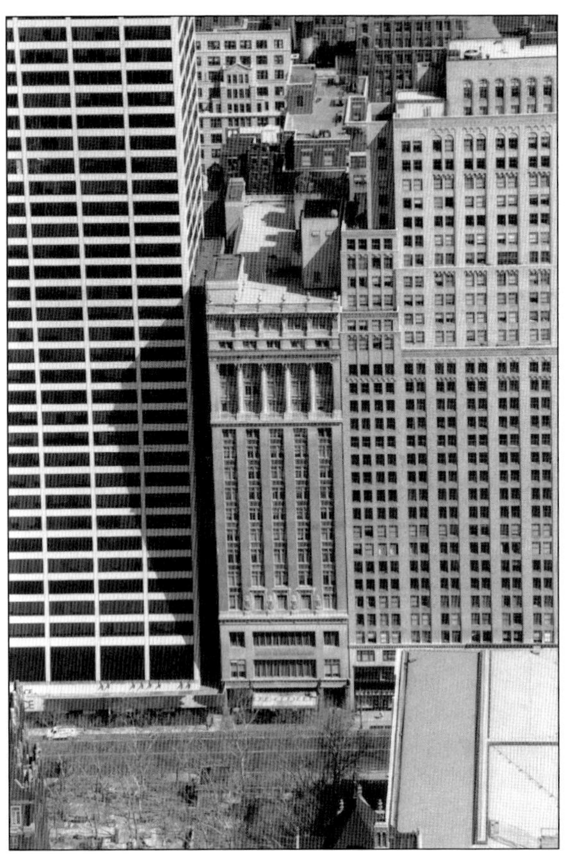

In 1989, the GC leased several floors in the neighboring Grace Building (to the left), designed by Gordon Bunshaft and completed in 1972. For a time, students moved back and forth between the buildings, though LGI offices and classes were eventually consolidated on the 15th and 40th floors of the Grace building. (Courtesy of the OBDE, CUNY GC.)

SLI students (from left) Jay Elliott, Jay Mueller (G 1997), and Robert Farrell (G 1997) enjoy the magnificent views afforded the Grace Building while on a study break in 1998. All three pursued careers in academe and remain close friends: Elliott and Mueller received doctorates at Chicago in Philosophy and at NYU in classics (respectively), while Farrell completed a master's in liberal studies (CUNY GC) as well as an MLS (SUNY Buffalo).

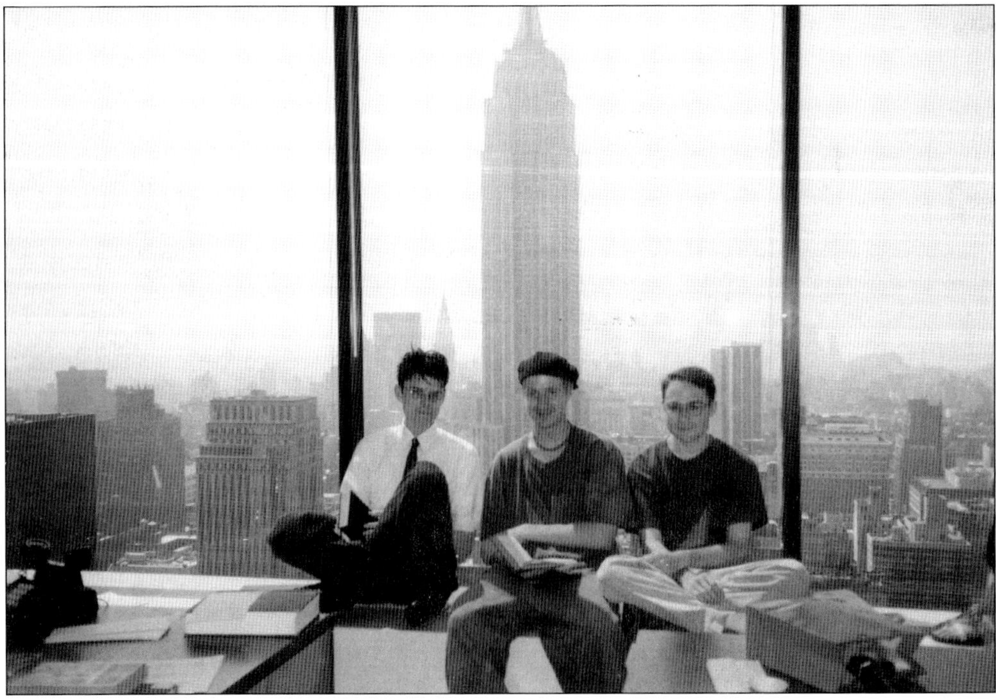

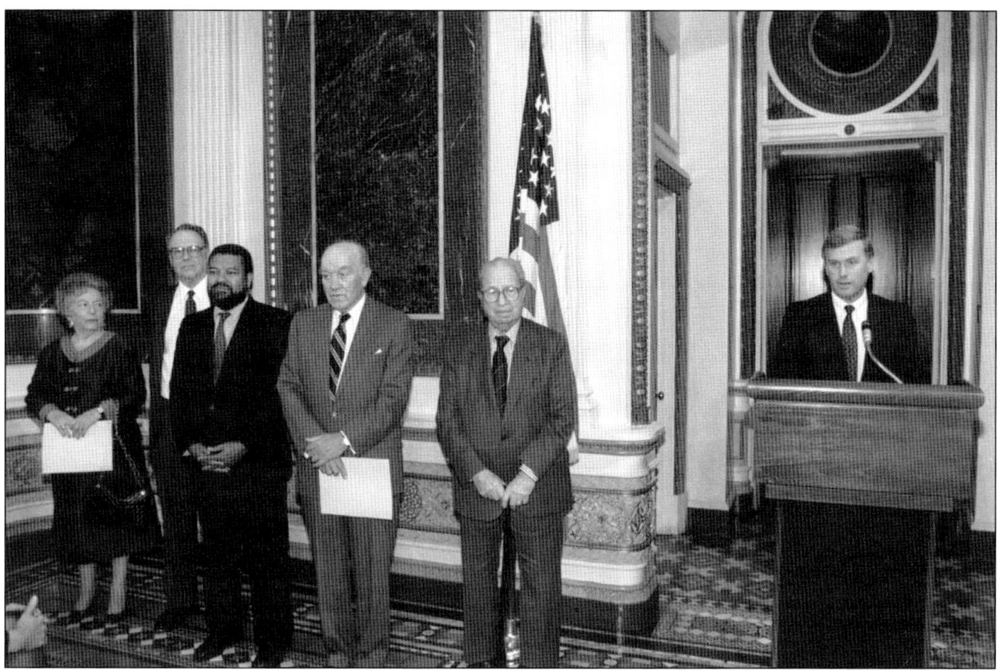

In an acknowledgment of her promotion of the humanities, Wolfe received the National Humanities Medal from Vice Pres. Dan Quayle in 1990. In addition to the LGI and Humanities Institute, her most significant contribution was the establishment of Brooklyn College's renowned core curriculum, which was shaped around a prescribed set of courses beginning with classical civilizations.

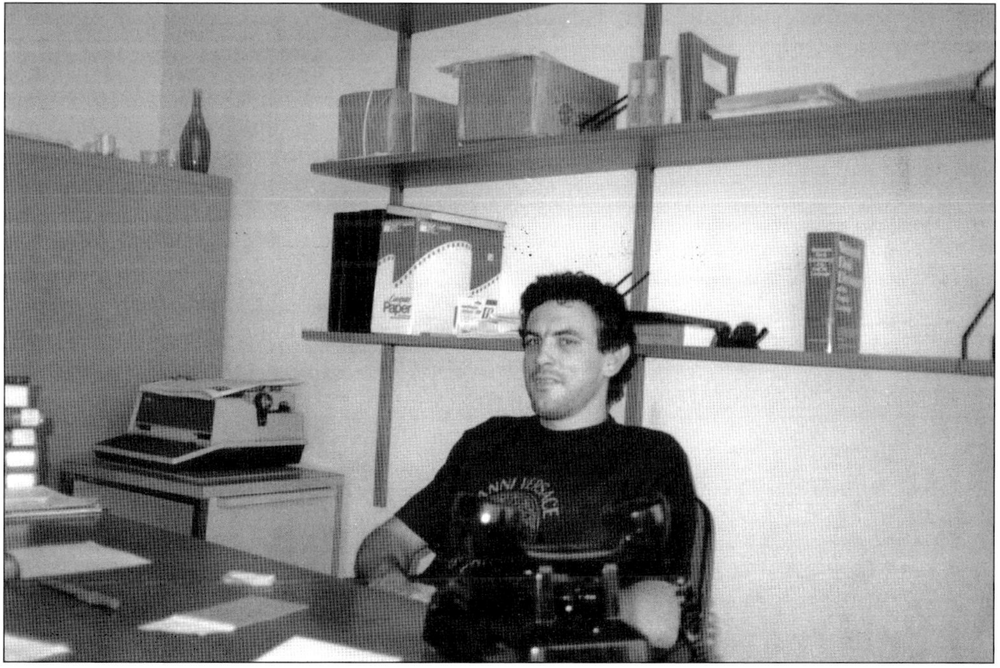

Alan Fishbone (G 1985) joined the Latin faculty in 1991. A talented Latinist, he supervised, chaired, and taught in both the basic and upper Latin programs through 2011. He was a charismatic instructor who very much defined the Latin program for the two decades of his leadership.

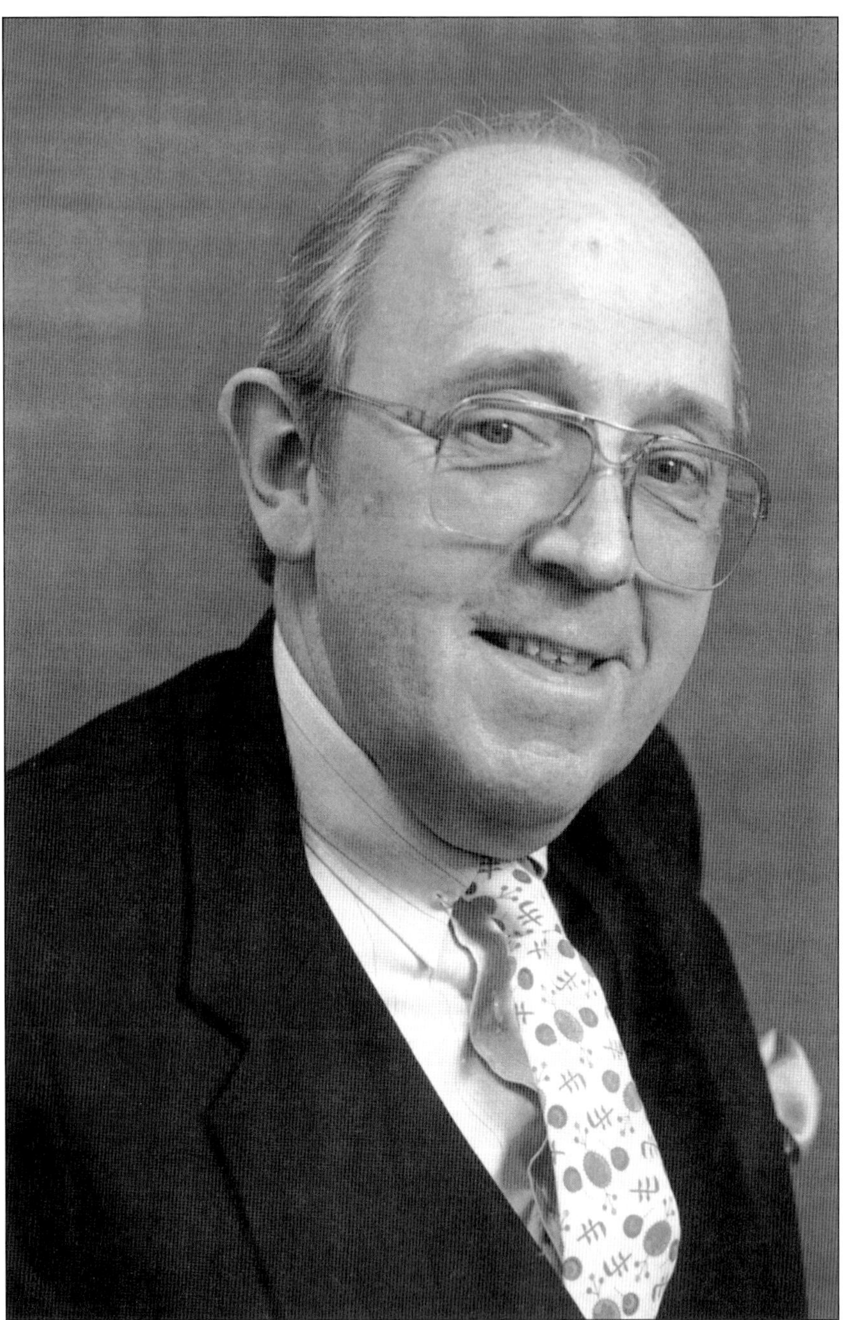

Gerald M. Quinn was Hansen's partner in developing the Basic Greek program. His premature passing created an absence in the tetrarchy of Moreland, Fleischer, Hansen, and Quinn—one felt acutely in this compilation of the LGI's history. Quinn was a Brooklyn native who completed his undergraduate studies at Fordham University and received master's and doctoral degrees in classical philology at Harvard. He taught at Fordham from 1967 to 1968 before moving to CUNY's Lehman College. In 1979, he rejoined Fordham as an assistant dean. Another adept administrator (there have been many in the LGI's history), he was promoted through the ranks and became dean of Fordham's Lincoln Center campus in 1989. (Courtesy of the Fordham University Archives.)

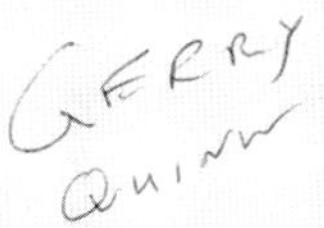

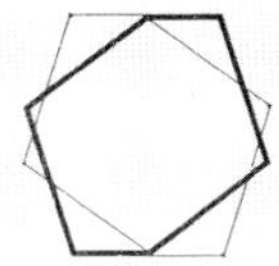

The Graduate School and University Center
of The City University of New York

Office of the Dean for Student Affairs / Box 650
Graduate Center: 33 West 42 Street, New York, N.Y. 10036-8099
212 642-2105

14 November 1991

Dear LGI Friends,

It is with deep sorrow that I share with you the news of the sudden death of Gerald M. Quinn. Many of you in both the Greek and Latin programs knew Gerry as an inspired teacher, a caring and compassionate human being, and a gifted administrator. He taught with us for many summers before his appointment as Dean at Fordham University. Even since then, Gerry came back now and again to spend a summer with us (those in the 1991 Greek Institute enjoyed the special pleasure of his guidance), and even when he was not able to identify an entire summer to spend at the LGI, he came back for visits: teaching an occasional class, competing at the annual Hoplite Challenge Cup, and celebrating the achievements of LGI students at our end-of-the-summer banquets. The Latin/Greek Institute was always special to Gerry, and even when he was unable to be here with us, the students and the activities here on 42nd Street were constantly in his mind. He generously contributed to the Scholarship Fund each year, and always generously gave of his time and wisdom when LGI people sought him out.

Gerry Quinn and Hardy Hansen crafted and shaped the Greek program in the winter of 1977-78, and many a student (both in this program and across country) have since been trained on "Hansen and Quinn." I remember vividly participating in practice classroom sessions that winter, tired from a long day of work, but amazed and invigorated by Gerry's (and Hardy's) energy and enthusiasm. The Greek Institute would come into being the next summer, but one could almost visualize it emerging and taking shape out of Gerry's energetic enthusiasm. He never seemed to tire of his work, especially when the nature of his work meant so much to him. And the Institute meant a great deal. He was a dreamer in the best possible sense of the word, for he worked relentlessly to make the dreams that mattered come true. The Greek Institute, for him, was a dream that mattered a great deal. We inherit the fruit of those dreams.

Gerry was killed suddenly in an auto accident on November 12. We are diminished by his absence, but we continue to be enriched by all he has given us.

Floyd L. Moreland

When the development of the basic program in Greek began in earnest, Gerry Quinn was teaching in the Latin Institute and had a thorough understanding of its methodologies and the depth of engagement required. He then taught full-time in the Greek program from its inaugural year (1978) through 1981, and again in 1988 and 1991, with guest spots in between. On November 12, 1991, he died in a traffic accident in New Jersey; he was only 50 years old. Moreland informed the LGI community in the letter presented here. His death occurred as the second edition of Hansen and Quinn (H&Q) was about to go to press; of his colleague, Hansen writes in its acknowledgments, "He was unique, and irreplaceable." Fordham subsequently raised $100,000 and renamed its Lincoln Center Library in his honor.

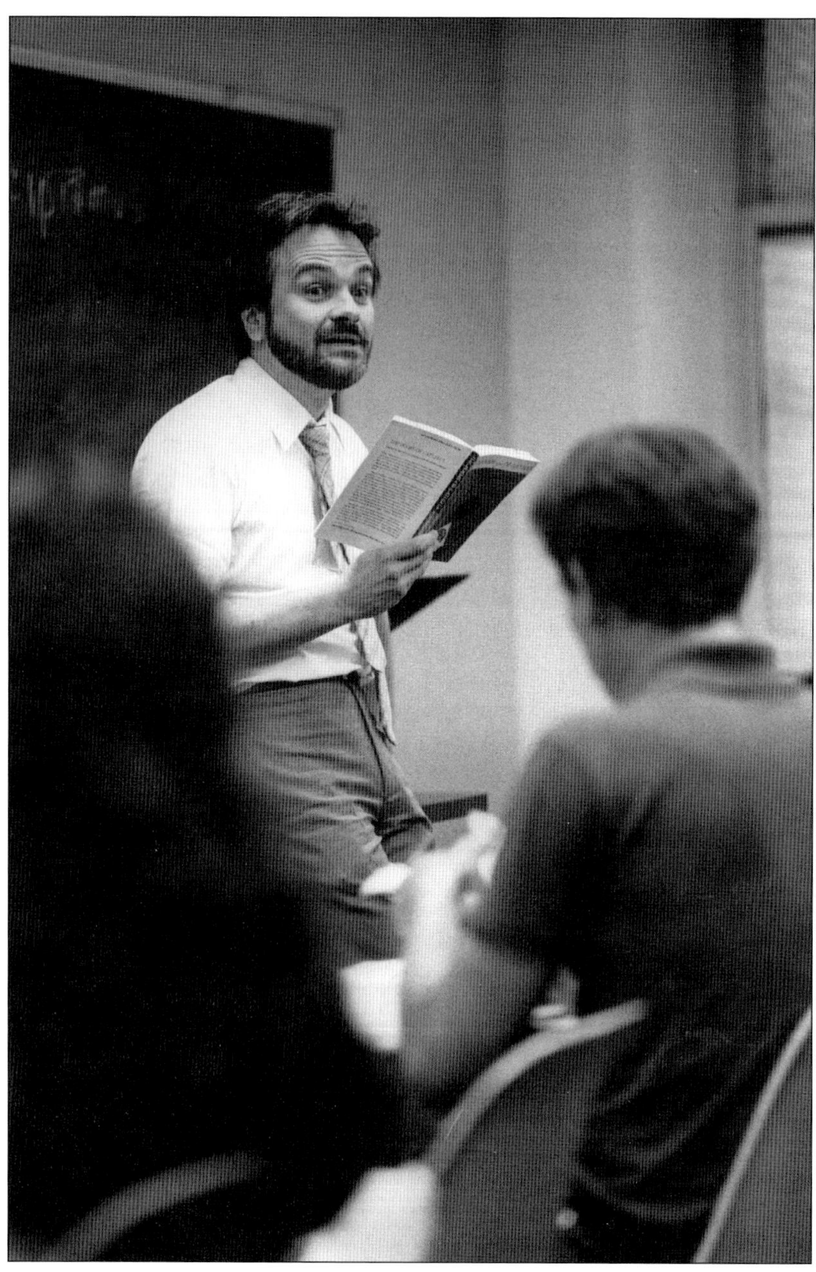

In 1980, CUNY appointed Floyd Moreland as director of the CUNY Bachelor of Arts program. Established in 1971, the CUNY BA is a nontraditional program that allows students to curate their own studies. By the late 1970s, the University Faculty Senate (UFS) had concerns about its quality and demanded better oversight. Moreland's success with the LGI was by then well and widely known, and he was considered ideal for the role. In only a few short years, he addressed the UFS's concerns, and additional appointments at the GC followed soon thereafter: associate dean of research and university programs, associate provost, dean of students, and, finally, as the newly created vice president for student affairs. In the fall of 1992, he stepped down from the directorship of the LGI, passing the reins to Hardy Hansen. He officially retired from the university five years later. Although he made only the occasional visit in subsequent years, the LGI remains a testament to his genius for curricular design and commitment to the highest instructional quality.

Michelle Kwintner, here enjoying a piece of Hansen's midsummer birthday cake in 1998, was a two-time graduate (L 1983 and AL 1986) and later an SGI faculty member (1994–1996 and 1998–1999). She was first introduced to the classics when, as a high school senior, she enrolled in an evening course at Brooklyn College. She received a BA and PhD in classics at Cornell and later published a Bryn Mawr Commentary on Euripides's *Medea*.

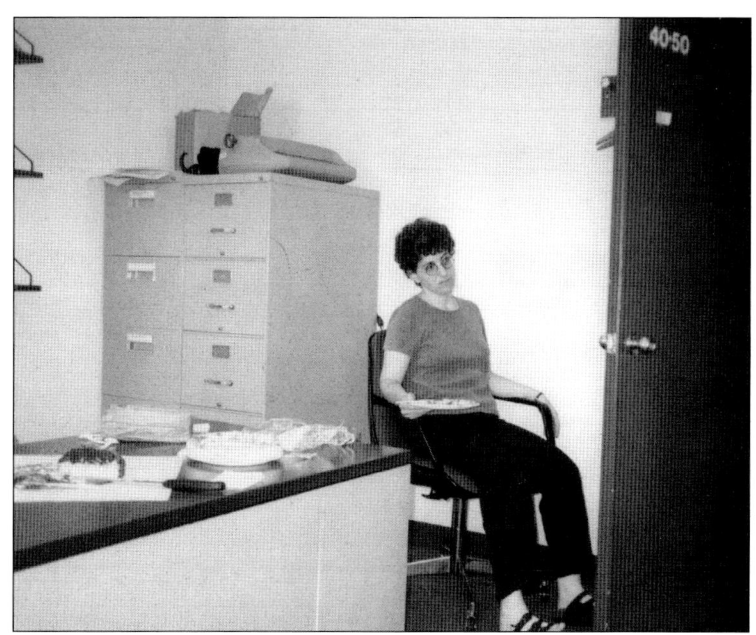

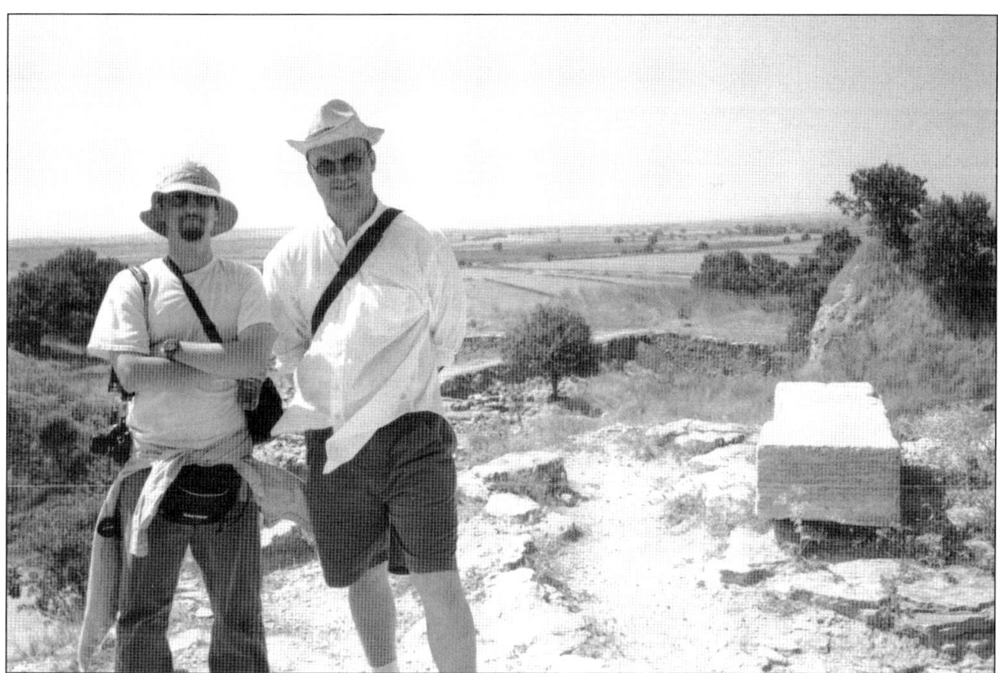

On a break from the American Academy in Rome's Classical Summer School, James Hunt (right) and the author visit the ruins of Troy in the summer of 1998. Hunt (L 1993 and G 1994) was a program assistant in 1996 and 1997 and subsequently SLI faculty (2001–2003, 2005). Hunt's appointment to the teaching staff reflects the increased alumni involvement as faculty, and the duo's trip highlights the durability of personal and professional relationships made at the LGI.

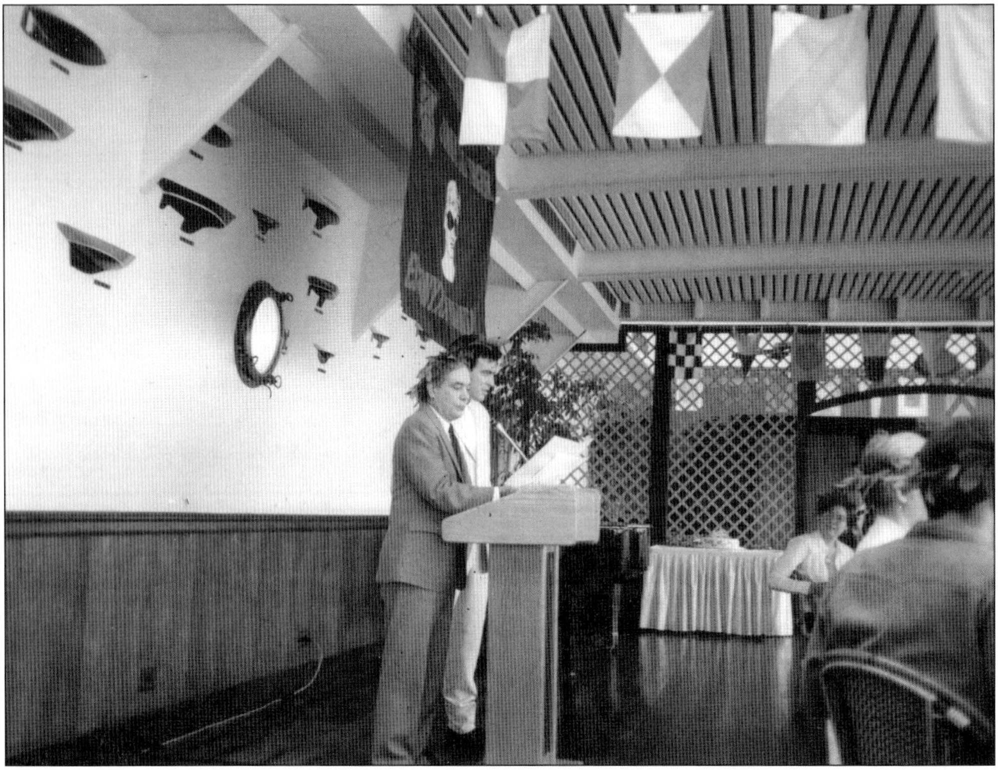

Hansen and Fishbone deliver remarks at the 1998 graduation at the Water Club. The venue, which hosted the event for almost two decades, is located at the easternmost end of 30th Street. It sits atop a barge in the East River and offers terrific views of the East River and Queens waterfront.

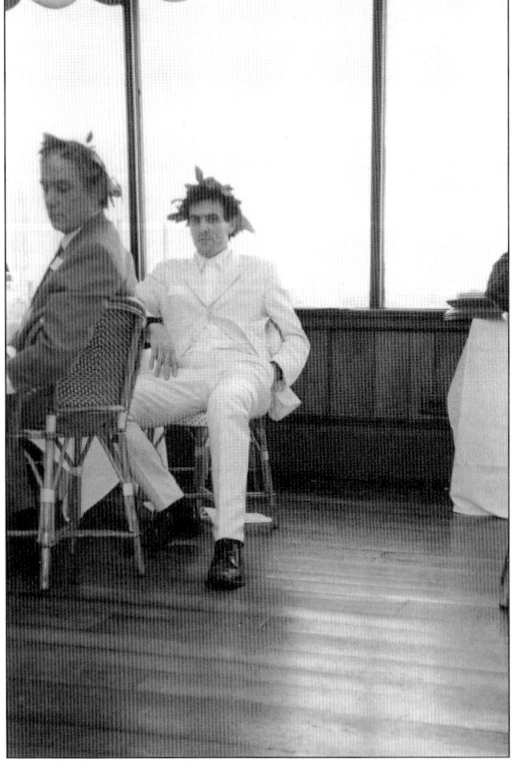

Hansen and Fishbone take in the event. There was much to contemplate: the decade—which, despite the transitions, had been a success—was coming to a close and a significant change was on the horizon, one that would usher in the next phase of the Institute's history.

Four

Monumentum Aere Perennius

The New Millennium 2000–2023

By the 1990s, the CUNY Graduate Center had outgrown its home on Forty-Second Street, and in 1995, the state provided $66 million to secure a new location. After an extensive search, the university identified a suitable edifice: the vacant B. Altman Building at 365 Fifth Avenue, which would provide about a third more space for the 4,000 students and 1,700 faculty who then regularly called the GC home. After renovation, the GC relocated in 1999, and the LGI welcomed the class of 2000 to its new home.

The first two decades of the new century brought other changes and developments—as well as its share of challenges. Most importantly, however, the LGI's strong and consistent enrollment has continued to reinforce its enduring importance to the teaching of the classical languages. In this regard, the circumstances that gave rise to its original foundation continue to drive its current enrollment: the limited (or, as of 2023, declining) availability of Latin and, especially, Greek; in this latter regard, it is worth noting that both the basic and upper Greek programs generate the strongest interest and, as of 2023, consistently enroll about double the number of students as their Latin counterparts.

At the same time, the changing demographics of LGI students indicate an important expansion of its mission. The number of students from historically underrepresented groups, including first-generation students, has grown steadily and consistently since the mid-1990s; accordingly, the LGI plays a role in helping to diversify the ranks of faculty, scholars, and K-12 teachers. Similarly, the number of international students has markedly increased—an indication in part, of the Institute's international reputation and reach. Over the past decade, students from Asia (especially China and South Korea) have been particularly well represented.

As of 2023, the Institute consistently offers four programs: basic programs in Latin and Greek (which assume no prior knowledge of the language) and upper-level programs, which require at least three years of previous study (or completion of a basic program plus additional coursework).

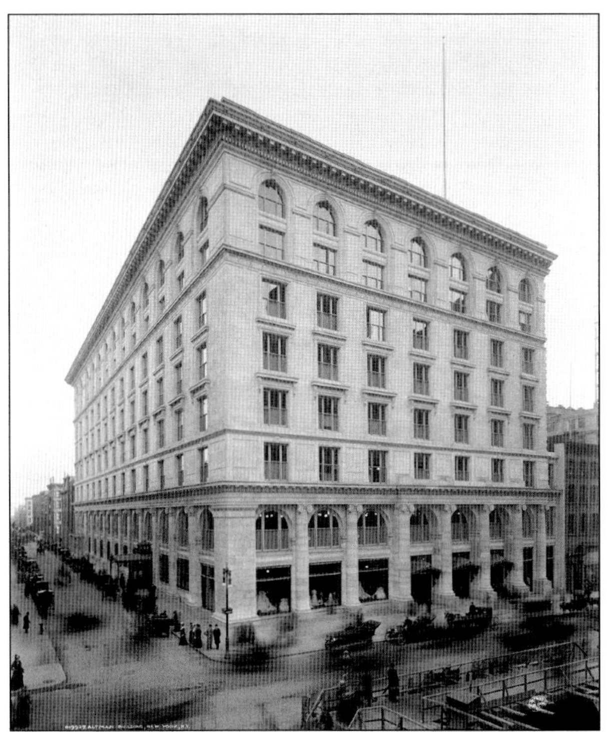

The B. Altman and Company Building was erected 1905–1913. Designed by Trowbridge & Livingston in the Italian Renaissance Revival style, the edifice, with its French limestone facade, occupies an entire city block. At the time of its construction, the department store's new flagship headquarters was located in a residential neighborhood outside the then-traditional Ladies' Mile shopping district to the south (Courtesy of Detroit Publishing Co. and the Library of Congress).

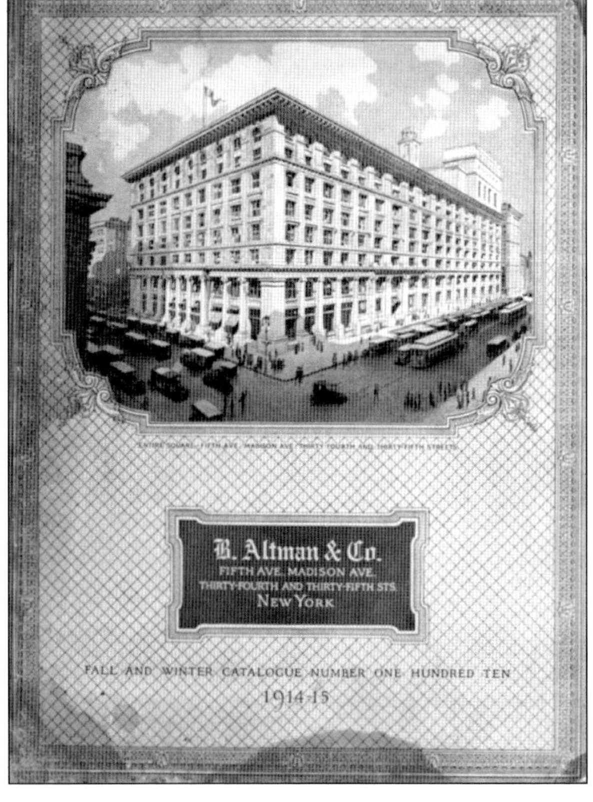

The company began as a small, family-owned store in 1865. Its founder, Benjamin Altman, struck a successful balance between quality, affordability, and outstanding customer service, and the emporium grew rapidly. It sold a large variety of products, as showcased in this 136-page catalog for 1914–1915. By 1989, its fortunes had waned, and the company declared bankruptcy—the same year its vacant headquarters was landmarked.

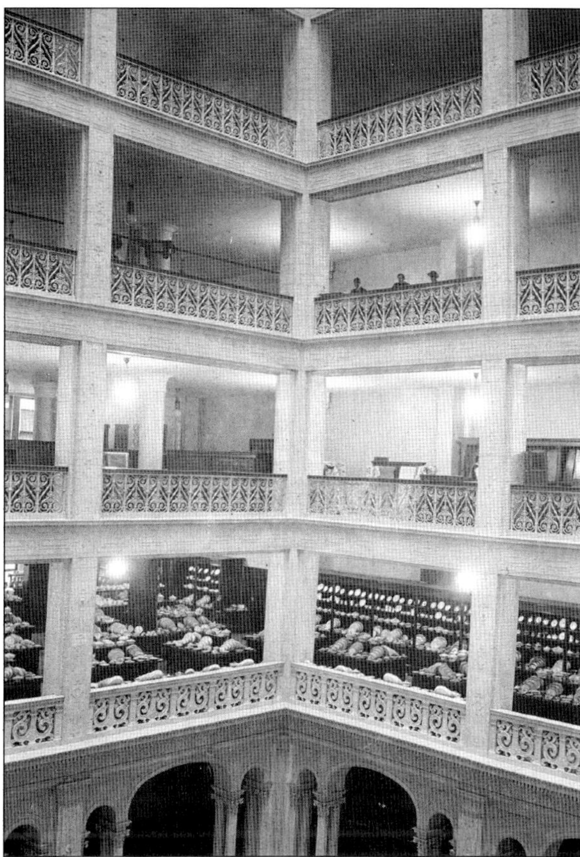

The building's entranceway along Fifth Avenue (the ornate details of which have been retained) originally opened to a large open-plan interior, topped with a magnificent glass dome that allowed direct light into the interior. The lower floors, with their high ceilings and spacious configurations, contained the salesrooms, while the upper floors were dedicated to administrative offices, storerooms, and workshops. The photograph below captures the once-ornate interior being gutted sometime in the late 1990s. The stairway shown is preserved in the Mina Rees Library. (Right, courtesy of Frank M. Ingalls Photograph Collection, circa 1901–1930, nyhs_PR028_b-06_430c, New-York Historical Society; below, courtesy of the OBDE, CUNY GC.)

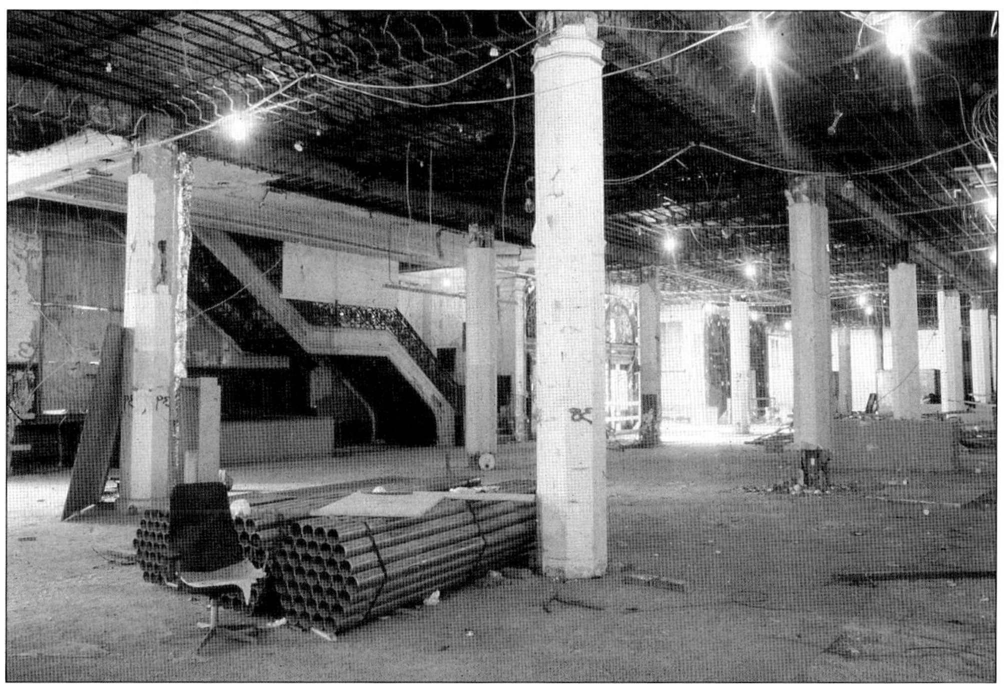

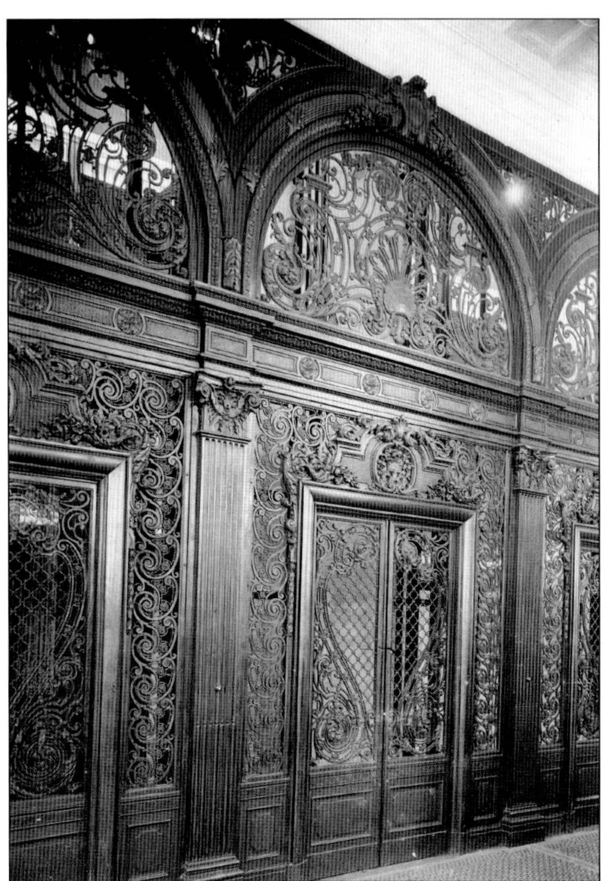

The building originally had 39 elevators: 22 passenger, 10 employee, 2 for trucks, and 5 private. The public elevators were originally detailed with elaborately carved mahogany surrounds, as evident in this photograph. Except for one small elevator bank in the library along the southern (Thirty-Fourth Street) side, most of these were gutted, stripped, and repurposed to their bare utilitarian function. To this effect, an image of the work during the building's reconfiguration in the late 1990s. (Left, courtesy of Frank M. Ingalls Photographic Collection, circa 1901–1930, nyhs_PR028_b-02_f-14_624-01, New-York Historical Society; below, courtesy of the OBDE, CUNY GC.)

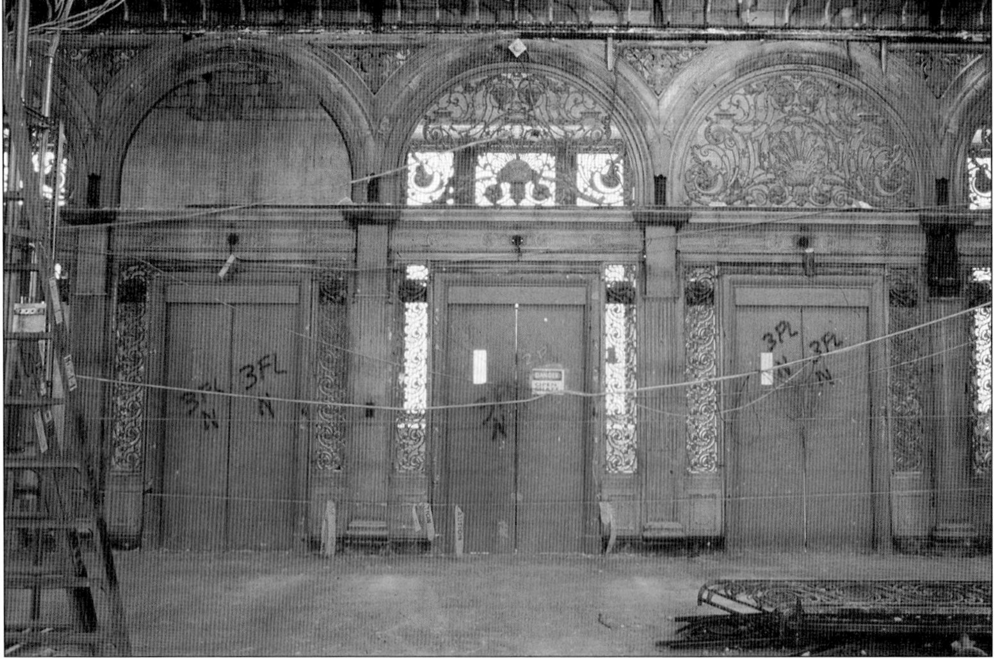

The poster for the summer 2000 Institute notes the new location. Having spent almost three decades in the Aeolian and Grace Buildings, the layout and amenities of the new GC required some getting used to.

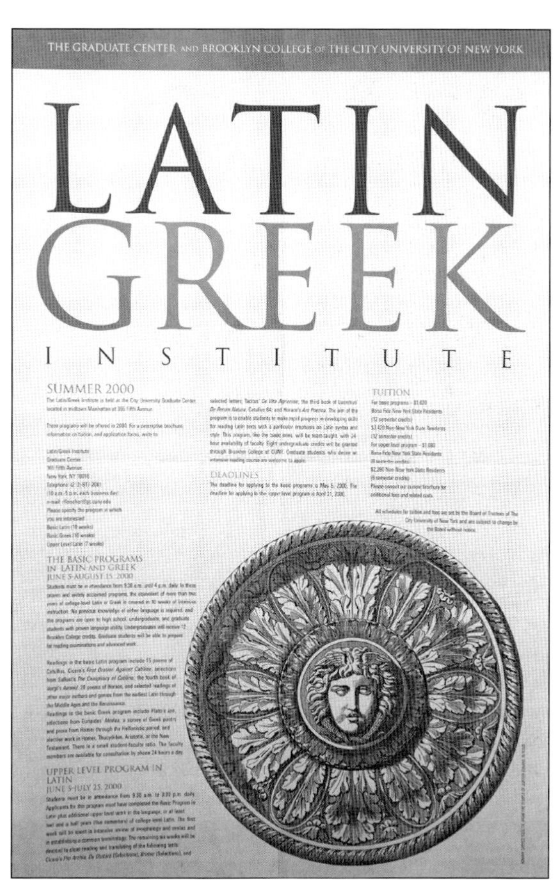

Following the move, the Institute was initially assigned room 4415. The office was shared with the Language Reading Program, of which Fleischer had become joint administrative director (in tandem with the LGI) some two decades before. Here, Arthur Imperatore (G 2013) accesses a Greek dictionary from the office library. To note, Imperatore's aunt India was a student in the inaugural year of Basic Greek. Family and (now) generational attendance are increasingly common. (Office of Communications and Marketing [OCM], CUNY GC).

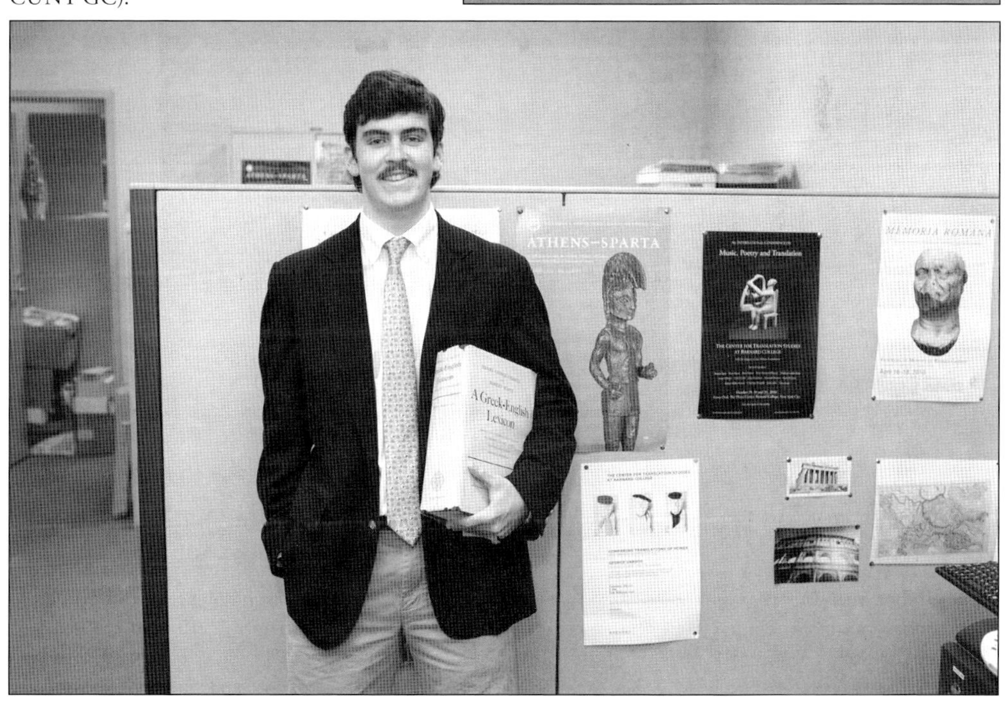

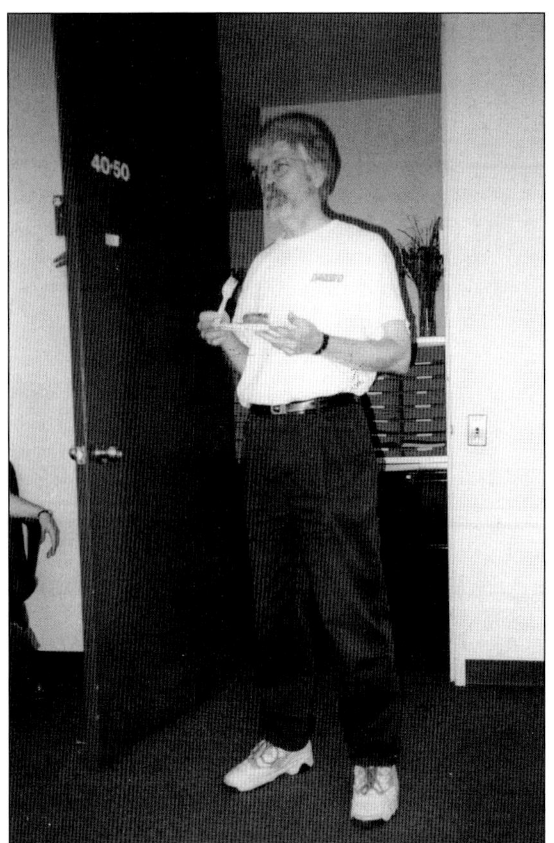

In 2002, the LGI suffered another loss with the tragic passing of long-standing faculty member Jack Collins, who fell ill only weeks into the start of the summer. His contributions to the Institute, both in-class and out, were significant: over 24 summers, he taught in both basic programs, Advanced Latin, and Upper Greek. A true LGI legend, his Institute career is highlighted in Chapter 5.

Ethyle Wolfe made her last appearance at the Institute's 2008 graduation and 35th anniversary celebration. Though she had retired almost a decade before, she continued to command significant respect at CUNY—and, at the LGI, enduring reverence for her inestimable importance: from her initial recruitment of Moreland (and others) to her longstanding and substantive support as a senior administrator. She passed away in 2010.

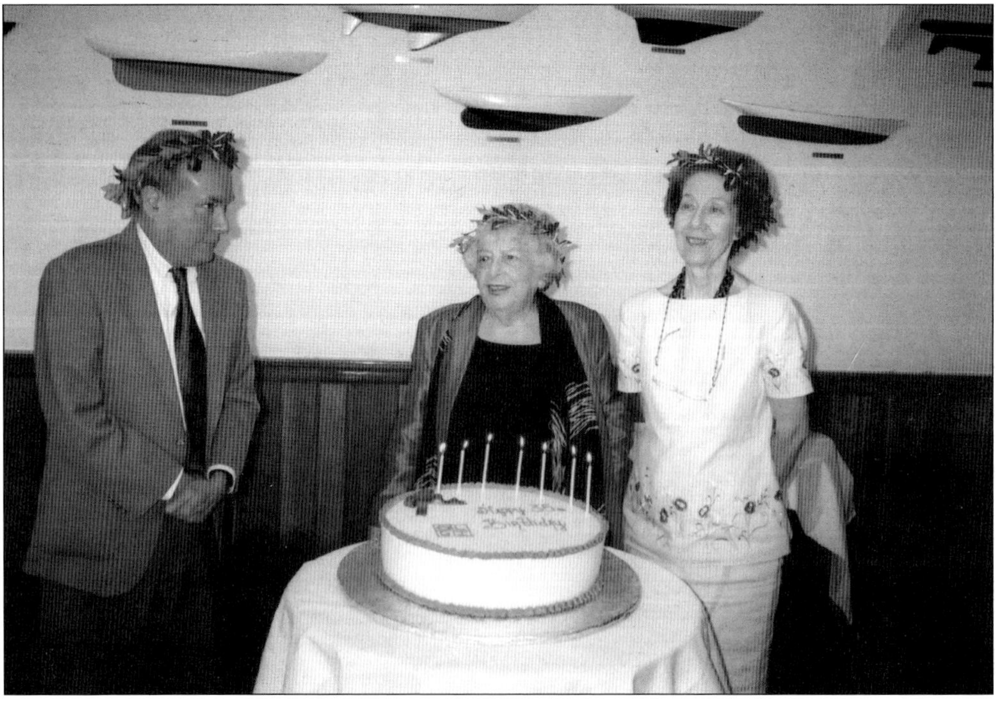

On every landmark year (usually intervals of five, from the founding of the Latin Institute), the occasion is honored with a cake. Here, Hardy and Rita flank that celebrating the aforementioned 35th anniversary held at the Water Club. Though he would continue for several years as LGI director, the year also marked Hansen's retirement from Brooklyn College.

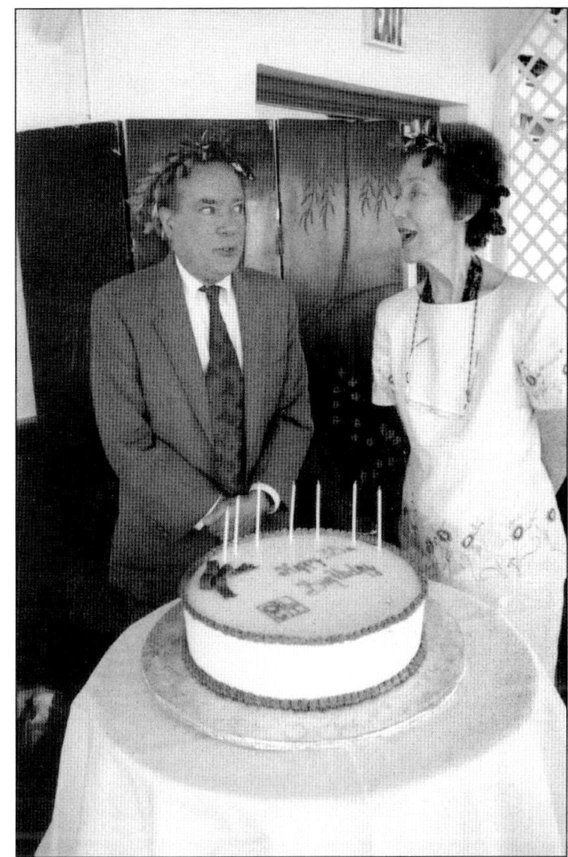

In 2013, Hansen retired as director of the Institute, though, like Fleischer, he remained involved in myriad ways: as an instructor, mentor to faculty, and adviser to subsequent directors and program chairs. His contributions to the Institute and the teaching of Greek are inestimable. At his 2014 retirement party, he was gifted with an antique print of a tapir, an animal for which he has a well-known fondness.

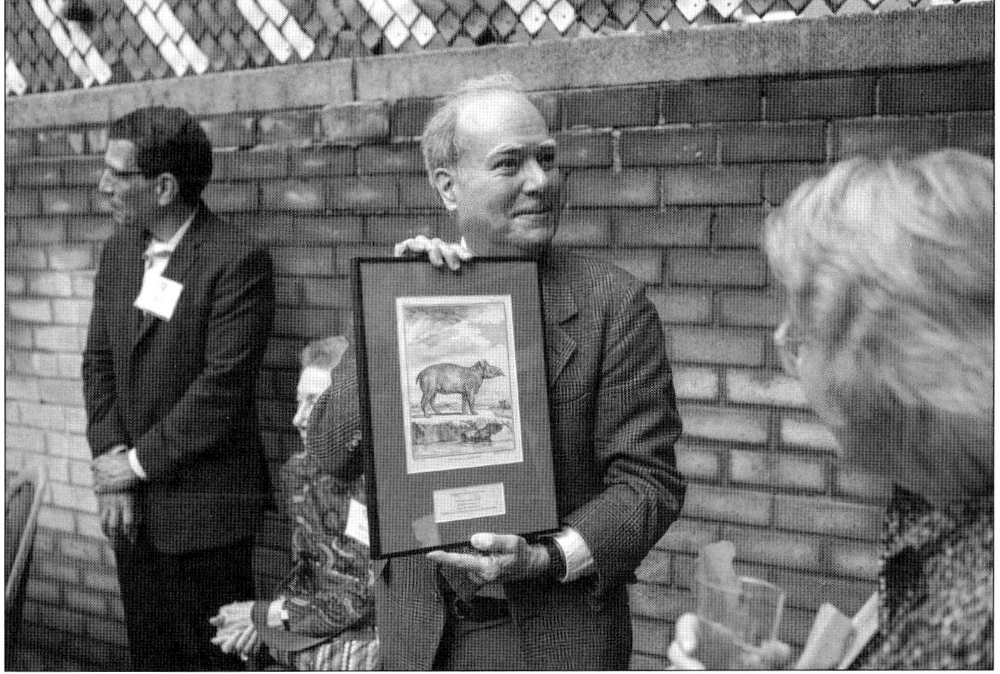

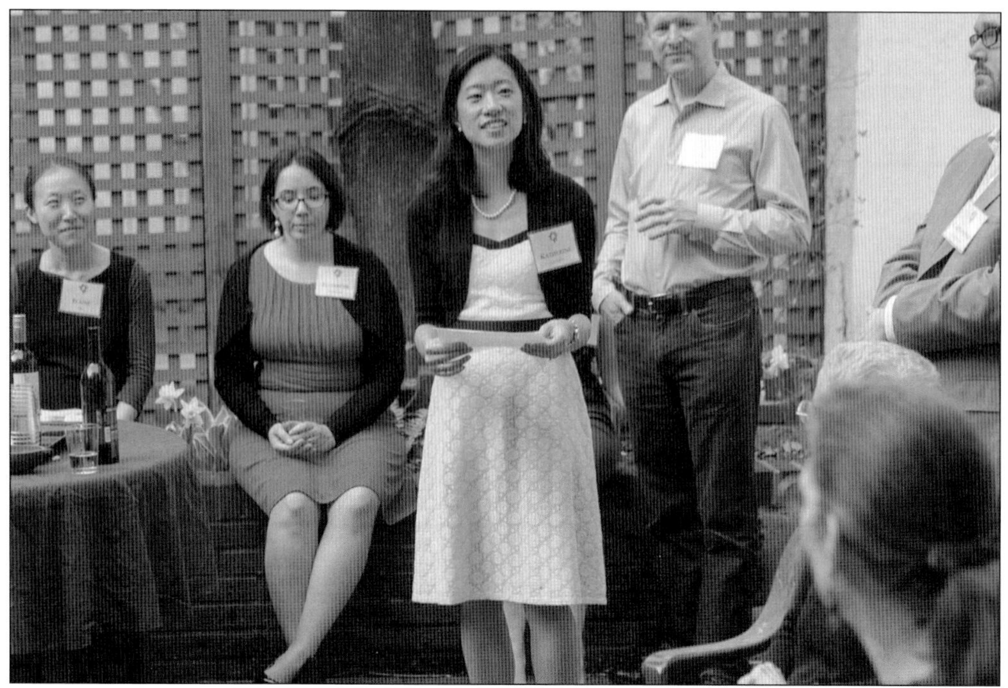

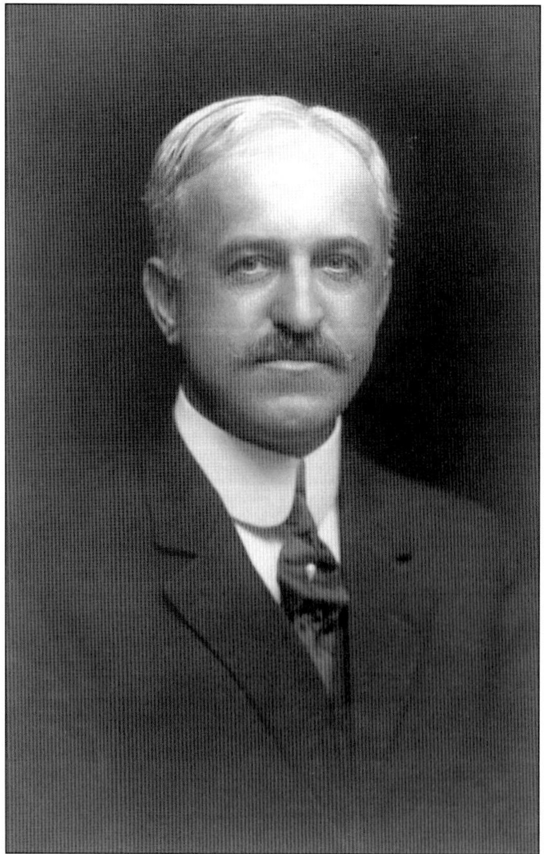

After a national search, Katherine Lu Hsu (G 2002) was appointed director in September 2013, the same year she received her PhD from the University of Michigan. Over the next eight years, she taught in the SLI and updated many of the LGI's administrative practices; most significantly, she received a $1 million scholarship endowment through the Stavros Niarchos Foundation (SNF) and deepened a critical relationship with the Kress Foundation.

Beginning in 2010, the Samuel H. Kress Foundation has provided scholarships for aspiring art historians; through 2023, the foundation has supported more than two dozen students. Samuel Henry Kress (1863–1955) was a businessman and philanthropist who made a fortune in retail and amassed an extensive collection of art. He later donated the bulk of this to museums across the country and established a foundation to continue his legacy of arts patronage. (Courtesy of the Samuel H. Kress Foundation.)

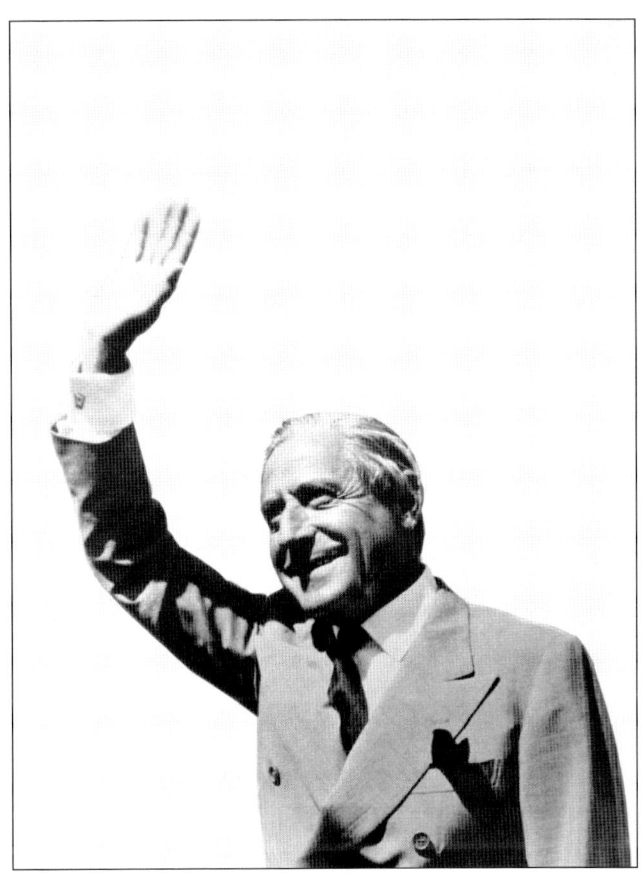

Stavros Spyros Niarchos (1909–1996) built a fortune in shipping and other commercial activities. A true global citizen, he designated a significant part of his estate to establish the Stavros Niarchos Foundation (SNF) which, as of 2023, has awarded over 5,300 grants to nonprofit organizations in more than 130 countries. SNF focuses on making positive and lasting change in various sectors including healthcare, the arts, and education. (Courtesy of SNF.)

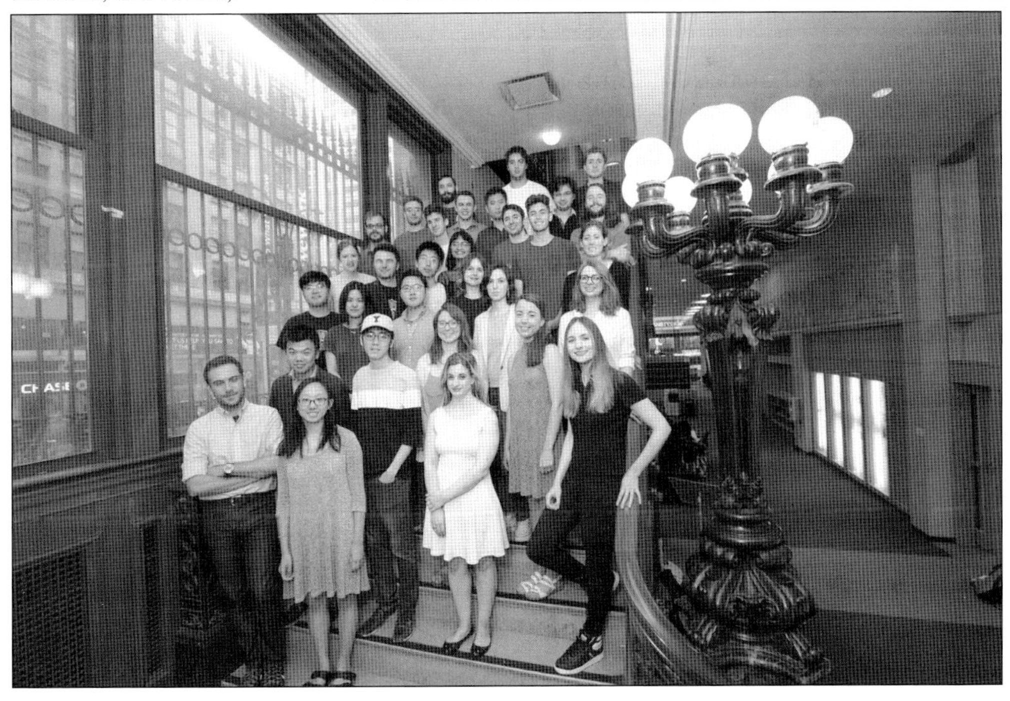

In 2014, SNF established a summer scholarship program at the LGI, with a specific emphasis on recruiting and supporting students from historically underrepresented communities. As of 2023, SNF scholarships have supported more than 150 students. Here, the 2017 recipients pose on an intact stairwell from the original B. Altman Building (see page 77). (Courtesy of the OCM, CUNY GC.)

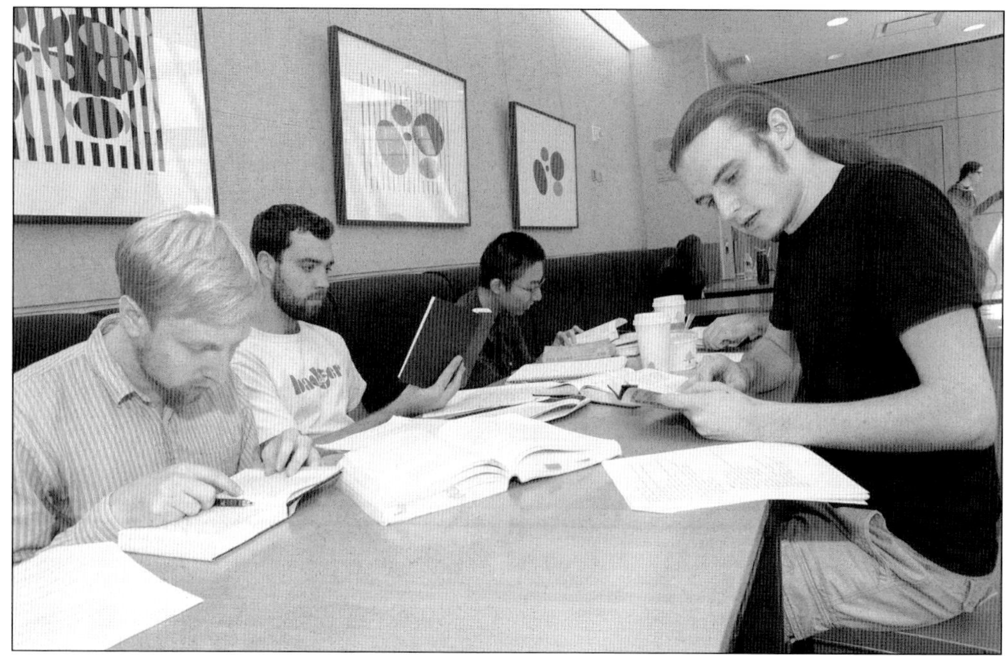

The intensive and immersive nature of the Institute often fosters strong and, in some cases, lifelong relationships (marriages included). Student study groups play an important role in this process. Here, 2013 SGI students read Greek together in the eighth-floor Dining Commons of the GC. (Courtesy of the OCM, CUNY GC.)

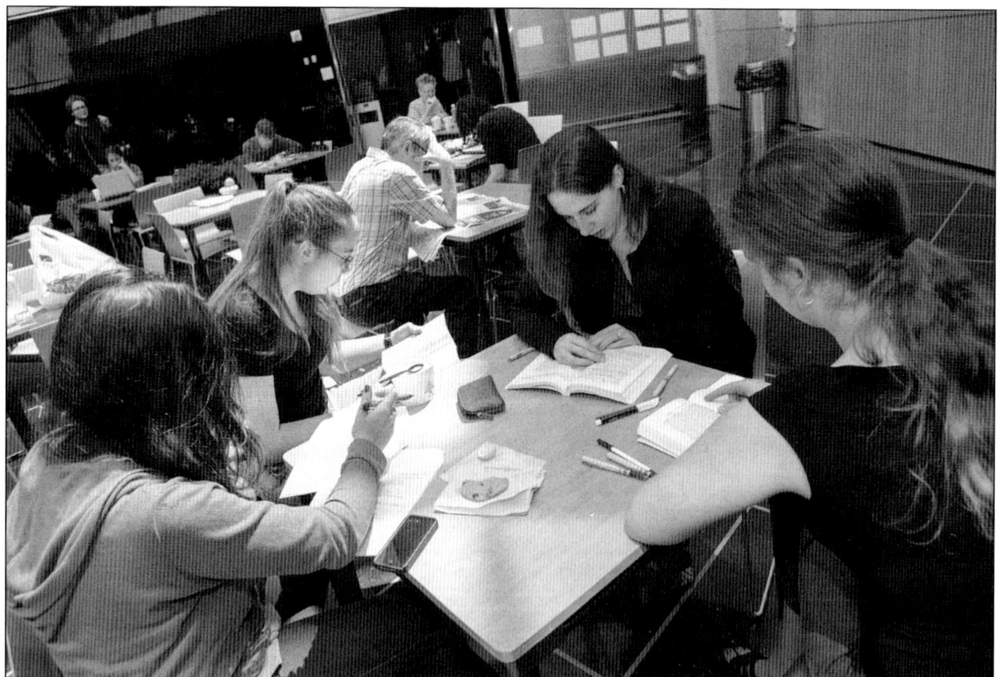

Another 2013 group reads together in the Dining Commons. As mentioned in the introduction, faculty and students are on a first-name basis. By the close of the first day, instructors are able to identify all of their students by name (Courtesy of the OCM, CUNY GC.)

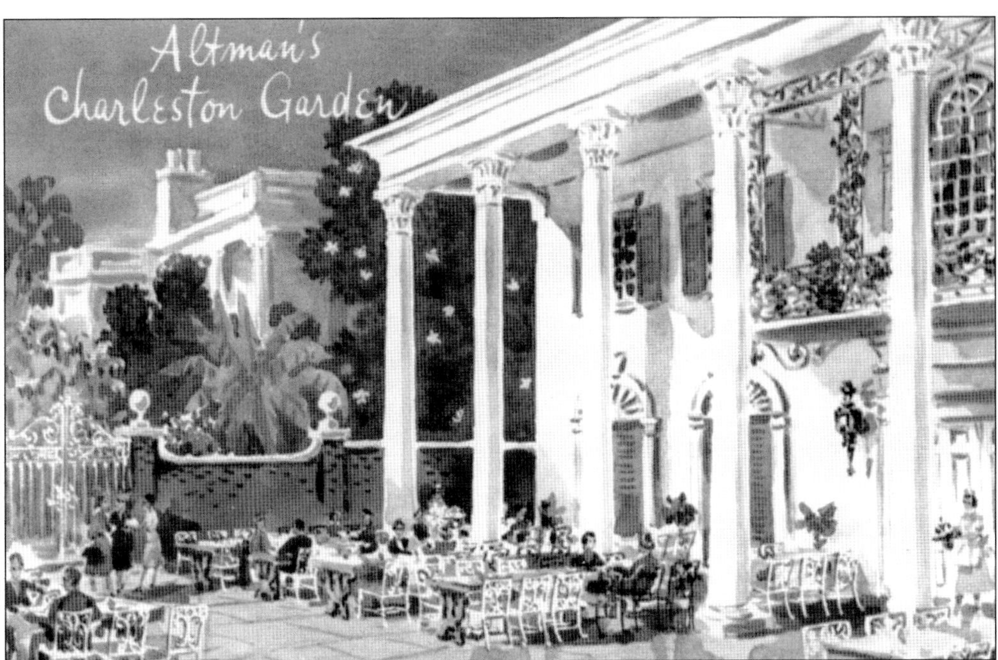

Fortunately for students, their summer is spent buried beneath textbooks, readers, vocabulary glosses, and flashcards. Following its renovation, the interior of the GC is now, alas, basic, bland, and utilitarian. The aforementioned Dining Commons, for instance, was once the location of B. Altman's Charleston Garden restaurant. Enclosed by decorated walls that simulated an outdoor garden, its centerpiece was the façade of an elegant mansion.

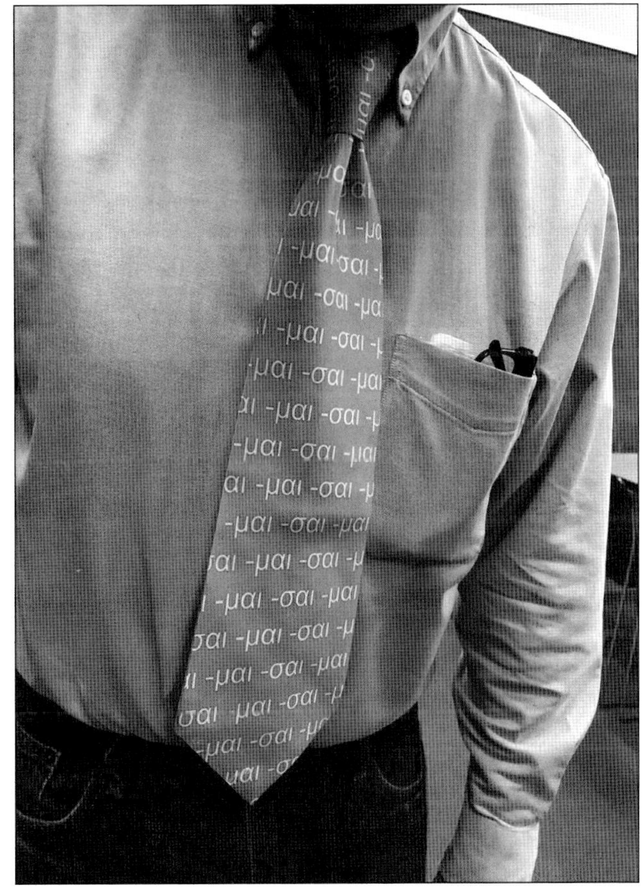

Hardy Hansen impresses in his μαι σαι (tie), a pun on the primary middle-passive person markers in the singular (-μαι, -σαι, -ται). The tie was conceived over drinks one evening early in the new millennium by SGI faculty members David Friedman (G 1992), Bill Pagonis (G 1990), and Hansen. At the time, Friedman was working for a marketing company. The tie continues to make an annual appearance on Day 8.

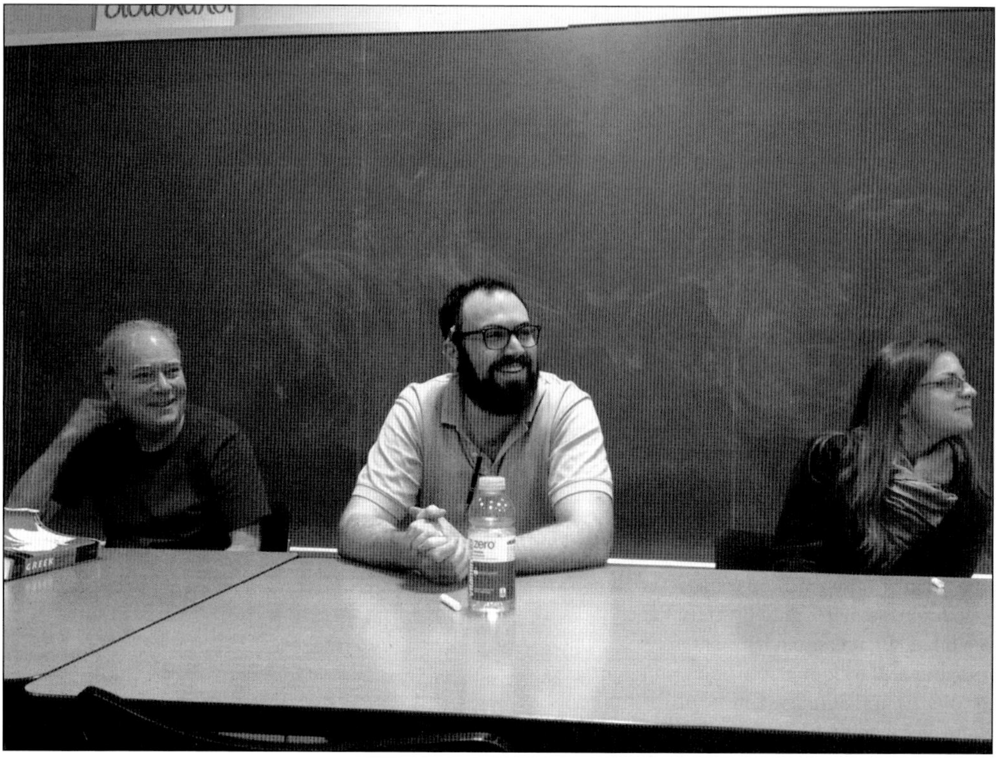

The 36th annual Hoplite Challenge Cup (2014) was a 17-round slugfest from which the students ultimately emerged victorious, 8.5 to 7. Above is a portion of the faculty team; from left to right, Hansen, Aramis Lopez, and Yekaterina (Katia) Kosova-Krauss (L 2005, G 2006, and UG 2007), await their turn. Below, Hansen generates the form requested by his student opponent. Lopez chaired the SGI from 2014 to 2019, providing it with leadership following Hansen's retirement from the directorship. Over the decades, student teams have devised strategies for taking on the faculty, the "easy" verb volley (e.g., λύω) for the half point among the most common. Though these have varied in success, most volleys—and indeed, competitions—are won (or lost) on simple errors.

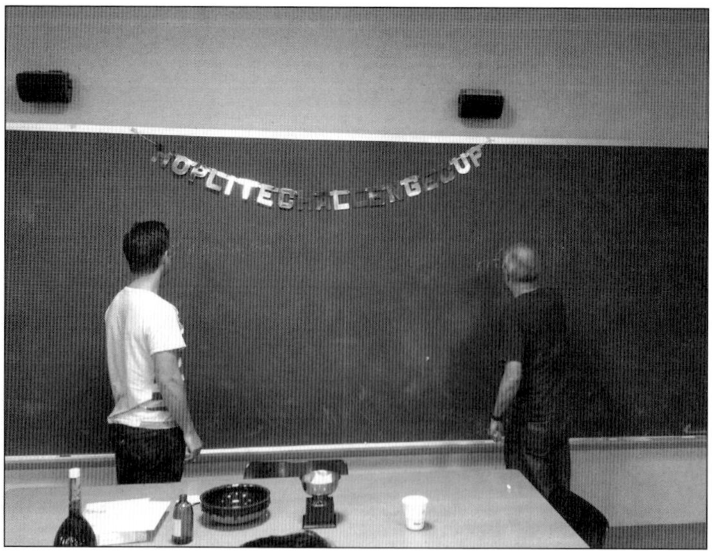

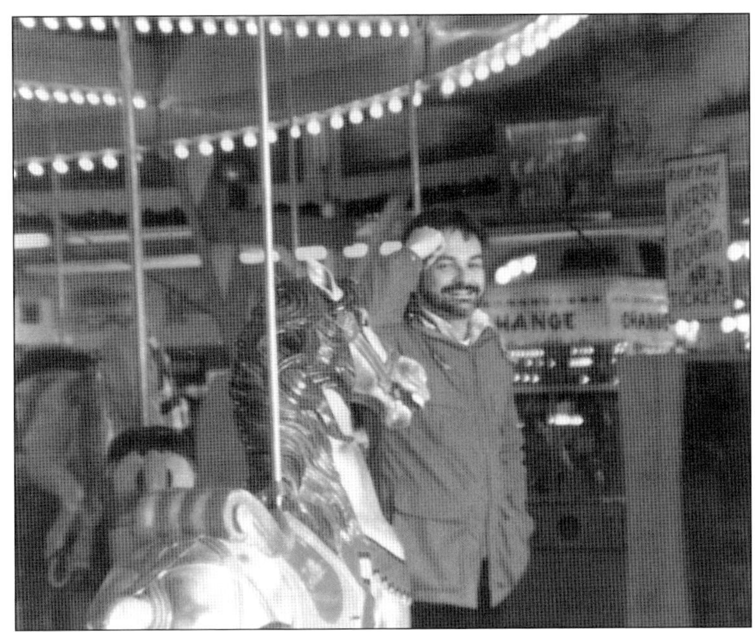

Floyd Moreland's retirement was a departure from CUNY (and the Institute) but not a disengagement from work; rather, he dedicated much time and energy to saving his beloved Seaside Heights carousel which, by the mid-1980s, had fallen on hard times. Its owners were considering dismantling the 1932 Dentzel/Looff attraction and selling off its coveted (and valuable) horses. Moreland stepped in, offering to rejuvenate and revive the attraction.

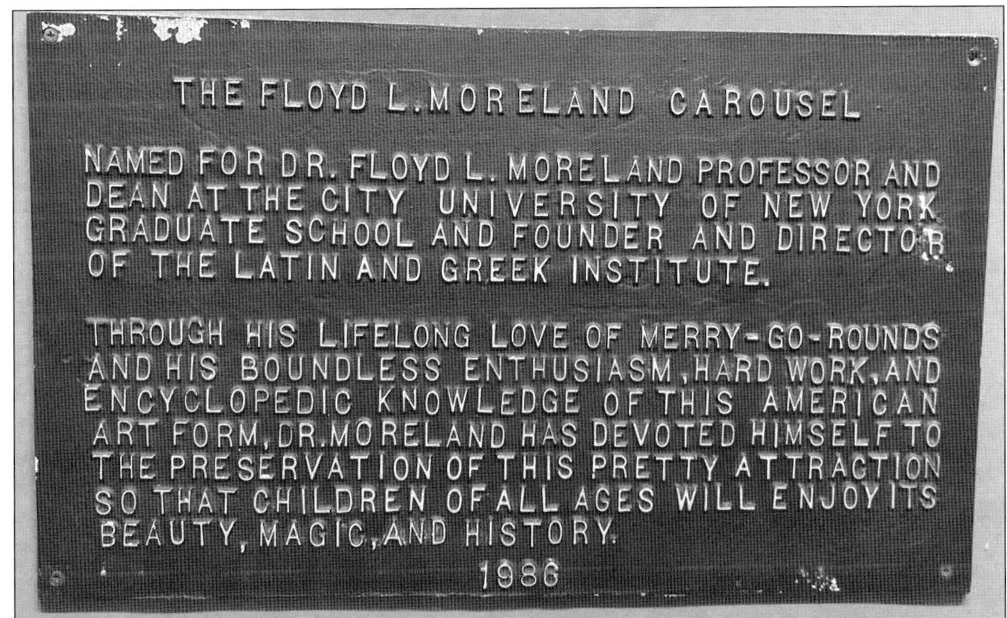

Applying his energy, creativity, and focus (and fundraising and networking), Moreland ultimately saved the carousel. In 1986, it was renamed in his honor; of note, its dedicatory plaque mentions the Institute. After a renovation in 2021, riders were once again able to mount a white horse named "Dr. Moreland" or one called "Rita." (Courtesy of the Seaside Heights Historical Society.)

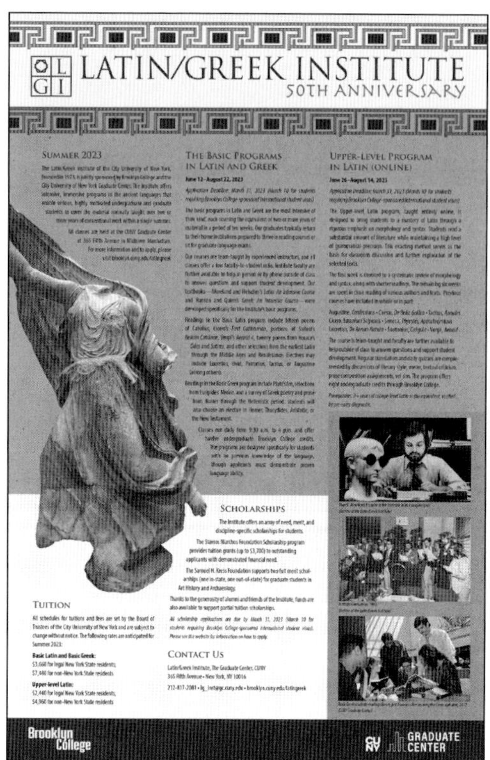

Summer 2023 marked the 50th anniversary of the Latin/Greek Institute. In addition to the basic programs in Latin and Greek, an online section of upper-level Latin was offered. Online uppers were an innovation of the 2020–2021 Covid pandemic. They proved a success and are now regularly offered in alternating summers. This attractive poster was designed by David Finkelstein.

Onward to the next 50 years: Christopher Simon delivers the first Latin lecture on Day 1 of the 2023 Summer Latin Institute. A highly accomplished philologist (PhD, Yale), Simon has taught in the SLI, UL, and UG programs and also served as deputy director. He, along with such faculty members as Carlo DaVia (UG 2010) and Jeremy March (UL 2000) have helped ensure the LGI's tradition of strong program leadership.

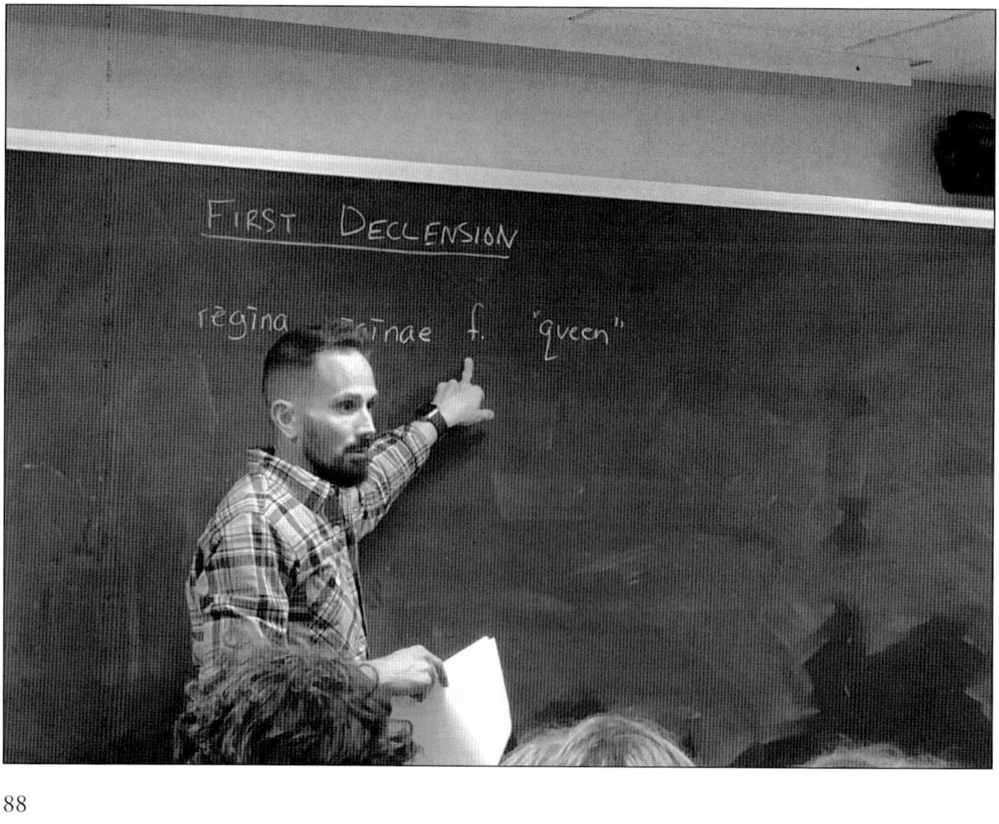

Five

Ἀλωτὰ γίγνεται ἐπιμελείᾳ καὶ πόνῳ ἅπαντα

The Curriculum

Mastering the equivalent of five to six semesters of Latin or Greek in only 50 days of study is a challenging and complex endeavor; Moreland described the experience as "beyond the intensive." The LGI's effectiveness, however, is not an exclusive consequence of its rigor but rather a reflection of the methodical and holistic way in which its programs are structured.

As pioneered at Berkeley, the Institute's pedagogy is based on two overarching concepts: (1) reducing and/or eliminating immediate barriers to learning, and (2) sequencing grammar and syntax not by complexity but by their necessity to read original texts as soon as possible. In Basic Latin, for instance, this approach is manifest in three primary ways: (1) faculty are on-call to provide students with immediate assistance; (2) to reduce time spent with dictionaries, all vocabulary is glossed—with embedded processes to memorize essential vocabulary; and (3) the subjunctive mood, necessary for reading unadapted Latin, is introduced almost immediately (something usually done later: *Wheelock's Latin*, for example, does so in Lesson 28; at the Institute, this happens on Day 2). This model, with necessary variations, underlies every LGI program.

The basic programs in Latin and Greek are similarly structured: the first half (five weeks in Latin, six in Greek) is dedicated to the mastery of morphology, grammar, and syntax while the latter half is shaped around intensive readings in prose and poetry, completion of a small but representative survey, and participation in an elective of the student's choice. In the first half, mornings consist of two drill hours which confirm mastery of the material presented the day before, followed by an afternoon lecture at which new material is introduced. During the second half, afternoon lectures acquaint students with various topics such as literary analysis, paleography, and digital resources. Each program is led by a faculty chair, who is responsible for the delivery of the curriculum.

Essential to the success of the LGI is the work of the faculty, who deliver the curriculum with consistency and precision. To this end, they continuously practice and refine their skills and, in a process known as pre-sessing, pre-teach the entire program in advance of the summer. By the 1990s, most faculty were also LGI alumni/ae.

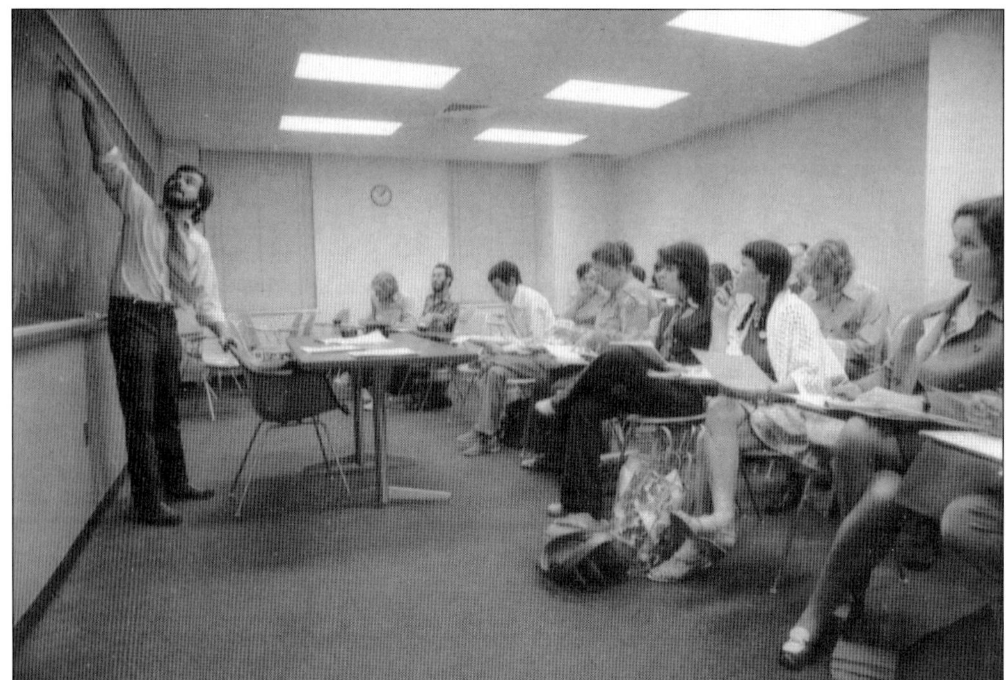

In the Institute's first year, Moreland delivered all the afternoon lectures on grammar, syntax, and morphology. It was not until he was waylaid by an earache that Fleischer stepped in to substitute. Within a few years, the afternoon lectures were shared across the faculty, though the earliest and most complex presentations continue to be the responsibility of the more senior faculty.

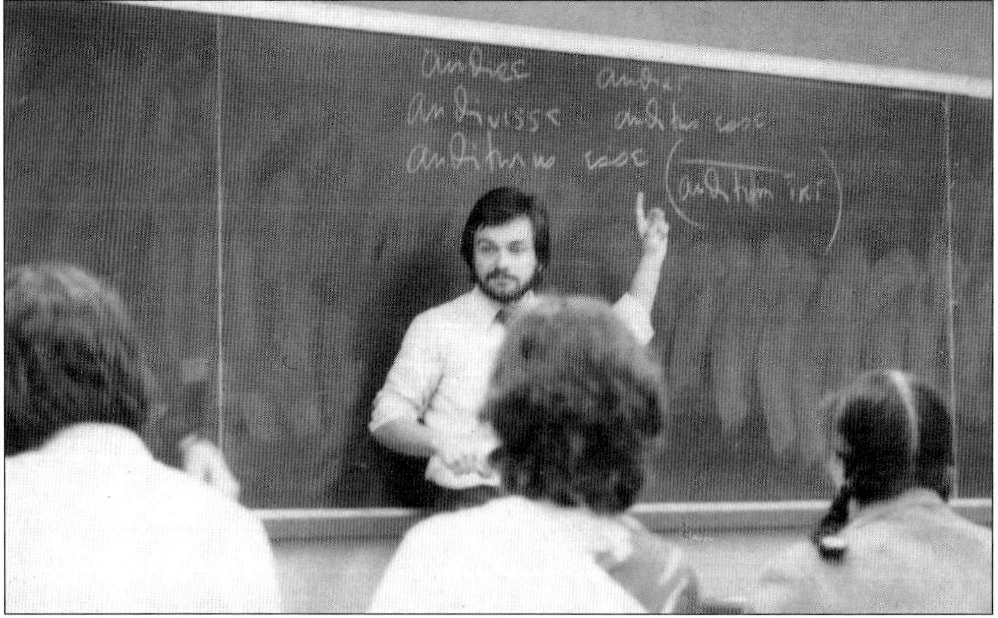

Although there have been modifications and adjustments to the basic programs, their architecture remains largely unchanged, and lecture and drill hours are theoretically interchangeable from year to year. The material on the blackboard in this 1973 photograph (infinitives and indirect statement, using the verb *audire*), for instance, indicates that this is the afternoon of Tuesday, June 19—day seven.

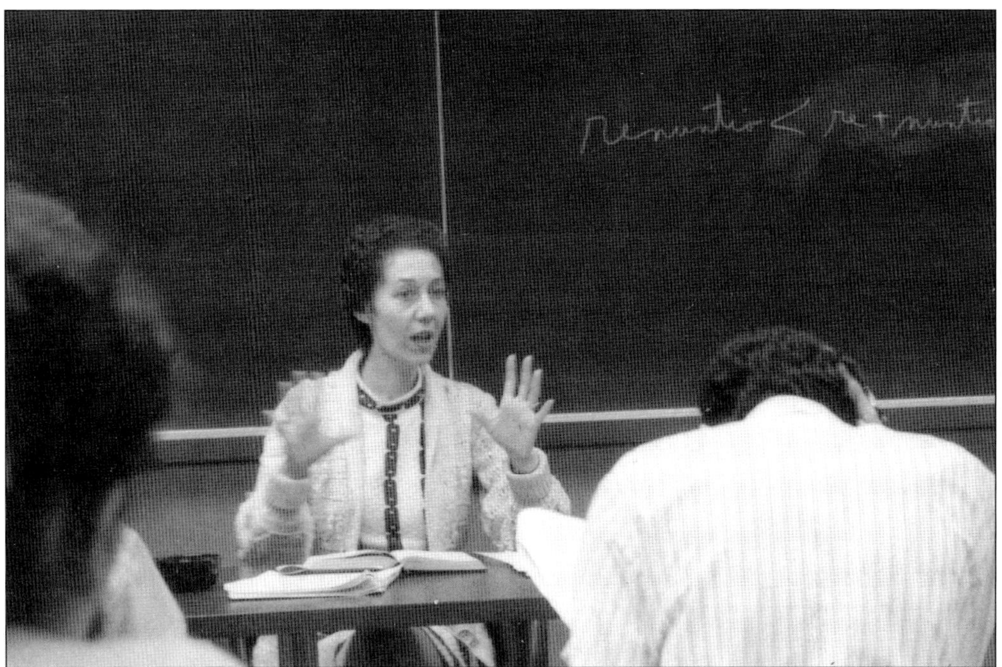

During the first half of the basic programs, a vocabulary presentation follows the afternoon lecture. Here, on Day 20 of the 1975 Institute, Fleischer introduces students to various techniques with which to expand and deepen their understanding and comprehension of vocabulary. In the summer of 2022, she delivered the same lecture, a reflection of the continuity and consistency of LGI pedagogy. The summer of 2022 marked a return to the in-person basic programs, which were suspended in 2020 and 2021 due to the Covid pandemic. Although an array of protocols ensured a safe and successful summer, the operational, administrative, and instructional challenges were significant.

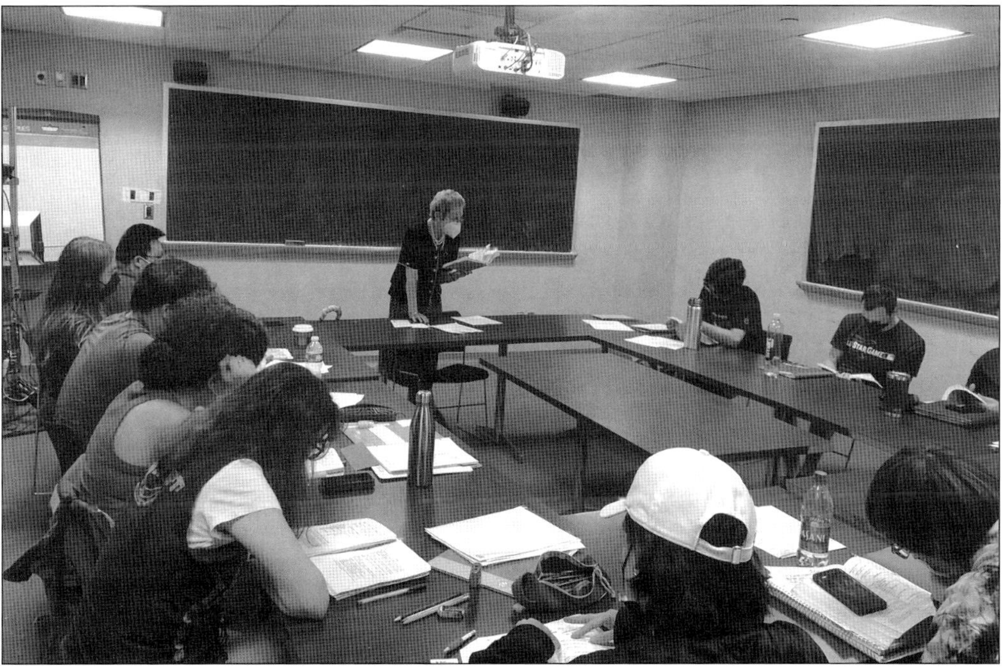

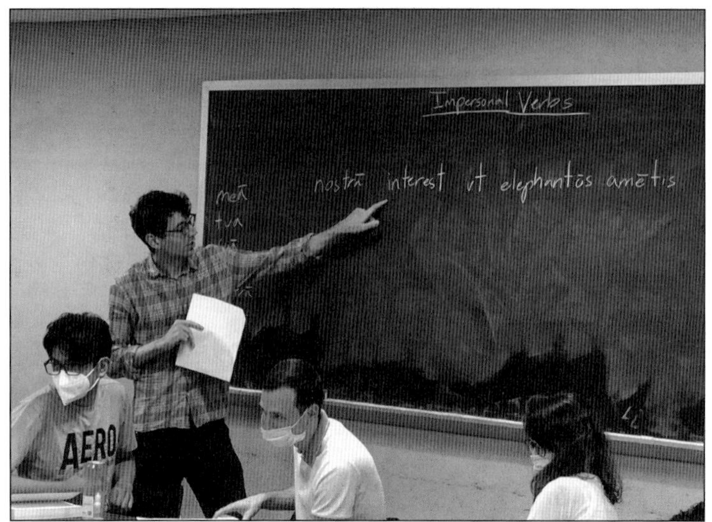

An update to the curriculum is reflected here, with Thomas Murphy (L 2019) presenting the longest piece of syntax currently taught in the SLI: "feminine ablative singular of the personal possessive adjective to express the person concerned, agreeing with an ellipsed *rē*, with *interest*, by analogy with *rēfert*." SLI Day 18, 2022.

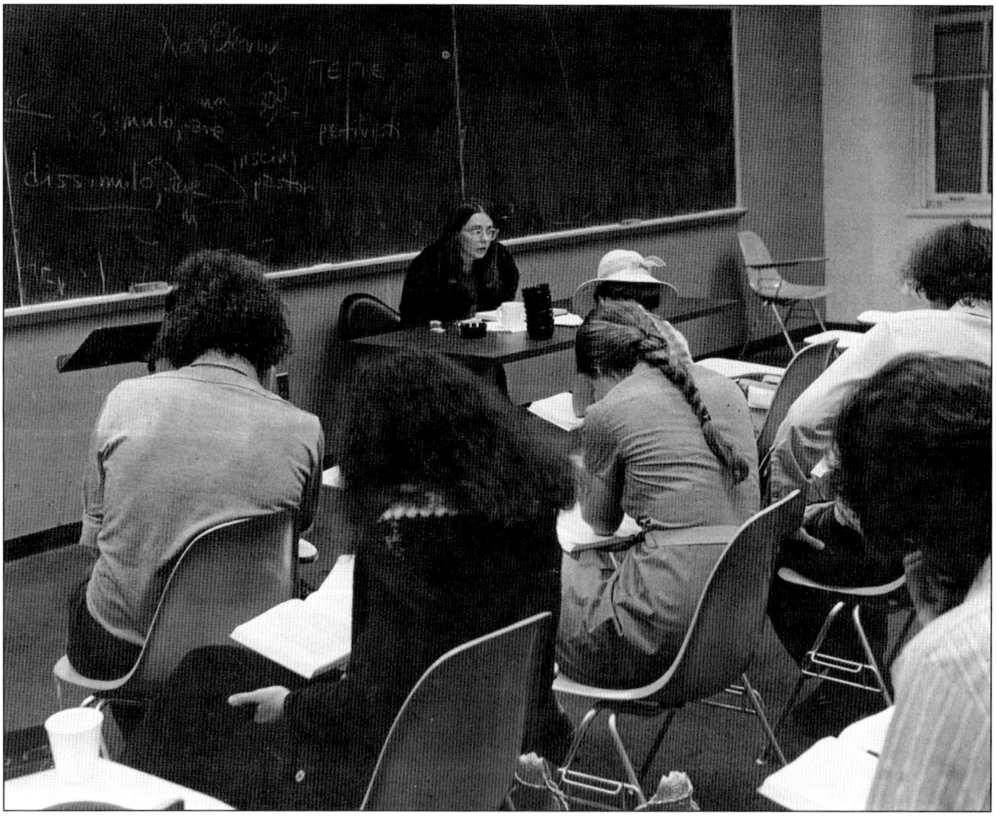

Students are divided into groups for morning drill, which allows more focused attention. The first hour opens with a quiz, and then a review of the previous night's assignment. It is designed to verify students' comprehension of the material and not to re-teach (extensive support is provided separately). The process is consistent across sections, an important aspect of faculty pre-sessing. A contemporary student would feel at home here in Russell's 1976 drill section.

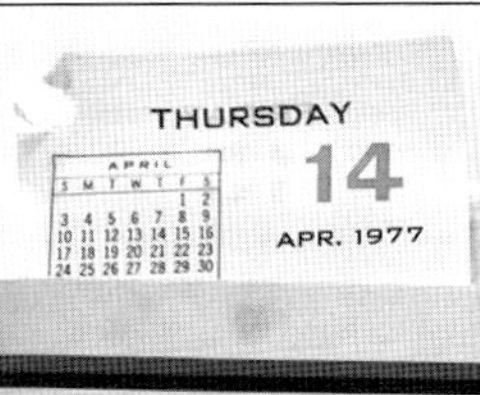

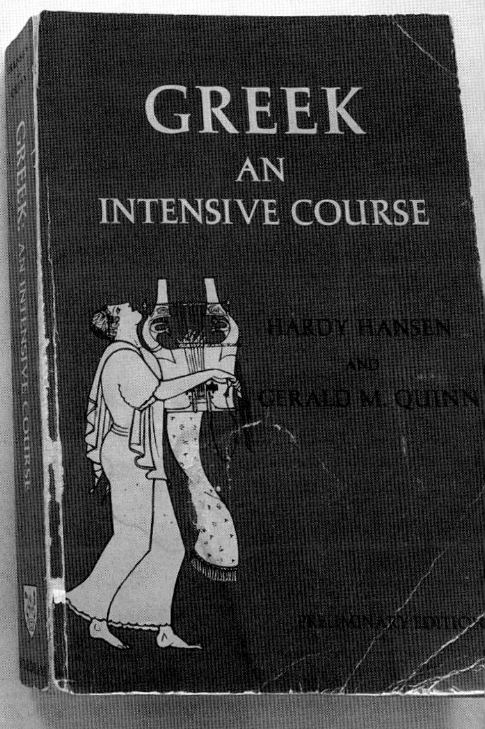

While he was still at Berkeley, the University of California (UC) Press had invited Moreland to write a textbook for the workshop. In 1973, he completed a manuscript that, even though he was no longer at Berkeley, UC Press published in 1974. Fleischer's copy of the preliminary edition is shown here; it is heavily annotated and indicates the sentences assigned for homework and to be drilled in class. Of note, many are the same as those that continue to be assigned. The Moreland & Fleischer (M&F) text is now in its third edition. As with its Latin counterpart, each chapter of Hansen & Quinn (H&Q, first published by Fordham University Press in 1980 and now in its third edition and reprinted multiple times) incorporates one day of material in the Basic Greek Program. If M&F sentences offered up numerous scenarios of sailors and queens (in anticipation of reading *Aeneid* IV), H&Q presented Homer and his brothers as recurring characters. The copy shown here is Hansen's original teaching text.

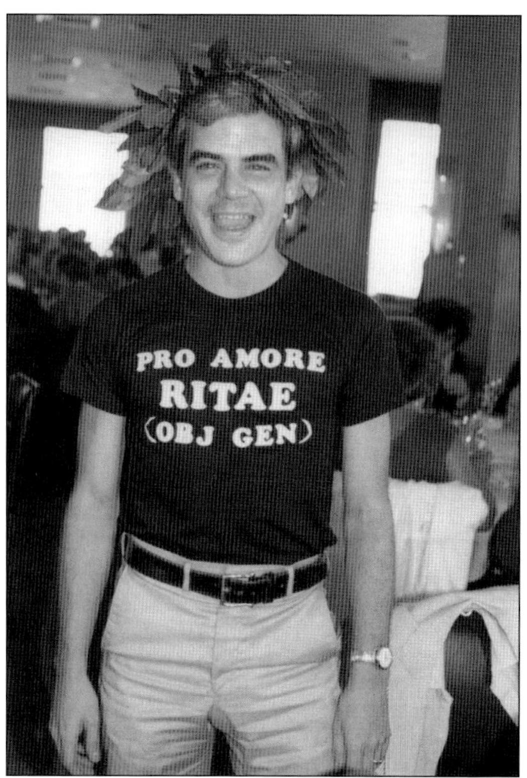

Though he only taught for two years (1983 and 1984), later generations know Clement "Clem" Dunbar (L 1980 and AL 1981 and 1982) for his name on the Latin reader, which he typed up in its entirety. The Latin reader, the focus of the latter half of the SLI, includes the text and glosses for the required prose authors (Sallust and Cicero) and a survey of prose and poetry. Dunbar was the first alumnus to become faculty.

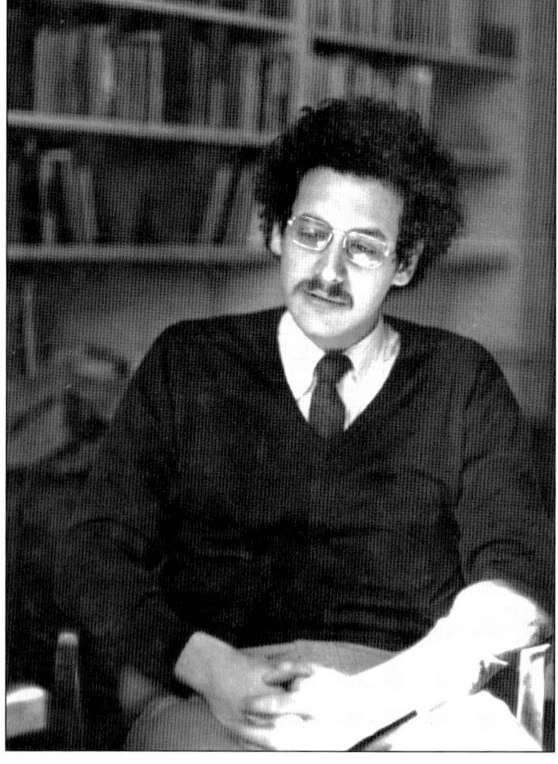

David Sider, a scholar of Greek poetry and philosophy, was on faculty from 1984 to 1996 (teaching in both the SGI and UG). Since then, he has continued to give a presentation on textual transmission and criticism every summer. In the basic programs, introductory lectures during the second half augment, expand, and deepen students' learning with such topics as epigraphy, paleography, and the use (and comparison) of dictionaries.

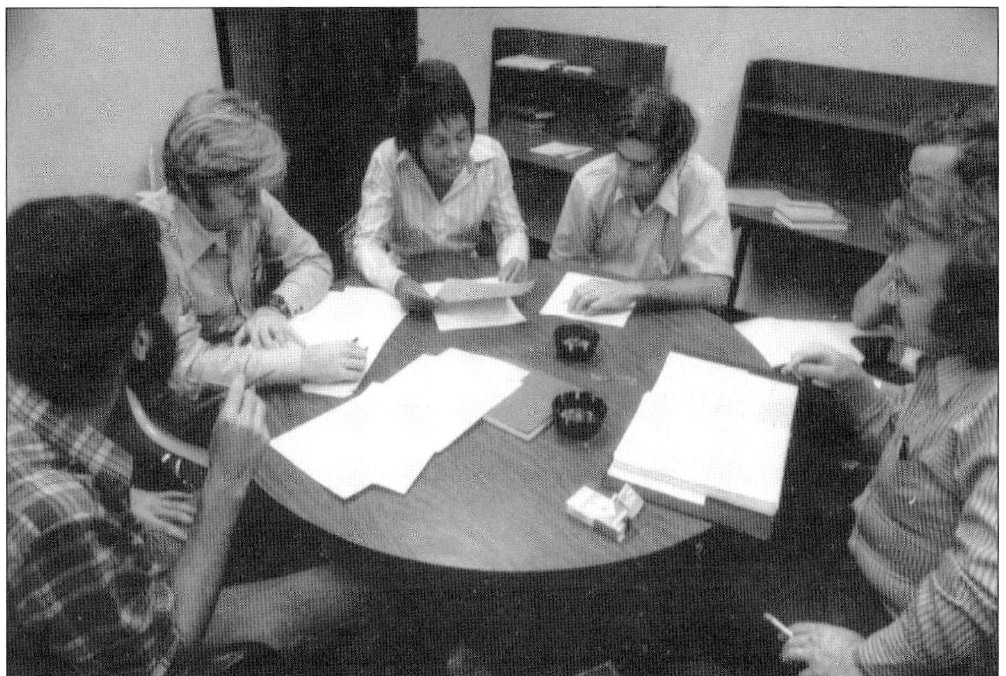

In the last two weeks of the basic programs, students choose an elective. In the Institute's inaugural year, the choices included Roman Comedy (Fleischer), Medieval Latin (Wyatt), and Tacitus (Smith), as shown here. This was a challenging selection that required not one, but two ashtrays.

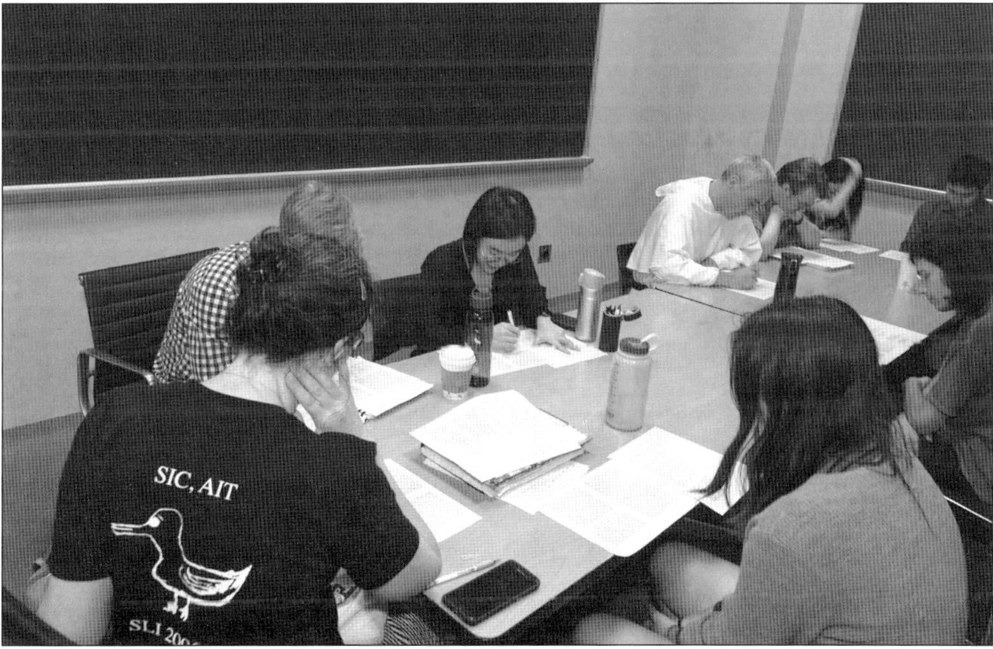

Alice Phillips Walden (G 2003, L 2006, and UG 2007) reads Lucretius with her 2019 elective students. Electives have changed over the years and often reflect individual faculty interests and expertise. One notable change in the Basic Latin program—in the electives, as well as in the reading survey—has been a reduction in the amount of Medieval Latin covered. (Courtesy of Alex Irklievski, CUNY GC.)

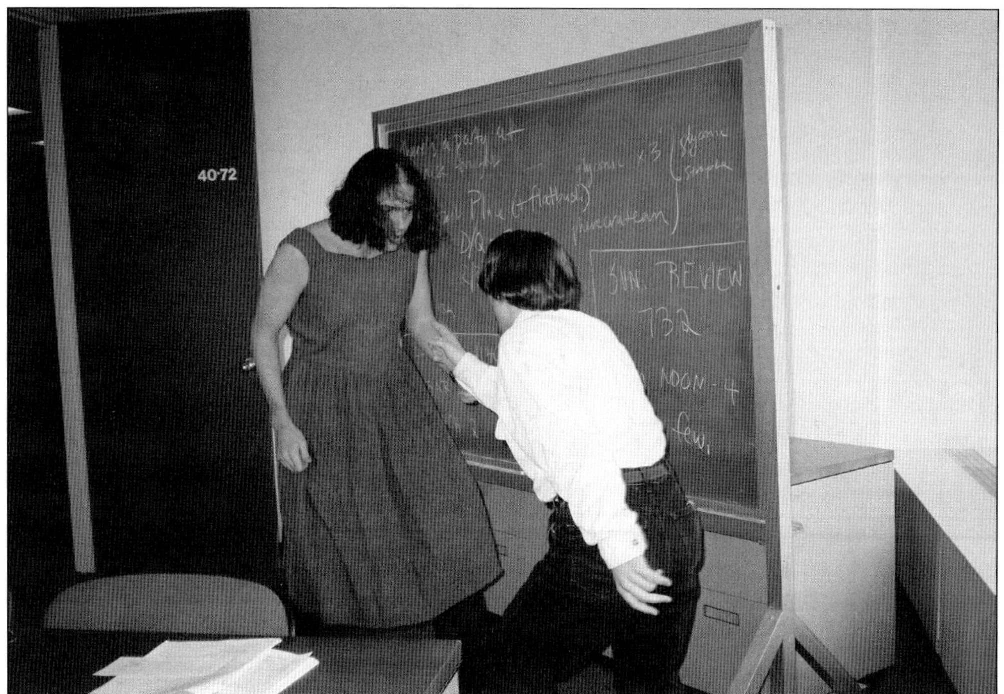

Christopher Long (left, as Medea) and Morgan Meis reenact Jason and Medea's confrontation in the 1995 SGI—a powerful scene, and ideal for the basic programs' memorization and recitation requirement. Long later received a PhD in philosophy and became faculty and dean at Michigan State University. Meis completed a PhD in philosophy and, in addition to being a faculty member at Detroit's College for Creative Studies, is a prolific writer. (Courtesy of Michelle Kwintner.)

SUMMER LATIN INSTITUTE —— CLASS SCHEDULE FOR SECOND HALF

	8:30-9:20	9:30-10:30	10:40-11:30	12:15-12:45	12:45-1:15	1:20-2:00	2:10-3:00	3:00-3:30	3:40-4:00	4:10-5:00
MONDAY 13 July Day 25		Introduction to Prose Unit A, B — SRR	Cicero A — ARK B — ABF	*(Optional)* Vocabulary Building: Prefixes and Suffixes SRR		Prose Composition A, B — SRR	Ennius, Cato A — ABF B — ARK			
TUESDAY 14 July Day 26	*(Optional)* ARK	Cicero A — SRR B — ARK	Cicero A — ABF B — SRR	*(Optional)* Subjunctive I ARK	*(Optional)* Genitive Case ABF	Prose Composition A, B — ARK	Cicero A — SRR B — ABF			
WEDNESDAY 15 July Day 27	*(Optional)* SRR	Cicero A — ABF B — SRR	Cicero A — ARK B — ABF	*(Optional)* Subjunctive II ABF	*(Optional)* Dative Case SRR	Sallust A — ARK B — SRR	**2:40—3:45** History of the Latin Language I ARK		*(Optional)* Sight: Caesar	
THURSDAY 16 July Day 28	*(Optional)* ABF	Cicero A — ARK B — ABF	Cicero A — SRR B — ARK	*(Optional)* Subjunctive III SRR	*(Optional)* Accusative Case ARK	Prose Composition A, B — SRR	Livy A — SRR B — ABF		**Hoplite Challenge Cup** (Greek Institute Morphology Bee) Observers Welcome Room 1500 Grace	
FRIDAY 17 July Day 29	*(Optional)* ARK	Cicero A — ABF B — SRR	Cicero A —SRR B — ARK	*(Optional)* Participles and Infinitives ARK	*(Optional)* Ablative Case ABF	Prose Composition A, B— ABF	Tacitus A — ABF B — ARK		*(Optional)* Sight: Livy	
MONDAY 20 July Day 30	*(Optional)* SRR	Cicero A — SRR B — ARK	Cicero A — ABF B — SRR	*(Optional)* Gerunds and Gerundives SRR	*(Optional)* Verb Morphology ABF	History of the Latin Language II ARK	Petronius A — SRR B — ABF		*(Optional)* Sight: Suetonius	
TUESDAY 21 July Day 31	*(Optional)* ABF	Sallust A — ARK B — ABF	Sallust A — SRR B — ARK	*(Optional)* Sight Reading: Tacitus ARK		Prose Composition A, B — ARK	St. Augustine A — ABF B — SRR		*(Optional)* Sight: Pliny	
WEDNESDAY 22 July Day 32	*(Optional)* ARK	Sallust A — ABF B — SRR	Sallust A — ARK B — ABF	*(Optional)* Sight Reading: Seneca SRR		Prose Composition: Characteristics of the Period SRR		*(Optional)* (At 3:10) Sight: Boethius		

Day Due	Morning	Afternoon*	Day Due	Morning	Afternoon
26	Cicero 1-6	Cicero pp. 88-89	**30**	Cicero 27-33	Petronius 27, 42, pp. 100-01
27	Cicero 7-12	Sallust 1-2, pp. 61-62	**31**	Sallust 3-6	St. Augustine I.1, II.1-2, pp. 107-08
28	Cicero 13-18	Livy I.29, pp. 91-92	**32**	Sallust 7-11 (to *facere*)	
29	Cicero 19-26	Tacitus XIV.5,8, pp. 96-98			

* Please read Introduction for each survey author as they are assigned.

This 1992 schedule for days 25–32 of the SLI demonstrates the highly choreographed nature of the LGI curriculum. Central to Moreland's philosophy was the generation of academic momentum, which reduces barriers to student learning, incorporates necessary remediation, and provides additional opportunities for engagement (such as sight reading). These detailed schedules help guide students through their programs.

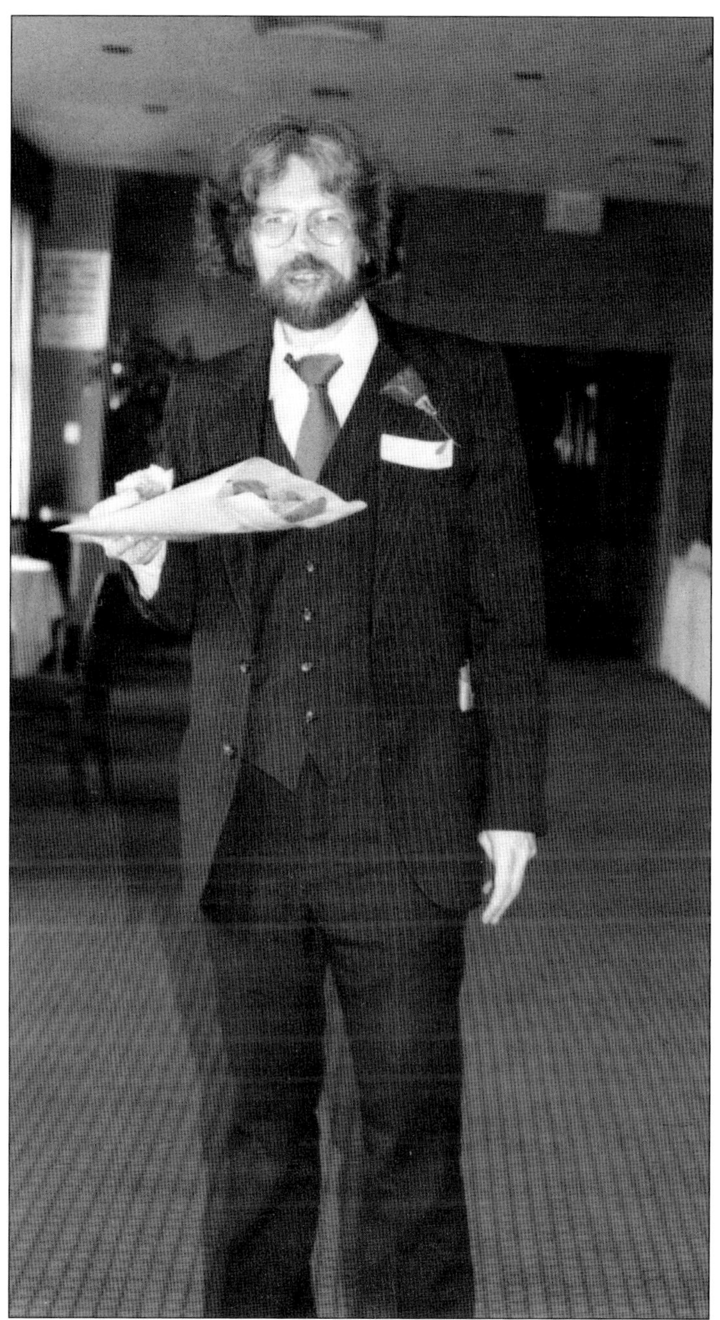

LGI faculty are central to every aspect of the Institute. They commit their entire summers (and beyond) as instructors, advisors, and—not infrequently—a shoulder to cry on. It is as grueling for them as for their students. Over the past half century, several faculty members have become legendary in the LGI community. Among them, John F. "Jack" Collins (shown here in 1978) perhaps looms largest. After majoring in classics and English at St. Peter's College, Collins received an MA and PhD in classics from Columbia. He taught at multiple institutions, wrote poetry in Latin and Greek, sang in a choir, and built his (large) family a computer from scratch (before kits and parts were readily available). Among his well-remembered aphorisms is "To row is human, to sail divine."

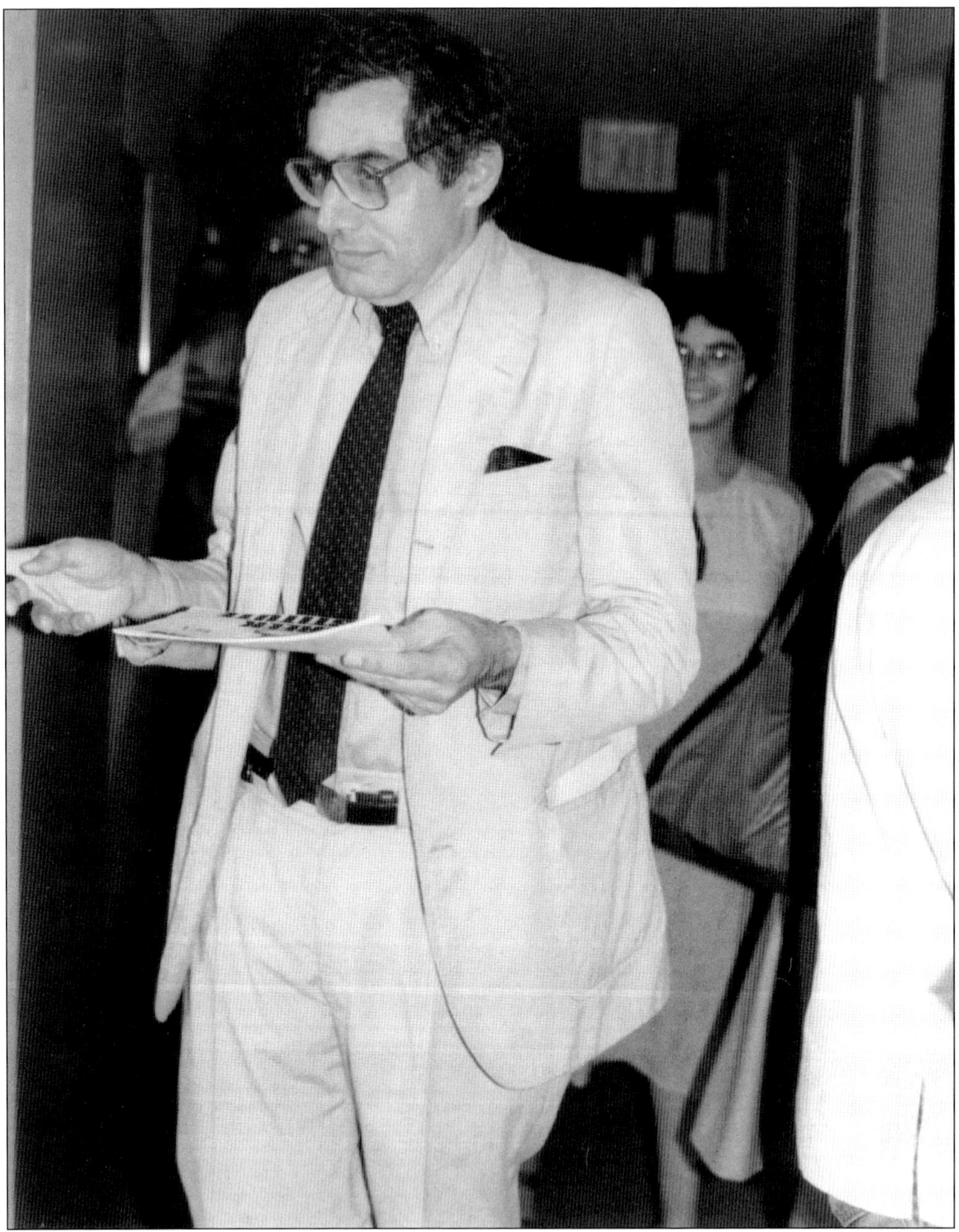

Seth Benardete (1930–2001) was a highly regarded classicist who taught in the first three years of the Basic Greek program. He was integral to the development and launch of the Advanced Greek program, in which he taught every year it was held (1981–1987). He also taught Advanced Latin (1986 and 1988, when Advanced Greek was not on offer) and, in 1982, taught in both advanced programs simultaneously. He was imbued from birth with a love of learning and intellectual inquiry, especially around languages and literature: both of his parents were faculty at Brooklyn College (his father, in Spanish; his mother, English). While a student at the University of Chicago, he studied with Leo Strauss and developed friendships with Allan Bloom and Stanley Rosen. He researched and wrote extensively, with an interest in the intersection of poetry and philosophy. The New School maintains an archive of his papers.

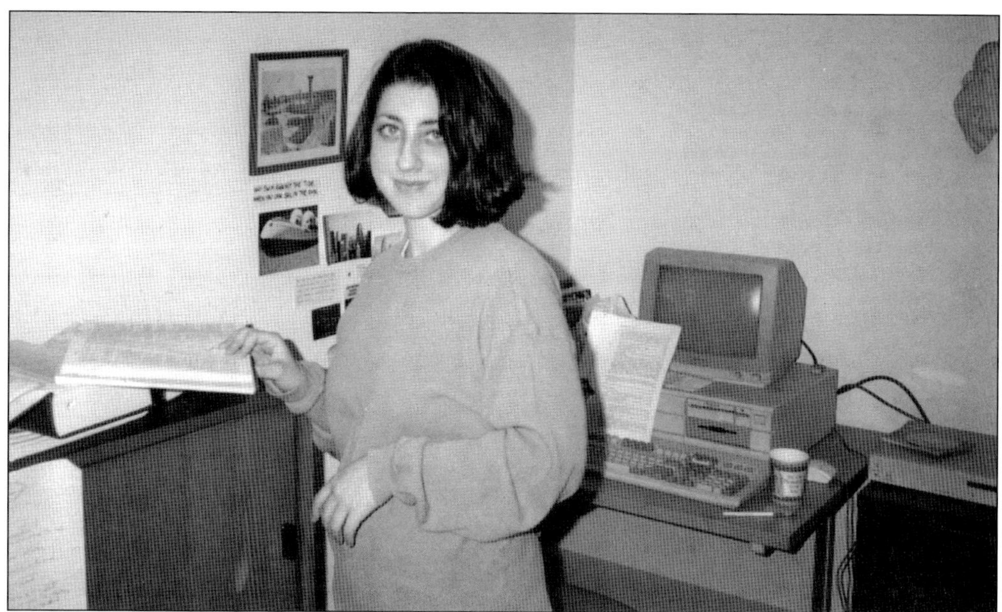

Valentina DeNardis (L 1991 and G 1992) taught in the SLI once and the SGI six times between 1994 and 2003. In the SGI, she exclusively taught the first three weeks. The three-week position provides additional support during the most challenging phase of the basic programs. DeNardis went on to complete a PhD in classics at NYU and was later appointed to the faculty at Villanova University.

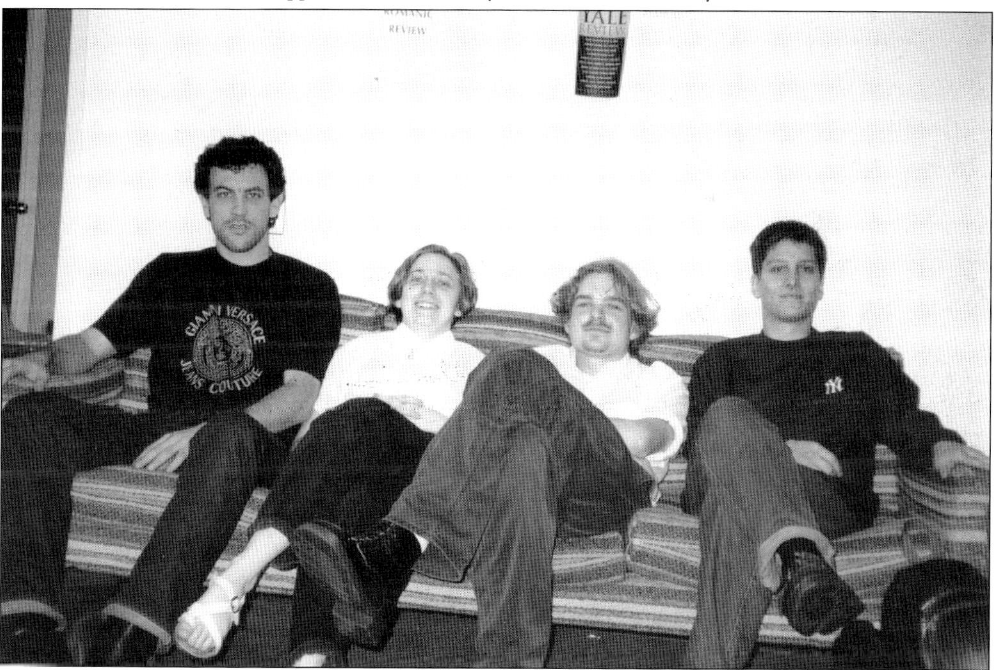

The advisor-advisee relationship is critical to the support system that facilitates student learning. In the early years of the Institute, students were assigned a faculty advisor for the entire summer. This was later revised to multi-week schedules to provide more frequent rotation. Here, Alan Fishbone and Dean Barker (farthest right; L 1993; SLI faculty, 1996–2000) engage SLI students Karen Nelson and Damian Fleming in 1998. Advisors closely monitor and assist their students.

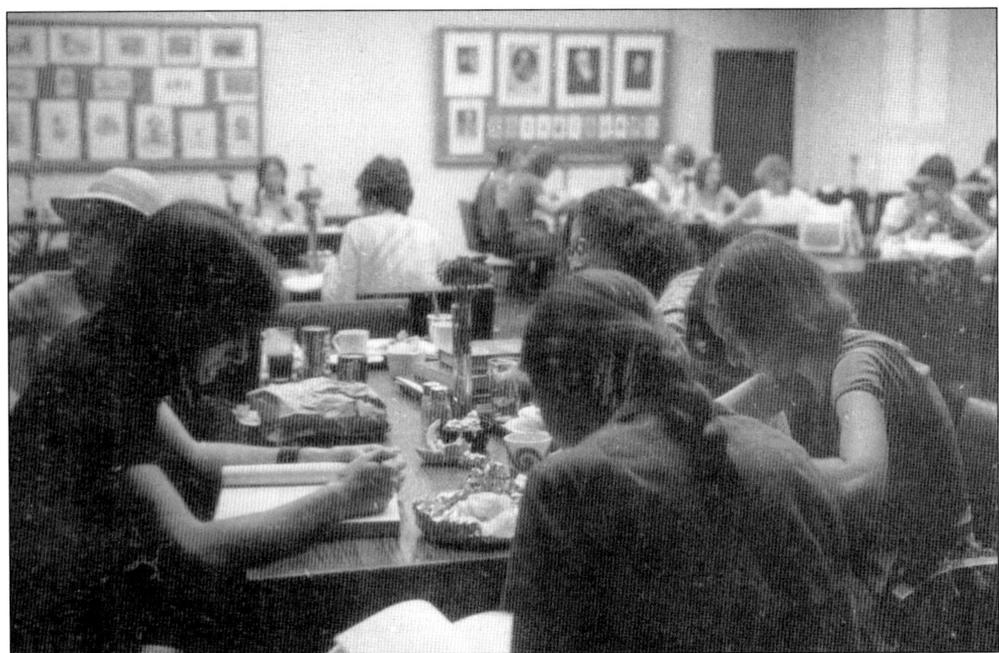

At the end of the day, students often gather in groups to take on their evening assignments. In the early years of the Institute, this happened organically, and more so in the latter half of the summer when reading became the focus of their studies. More recently, group work has been emphasized at the start, especially in the SLI. Although the GC has historically been largely unoccupied in the summer, designated group study rooms are now part of the schedule. Each program also designates a faculty member to stay on-site through the early evening to help support students—a reflection of Moreland's emphasis on reducing immediate barriers to learning and acquisition. Here, student groups are seen at work in the early 1970s and 2013. (Below, courtesy of the OCM, CUNY GC.)

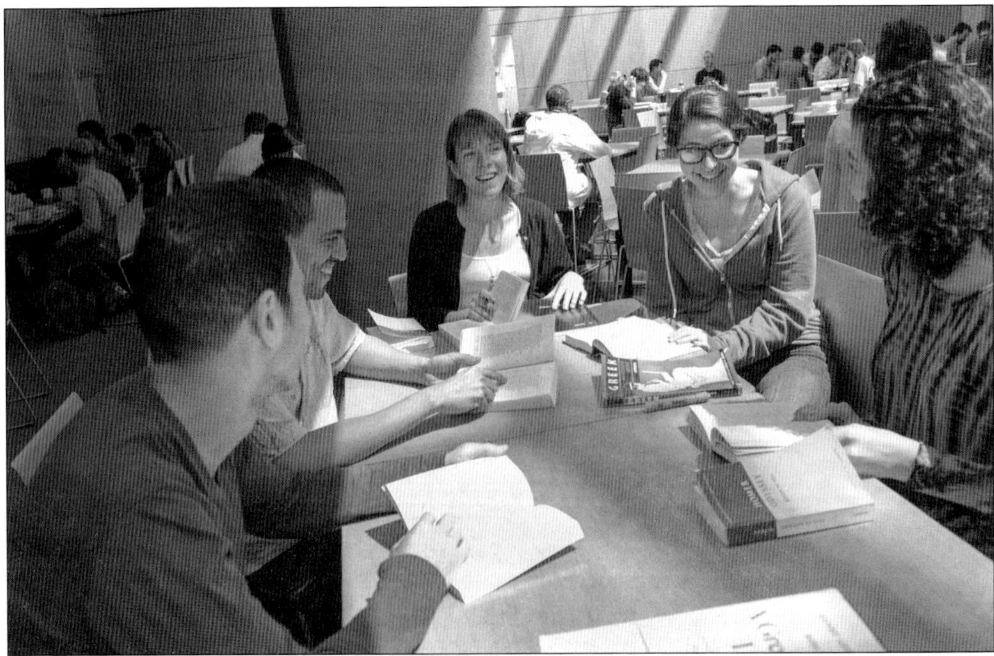

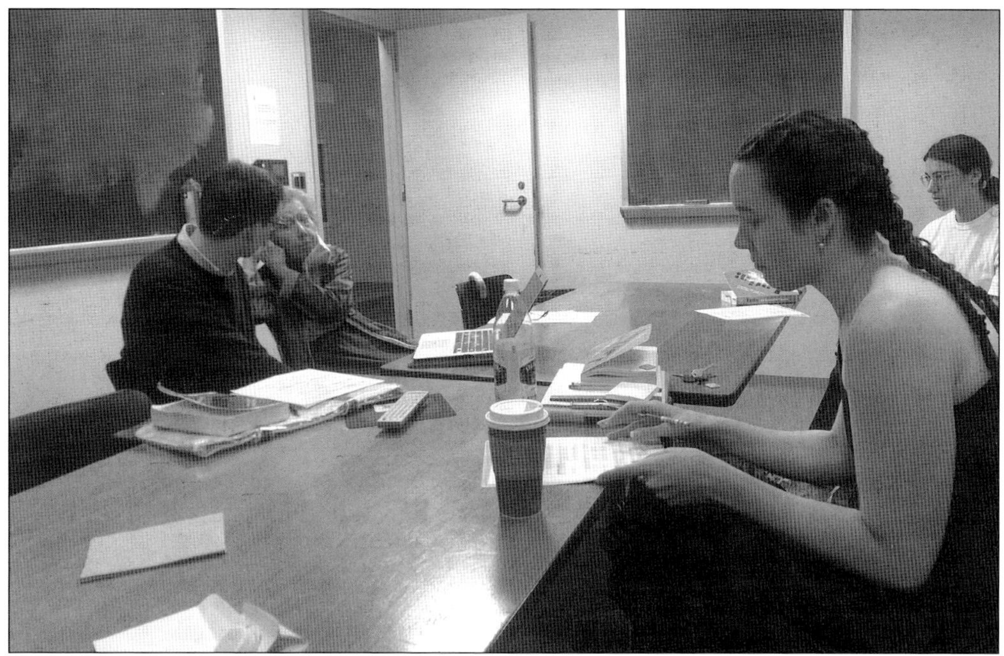

Pre-sessing ensures accuracy and uniformity in the faculty members' delivery; the curriculum is analogous to a symphony, with a score that must be performed as perfectly as possible. It is required of all instructors, regardless of their years of experience. Here, Fleischer critiques the work of the 2023 Latin faculty; from her left are Elizabeth Raab (L 2019), Madison Forbes (G 2019), and Murphy (program chair).

Though the Institute's basic curricula are fixed, continuous adjustments and modifications help ensure their optimal delivery; as Hansen has remarked, the LGI will forever remain a work in progress. Improvements are facilitated by an array of assessment mechanisms, including an open-door classroom policy that permits peer-to-peer faculty feedback and confirmation of uniform delivery. Not even Moreland was exempt: here, Fleischer observes the *conditor* in action in the early 1970s.

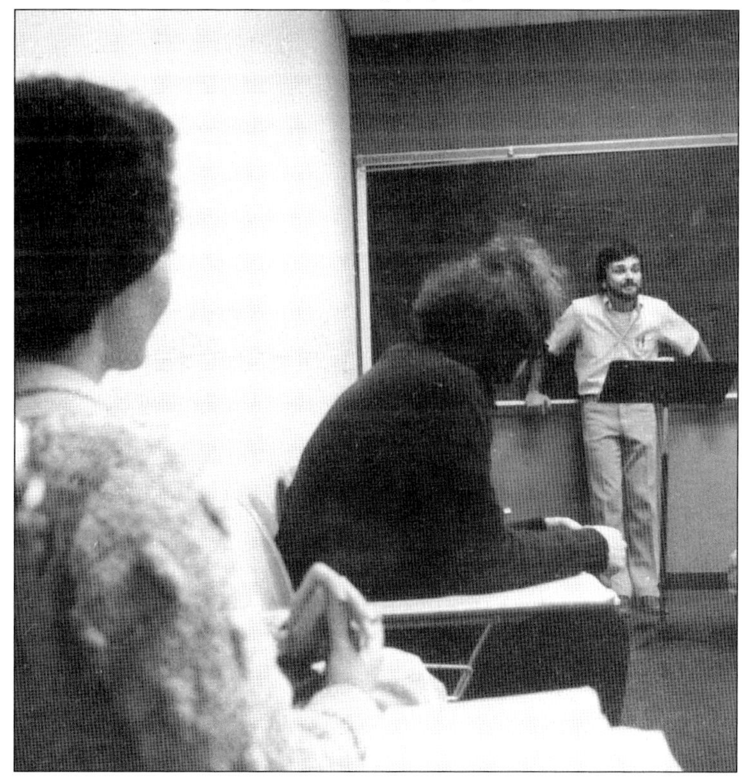

Brooklyn College and the Graduate School
The City University of New York
THE SUMMER LATIN INSTITUTE, 1973

FINAL REPORT

A. ENROLLMENT

Although 27 students were expected to continue into the second half of the Summer Latin Institute, 29 actually did so. Of these 29, 25 completed the program. Several of the students whom we had advised to drop because of academic deficiencies chose not to do so and to remain in the Institute. Our original estimation was correct, for none of these did well at the end. In two instances, students who we felt were improving and showing evidence that they might complete the second half successfully suffered a reversal and did not perform as we had projected. In one case, at least, this reversal resulted from problems of a personal nature which were not related to the course. During the second half, four additional students dropped, either by encouragement or because of personal reasons, again not related to the course. In three of these cases, there was every indication that the students would complete the Institute successfully, if not with distinction, given the proper circumstances and frame of mind.

It is instructive to note that almost all the serious problem students had been spotted by our staff after the first major grammar exam at the beginning of the second week of the program. Given this information, which is consonant with my previous experience at Berkeley, students in future years who cannot receive a grade of B+ or better on the first grammar exam should be urged to drop at once, except in very special cases. The speed and compression of the Latin Institute make it most difficult to correct major deficiencies and misconceptions after the fact; provision should be made for such students to transfer into another summer Latin program in the CUNY system so that the opportunity to learn Latin is not terminated, but rather is channelled into a route which is more realistic for the individual student and consonant with the level of his ability and motivation.

That 25 out of an original 40 students completed a program of this intensity is a reasonably good statistic; we should nonetheless like to see the attrition rate diminish in future years. Part of the problem lay with the selection of candidates for the Institute. The admissions committee will meet this winter and study carefully the applications of those students who were not able to finish the program in order to determine what, if anything, in their records might have foreshadowed their problems, and to establish more effective guidelines for future evaluation and action on admissions. There is also a problem inherent in the sheer nature of the course and the absolute impossibility for candidates to understand exactly how much time, effort, and emotional energy must be invested in order for the Institute to function. No amount of advertising or warning is sufficient for this purpose; word-of-mouth reporting should be. At Berkeley, the Latin Workshop has the reputation of being one of, if not the, most difficult and demanding programs on the campus. Students either shy away from it totally or are intrigued by the unique and invigorating possibilities of participation in it. Given one or two more years of operation,

two

At the conclusion of the Institute's inaugural summer, Moreland authored a comprehensive two-part report detailing almost every aspect of the program. These annual reports continue to be produced and, as part of the ongoing assessment process, help inform enhancements and improvements to the LGI's various academic and administrative functions.

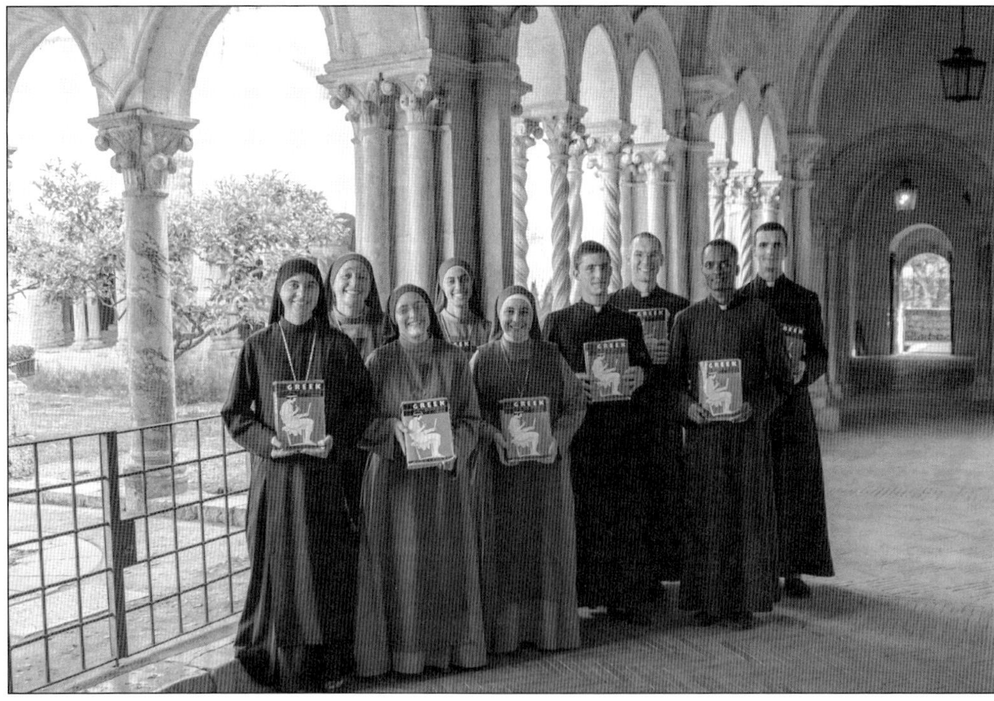

The LGI's methods have had an impact beyond the Institute itself. Here, Sister Maria del Fiat Miola uses Hansen & Quinn to teach Greek to international students (religious brothers, sisters, and priests) at the Servants of the Lord and the Virgin of Matará in Fossanova, Italy. The course uses a modified Institute-inspired curriculum taught entirely in Spanish. (Courtesy of Sr. Fiat.)

Six

Nil Adsuetudine Maius

Institute Traditions

A summer at the Institute is as much an experience as a program of study. Although it confers no standalone degree, graduates are considered (and consider themselves) alumni/ae. This autonomy is further reflected in an array of trappings, customs, and traditions that have come to define a summer at the Institute. Some of these came about by design, with specific curricular connections, while others developed organically. Over time, some have disappeared and new ones have been introduced, while others have evolved, changed, or taken on greater or lesser significance.

Each summer opens with an orientation and, on the Friday before final exams, closes with a party (a "graduation" of sorts). In between, every hour of every day is meticulously planned to ensure student progress. With one exception (the caesura between the conclusion of the grammar portion and the start of the reading sequence), weekends are given to study and review. Early on, Moreland recognized the challenges posed by such an unrelenting pace and embedded opportunities to provide students an outlet to socialize and interact.

To this day, there is an all-program mixer at the end of the first Friday. Begun in the first year of the program, it remains an important capstone of the first week, providing the first opportunity for extended social engagement among students and faculty and across the programs. One early tradition, a communal coffee hour at the conclusion of the morning drill, was eliminated in 1983 at the request of the administrative staff, who found it a time-consuming distraction.

In this latter regard, though less visible (and perhaps less heralded), is the work of the LGI administrative staff, which, with its own precise and time-delineated responsibilities, facilitates and supports curricular momentum. The office manages almost every aspect of students' non-academic responsibilities (such as registration and enrollment), which can be onerous and burdensome. For most attendees, LGI staff are their only engagement with CUNY; in many cases, it is their only experience with public higher education.

No matter the year they graduated, almost every LGI graduate would recognize the elements that follow.

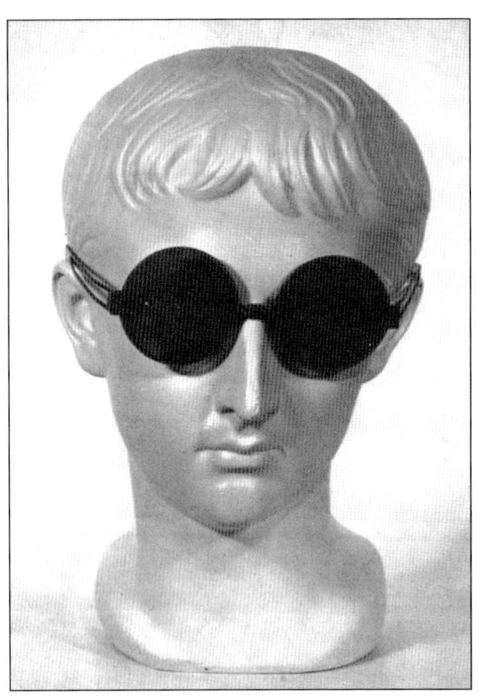

Augustus in sunglasses has served as the Institute's mascot from the start. Moreland had asked his cousin, who worked in advertising, to help design the first promotional poster. He sourced the bust and added the sunglasses which, adding a touch of whimsy, were meant to evoke the summer. Some felt that the sunglasses bordered on the sacrilegious, but they were retained, and the bust has been ubiquitous on LGI materials ever since.

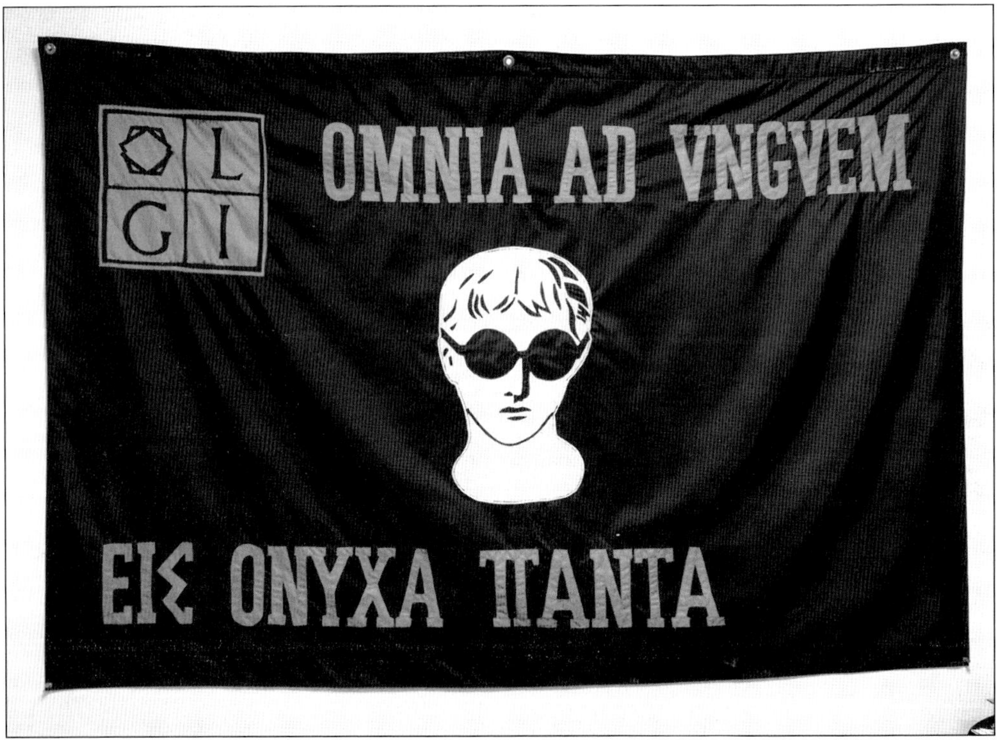

The LGI motto, *omnia ad unguem* ("everything to the nail") conveys the precision of the curriculum by invoking the craft of the ancient sculptor, who would ensure the quality and finish of their work by running a fingernail over its surface. The practice is referenced by Horace (*Ars Poetica* 294), while the Greek (εἰς ὄνυχα πάντα) has been ascribed to a lost treatise of the sculptor Polyclitus of Argos.

For many alums, a large format poster was often their first introduction to the LGI. From the Institute's initial summer to the present, they have been a common sight in humanities departments nationwide (in addition to a small Canadian distribution). Even after word of mouth and electronic distribution came to predominate, LGI posters continue to provide essential and readily accessible information about dates, application processes, scholarship opportunities, etc. in a highly visible and engaging manner. In this regard, the posters themselves have become something of an LGI tradition. The poster at right is from 1987, and the one below is from 1992. Over the years, several have received accolades for their design. The 1987 poster reproduced here won a bronze medal for in-house publications by the Council for the Advancement and Support of Education.

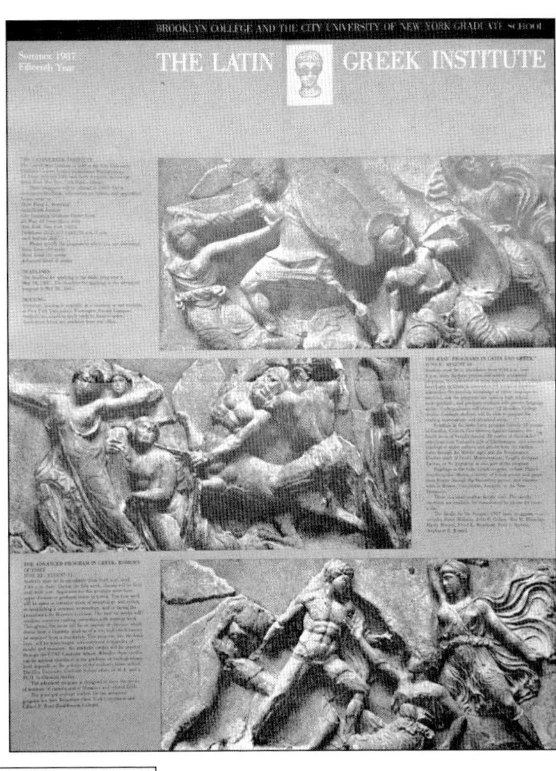

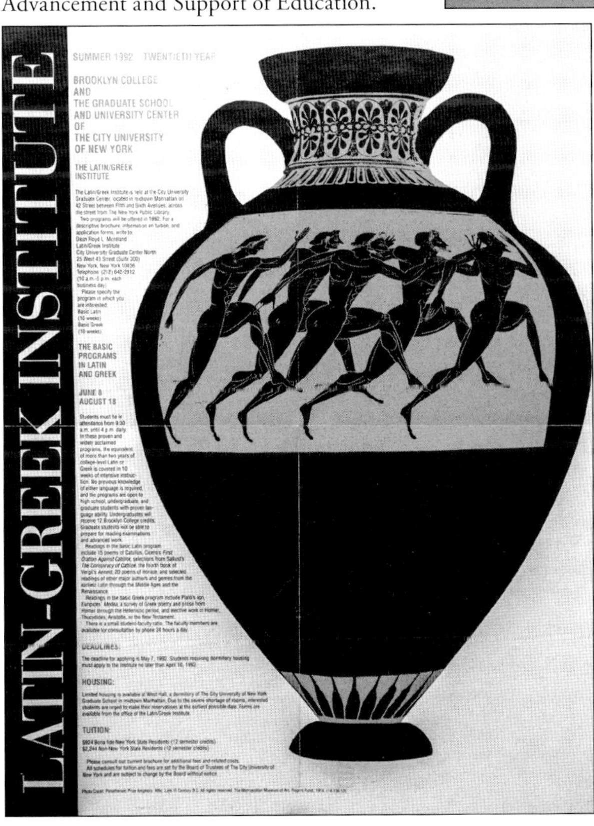

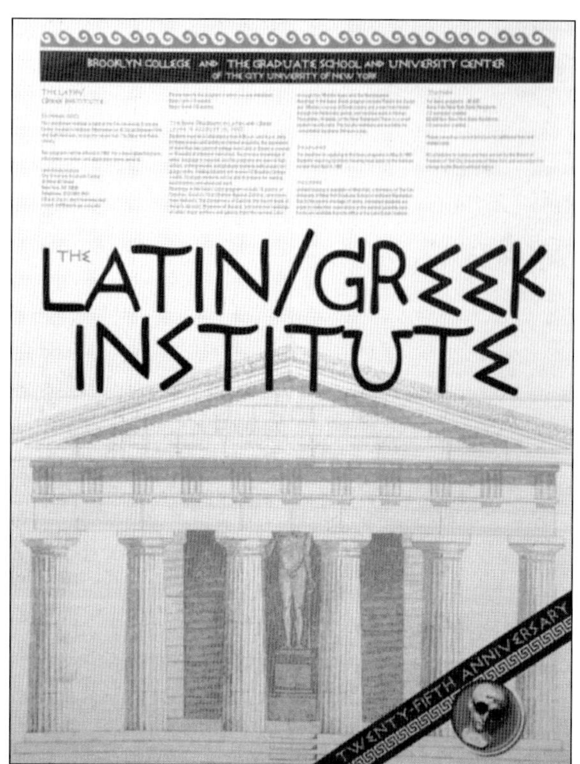

Since 1973, there have been about 10 distinct styles (many with their own subsets that vary in color and imagery). Several of these have been previously introduced in their larger historical context: in 1973, the foundation of the Latin Institute; in 1978, the introduction of Basic Greek and subsequent name change to the CUNY Latin/Greek Institute; in 2000, the Institute's move to the B. Altman Building; and finally, in 2023, marking the Institute's 50th anniversary. The 1973 and 1978 examples were two distinct styles, each lasting several years. The posters reproduced here (left in 1997, and below in 1998) are two examples from a decade with significant stylistic variation: four unique styles, each with several versions.

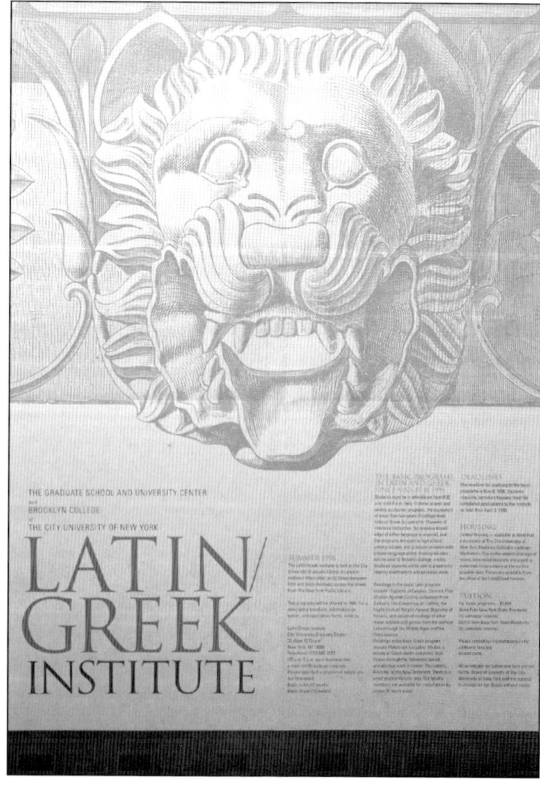

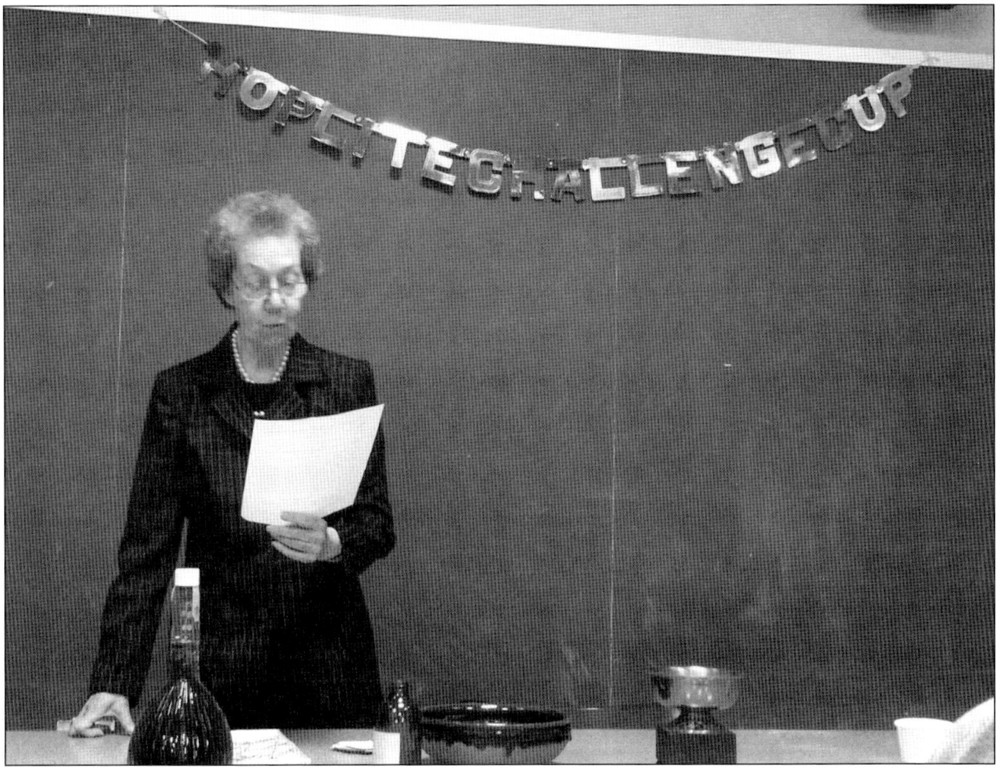

After the improvised 1978 Hoplite Challenge Cup proved a spirited and worthwhile success, Hansen and Quinn developed an official set of rules. These have been modified over the years to clarify issues as they arose. At present, the competition consists of a three-round duel between a student and faculty member (and the occasional alum and/or guest), with play continuing until all students have competed at least once. Here, Fleischer reads the rules for the 2014 cup.

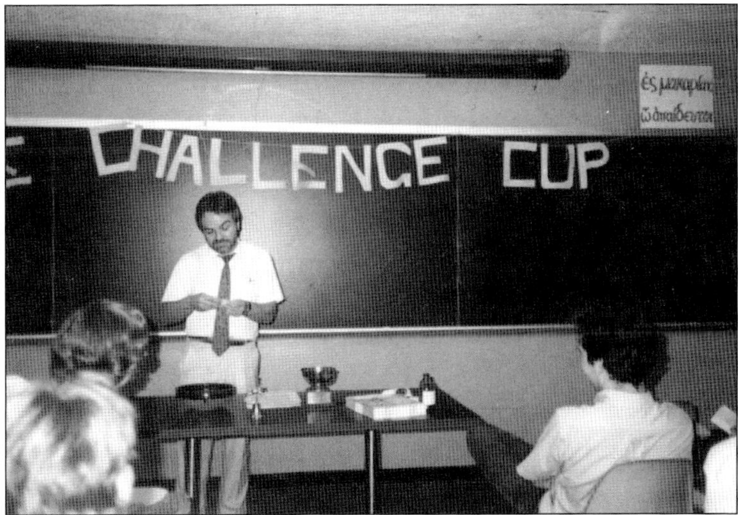

The competition is open to the public and invariably crowded with Latin students. Also present are a judge to verify the accuracy of forms and adjudicate any disagreements, a timekeeper (students have 30 seconds, and faculty have 20), and a scorekeeper. In this photograph from the 1986 contest, Moreland reads out the order of the competitors, selected at random.

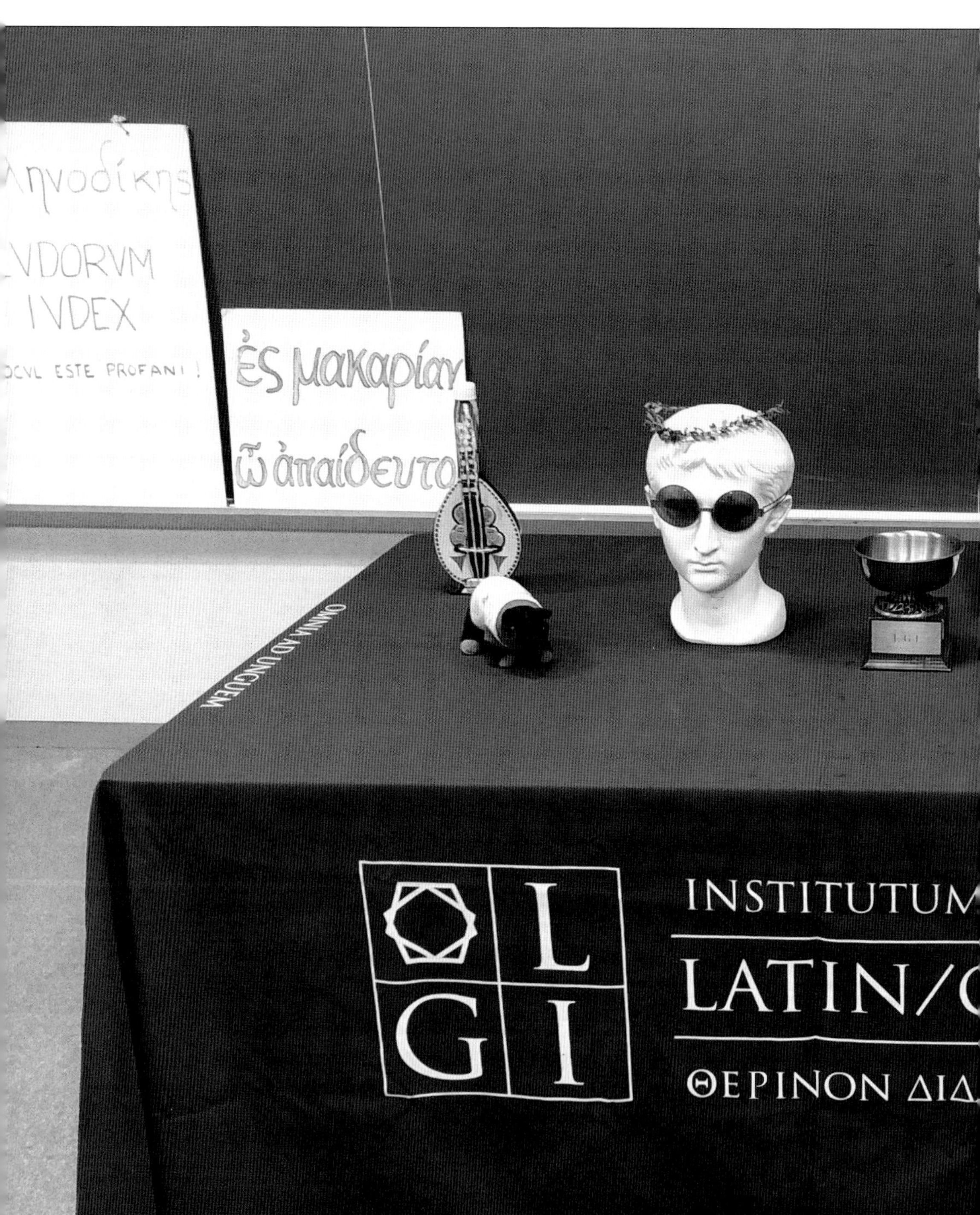

As the contest was increasingly formalized, an array of implements became associated with the event and displayed on a table at the front of the room. Two of the most important are the trophy and the sorting bowl, used for the random selection of the student competitors and the faculty team (distinguished by color-coded paper). The vessel, redolent of a *phiale* (a Greek ritual vessel), was made by Thomas Turnbull (L 1979), a

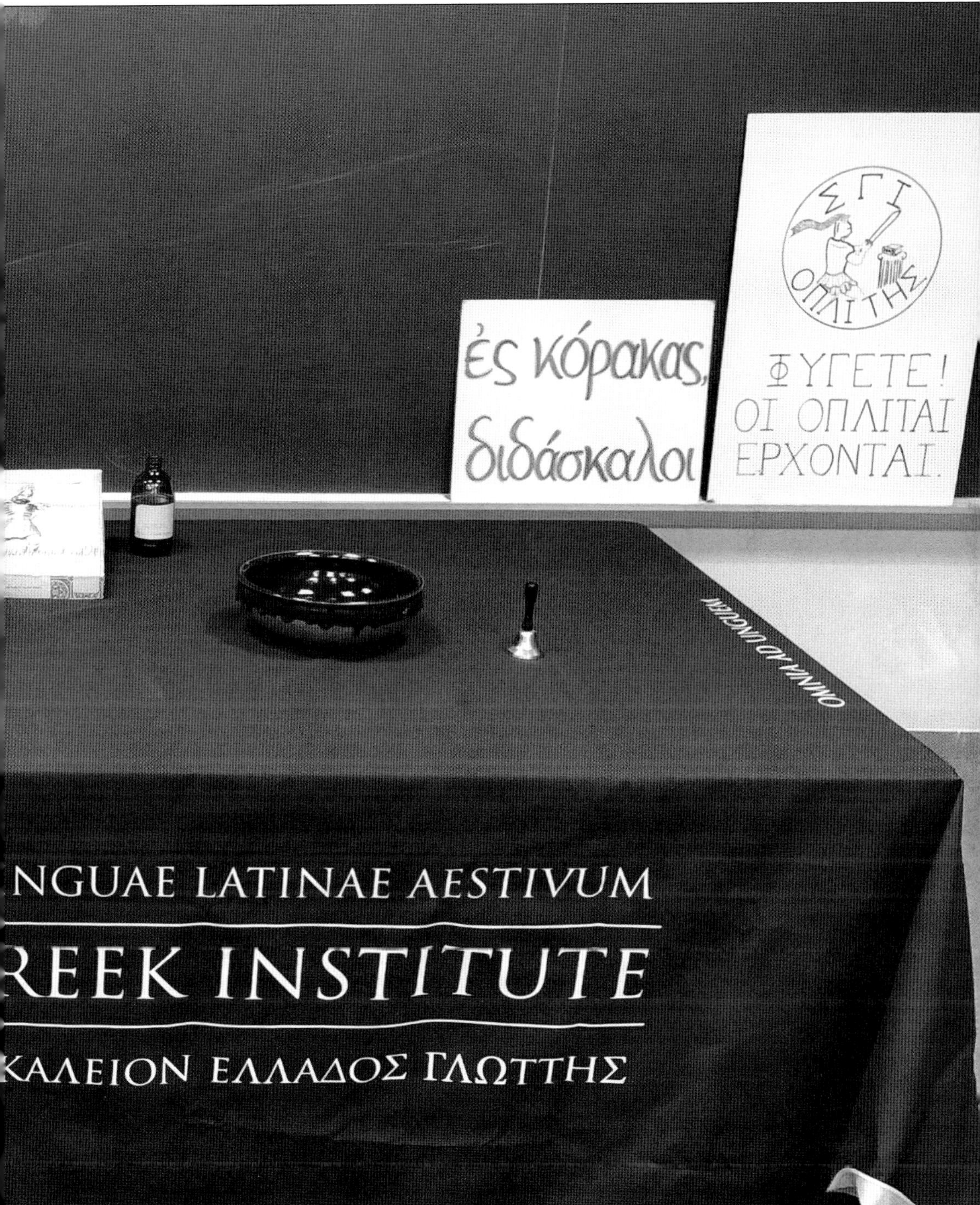

professional potter. Also regularly displayed are Collins's 1980 home edition of the Hoplite Challenge game (limited to 15 verbs) and the LGI "hop"-lite beer bottle. Although present here, Augustus has long since been retired, having grown fragile over the years. To the left is Hansen's tapir, in a t-shirt that quotes the opening of the *Odyssey*. On the right is the timekeeper's bell.

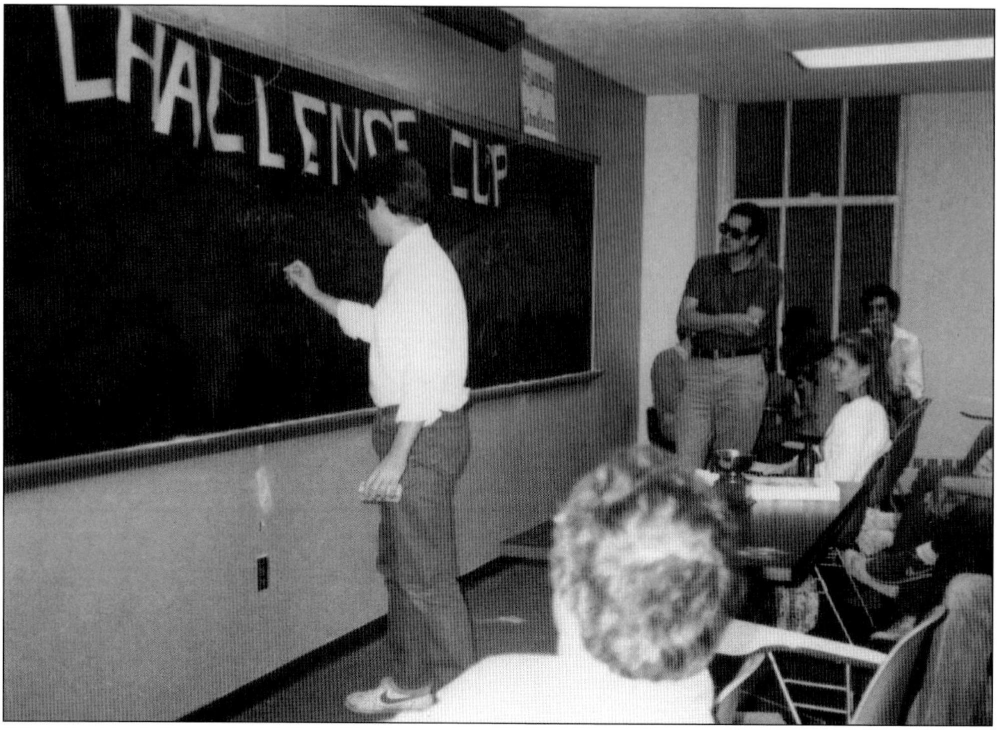

A duel begins with a student asking the faculty opponent to generate a Greek verb in a specific form (tense, mood, person, number, and voice). If the answer is correct, the faculty opponent requests two changes be made to its morphology; if either errs, one point is granted by the opposing team. If no mistake is made after three rounds, a half point is awarded to the student team. Here, David Sider watches his 1986 student opponent complete the requested form.

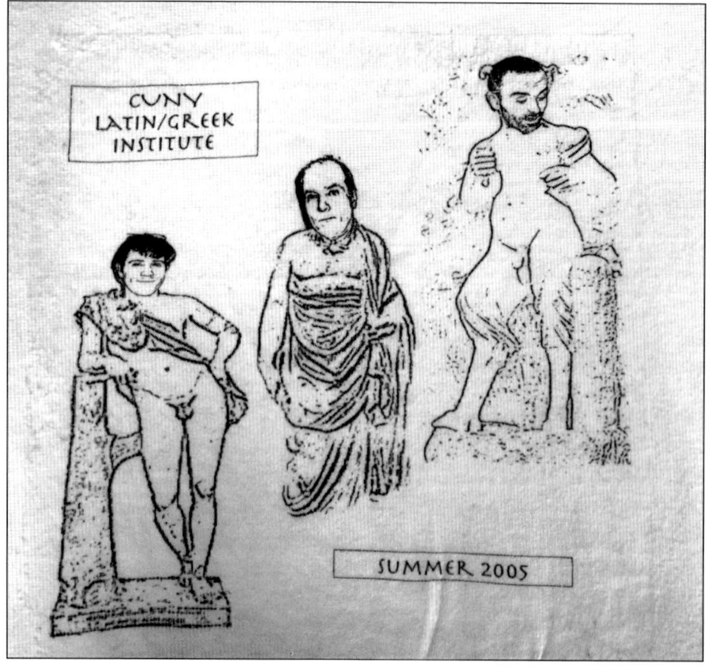

Of all the strategies deployed over the years, that of the 2005 SGI students was perhaps the most creative: the faculty arrived at an empty room, and all the students—after a calculated delay—silently entered wearing this t-shirt, portraying faculty members (left to right) Steve Pigman, Hansen, and Bill Pagonis in Greek guise. The students won (9-8), and the t-shirt became legendary.

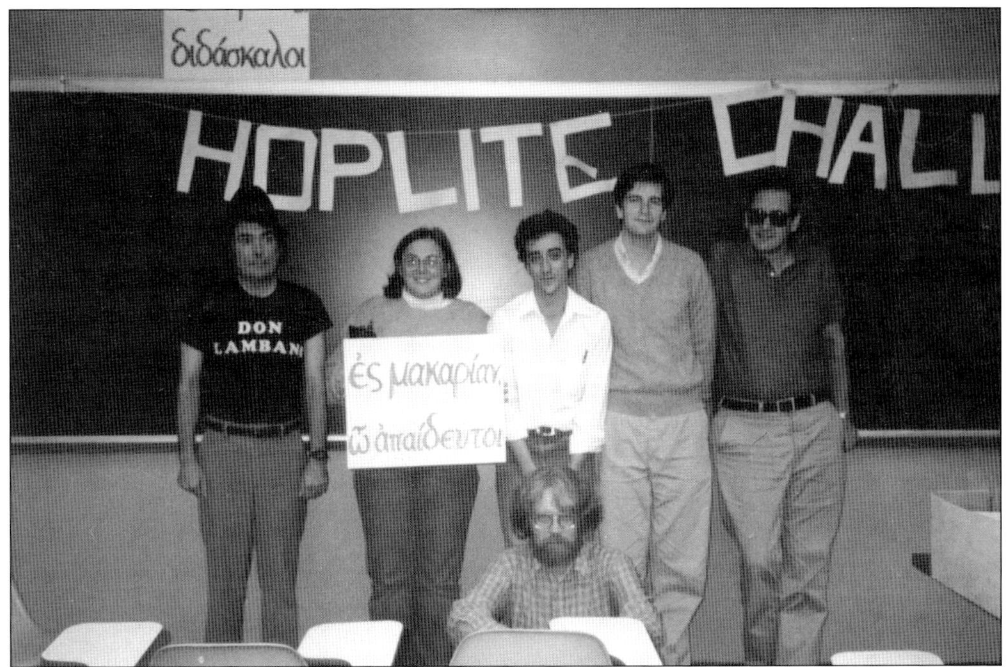

The Hoplite Challenge Cup has been contested 43 times as of 2023. Of these, the Institute has definitive information for 26, with the faculty holding a winning record of 17-7-2. Here, the 1986 faculty team poses for a group photograph. In 2016, faculty member Jeremy March created the Hoplite Challenge app, which simulates the competition and—unlike Collins's home edition of the game—uses every H&Q verb.

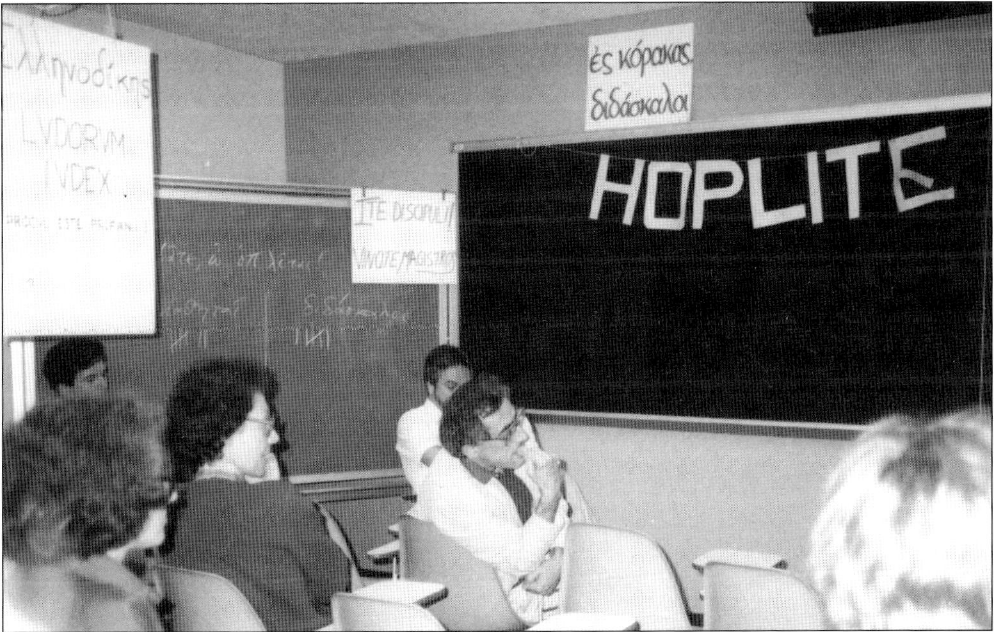

In addition to the table objects, a motley collection of signs has been collected over the years and displayed during the competition. Mostly in Greek, a few in Latin, they offer encouragement and support to one side or the other. Except for a new "Hoplite Challenge Cup" banner (visible on page 86), those present here in 1986 continue to cheer on the combatants to the present day.

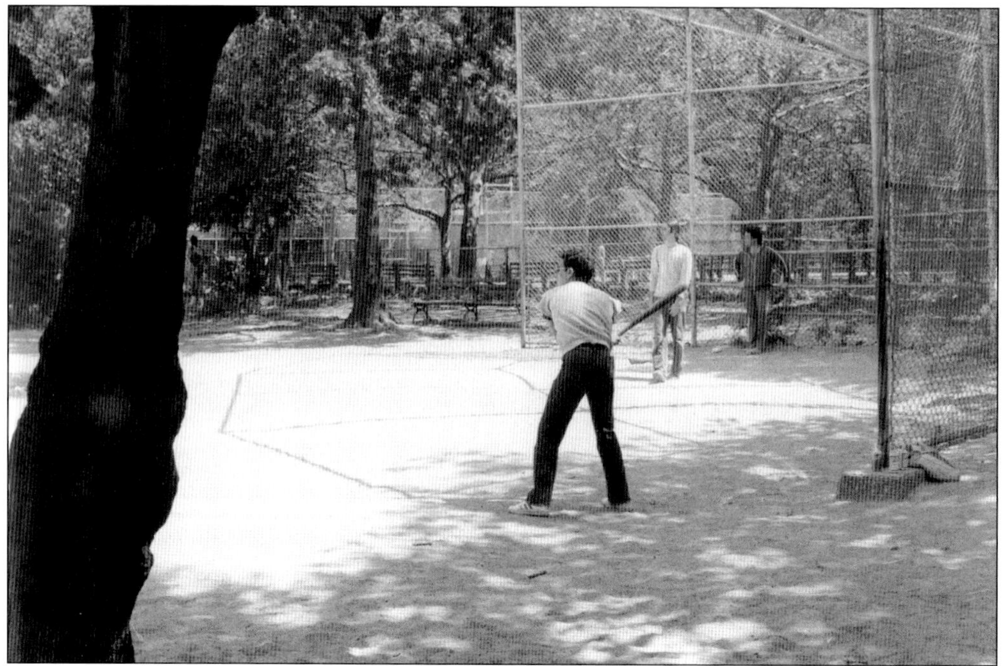

One short-lived tradition was Dido's Cup, a softball game between the Latin and Greek programs, only played twice (1980 and 1981). The 1980 game, contested on August 17 in Riverside Park, was a runaway victory for the Greeks (15-0).

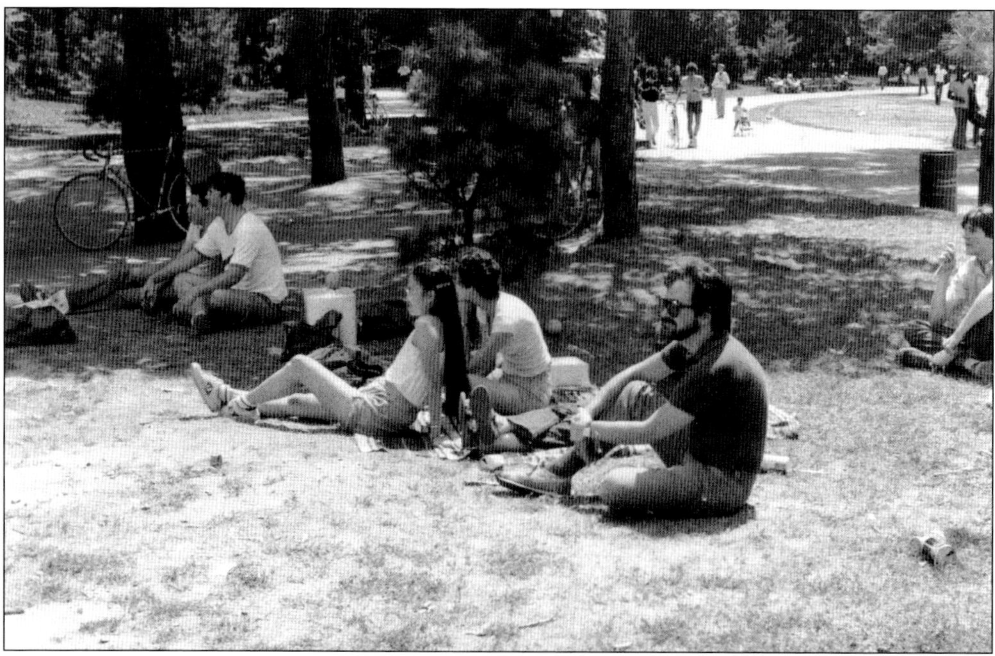

In 1981, a student was hit by a ball and injured, thereby ending the annual game. The competition's name, which echoed that of the Hoplite Challenge Cup, was inspired by the tragic tale of the Carthaginian Queen Dido, magnificently recounted in Book IV of Vergil's *Aeneid* and read in weeks 8-9 of the SLI.

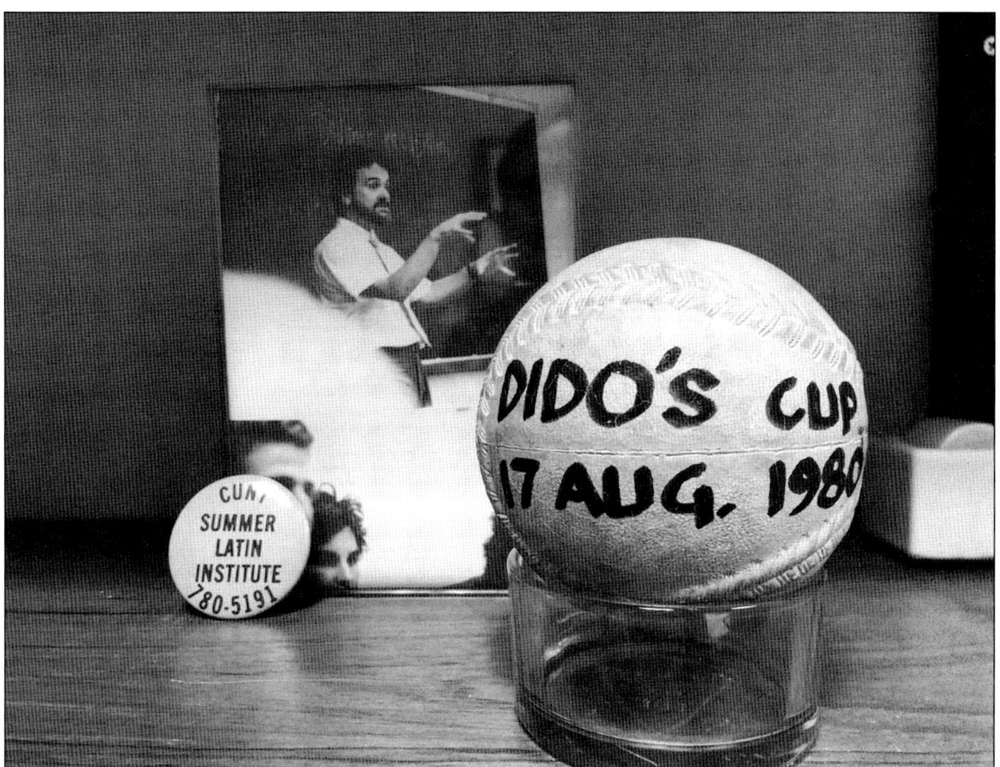

Both current LGI offices (4206 and 9127) contain various artifacts and ephemera retained over the last half century. One small display includes the 1980 game ball, commemorating the triumph of the Greeks. In the background is the 1973 Institute button mentioned on page 37.

Nero – Section A – Stephanie

10/10 excellent!

SEI--Day 33

Here is a passage from In Ciceronem by the famous Roman orators, Principes Institutonis, in which the consuls, having exiled Cicero ex institutione, defend themselves with a striking prosopopeia from the charge that they should have killed Cicero before a) he could organize a revolt freom the nearby Castra Bryantina, or b) he had the chance to finish his speech:

Quae cum ita sint, quid dicamus si patria nobiscum sic loquatur: "O Floedi Ritaque, quid agitis? Ego in manus vestras posui hunc Ciceronem, hunc discipulum, ingenio disertissimo sed moribus sceleratis, ad vel edocendam vel delendum, hunc mensem his muris in vestris luce, cibo sano, sole aestatis prohibitum. Sed 'Nihil disco,' inquit Cicero, 'nisi in Studione LIV.' Quasimodo nihil agitis. Cur non interfectus est? Nemo sit tam Clemens ut Cicero supersit. Multa ab amicis occultis mihi feruntur. Si mihi pinocchiatum erit, undique usqueque deniqueque voces audietis; esse videbatur; Romulus Remus; Stephanie Russell; clausulas amo."

Floedius, -i, M., a man's name
Rita, -ae, F., a woman's name
Stephanie Russell, (indeclinable!), a woman's name
clemens, clementis, resembling Jack Lemmon a little
pinocchio, pinocchere, pinochle, pinocchiatus, to stick one's nose into
quasimodo (adv.), here, "On July 26th in midtown while running a red light"

1. Give the syntax of pinocchiatum erit: Future perfect indicative in a Future More Vivid Conditional with an Emphatic Proboscis

2. Give the syntax of amicis occultis: Ablative of the Double Agent

1. Of which of the five parts of an oratio is this passage a part? Refutatatatio

2. Give an example of a clausula: aestatis prohibitum (although long by position, of course Cicero would shorten this to for greater effect) yes, of course

3. Give me an example of a tricolon: The end section – although it seems as though there are five pieces of syntax after 'deniqueque,' the first and the last ones of course are not counted. yes – although Quintilian says it's a double tricolon with "Romulus Remus" counted twice, your interpretation is really better

4. Give an example of a hendiadys: Floedi Ritaque

In both basic programs, students are surprised with a gag quiz. Though meant to provide a small measure of (humorous) relief, it has sometimes caused consternation among unsuspecting students. Hansen started the tradition by distributing a tiny, postage-stamp-sized quiz in the inaugural SGI (apologizing that "it got stuck in the dryer too long"). This 1984 gag quiz from the SLI is the earliest on file.

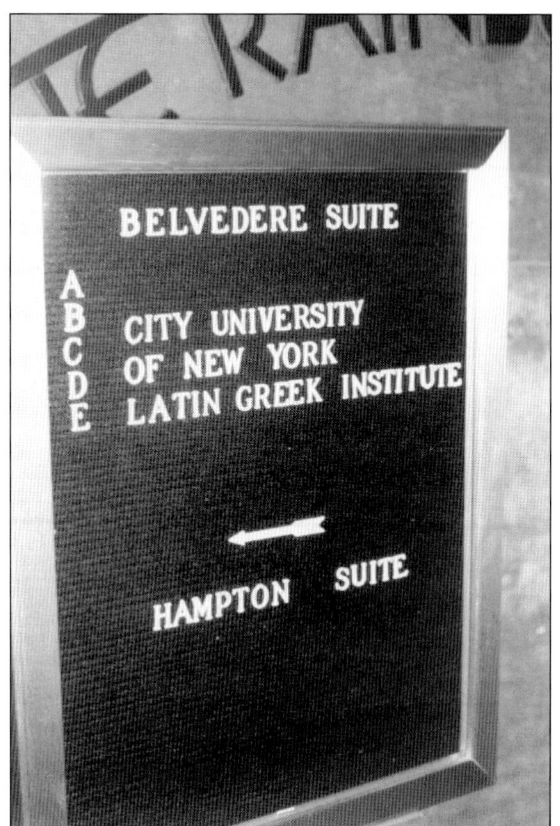

The end-of-summer party has been held at some of the city's best-known establishments, including Tavern on the Green (1980), the Rainbow Room at Rockefeller Center (1981–1985, as shown here), Fraunces Tavern (1999), and Windows on the World (1986–1990). The most frequented venue was the Water Club (1991–1998 and 2000–2013). Only one summer, 2003, was without a ceremony, as it followed a massive regional blackout the day before (on August 14).

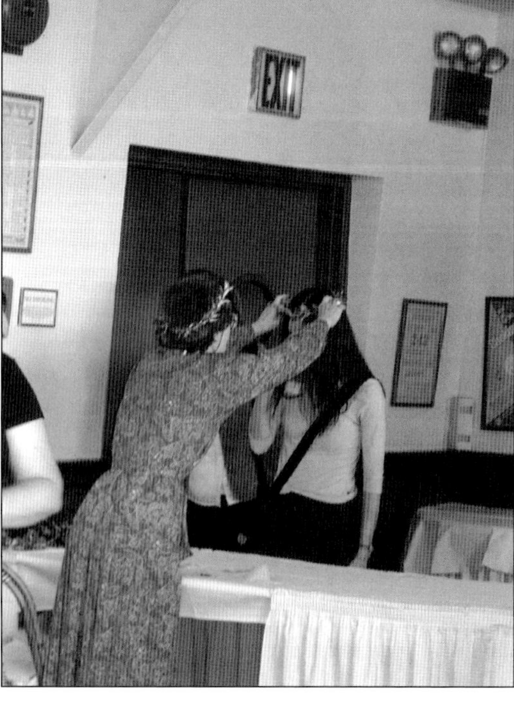

Fleischer crowns each celebrant with a laurel wreath as they arrive. Here, she does the honors at the Water Club in 2004. Stephanie Russell introduced the tradition around 1980. Until 2019, the wreaths were made by the same florist who, delighted by the tradition, helped keep costs reasonable. Following his passing, the only affordable replacements were, alas, made of plastic.

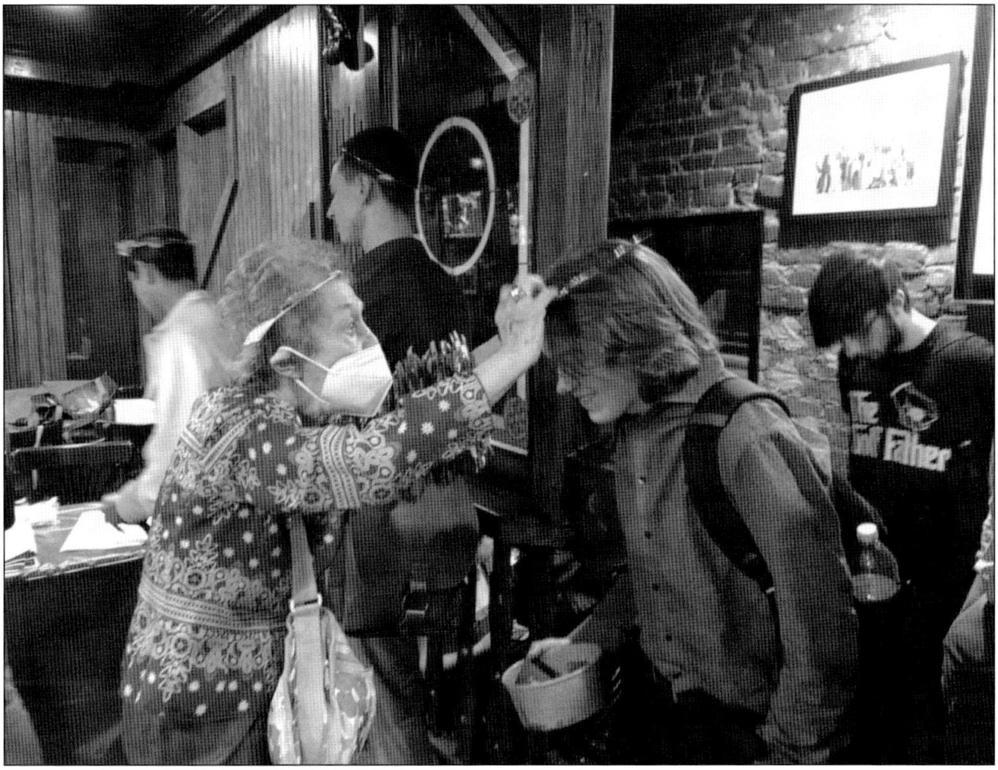

In recognition of the Latin/Greek Institute's 50th summer in 2023, the wreathes were gold in color. Rita Fleischer, as always, crowned the arrivals. As the SLI and SGI have different schedules, students usually arrive in separate groups; here, SLI students are the first to make an appearance. As per tradition, the milestone was also celebrated with a birthday cake.

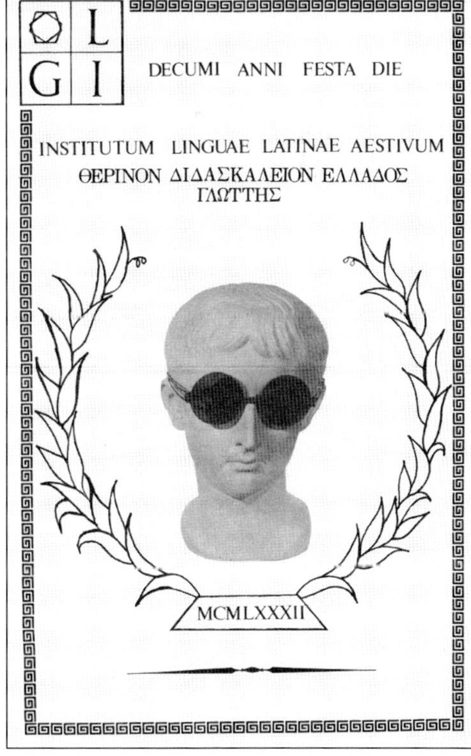

The afternoon's festivities are detailed on a bilingual program; in decades past, these were printed in large format on hard cardstock. The proliferation and ease of desktop copiers have introduced some variation in size and format in the new millennium. The 1982 program, shown here, was one of the first large-scale, high-quality productions.

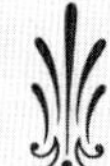

CENACULUM ARCUS PLUVII

FERCULA FESTIVA

IDUS AUG. MCMLXXXII

Multos post operae dies et horas
advenimus ad cenulam modestam.
Combibonibus, o, salutem et omnes
propinemus eo die magistri.
"Hic finges nihil audiesve fictum
et voltu placidus tuo recumbes."
Haec vatis moneant ut gaudeatis:
diem carpite tempus ante cedat.
Iam discedimus, et "valete" fandum:
fugaces abeunt dies laboris.
Discedunt comites amabilosi,
quod iam conficietur Institutum.

Carissimis amicis--discipulis egregiis collegisque--Dennis, Floyd, Gail, Hardy, Jack, Joel, John, Karen-edis, Ken, Rita, Roberta, Ron, Seth, Stephanie, Tony S.P.D.

PARTES EPULARUM

PRIMO

Gallicaudae Diversae

(potiones--nos miseret--prandiis non includuntur; quisque ipse suas petat)

Promulsides Parvulae

PRIMA MENSA

Pomorum Novorum Lanx

SECUNDA MENSA

Gallus modo diei Sabbatorum praeparatus, cum holeri foliorum viridium atque placenta palmae appositus

Lac Glaciatum cum racemis passis liquore inebrianti perfusis

Vinum Scintillans

Caffeum vel Thea

Multos per menses et multa per aspera pulsi
Aggredimur tandem sidera ad alta supra.

The interior of the program includes one page in Latin and another in Greek. Both detail the menu in the respective language and include a poem. Moreland wrote that in Latin, which is perfectly calibrated to an SLI student's sight-reading ability by the day of the party (and also contains a wonderful Latin neologism: *amabilosi*). The 1982 celebration included several courses but drinks (except for champagne—*Vinum Scintillans*) were not included.

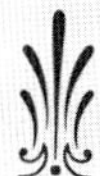

ΙΡΙΔΟΣ ΜΕΓΑΡΟΝ

ΣΥΜΠΟΣΙΟΝ

ΠΕΜΠΤΩΙ ΕΝ ΘΕΡΕΙ

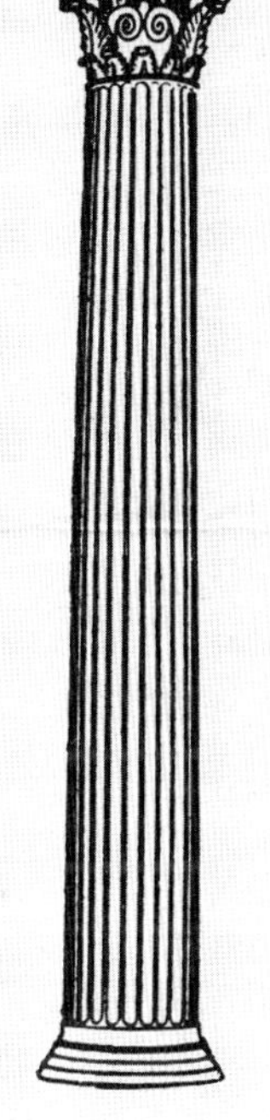

φαίνεταί μοι κῆνος ἴσος θέοισιν
ἔμμεν' ὤνερ ὅττις ἐπισχερώ τοι
πιδύει πᾶν ῥήματος εἶδος ὑψί-
φρων μέγα φωνῶν.

καὶ γελάσας σαρδάνιον κελεύει
σπέσθαι ἡμᾶς ἐκπαταγοῦνθ' ἑαυτῷ
αὖ τε τευτάζειν καθ' ἕκαστον ὧν ηὔγ-
μην λελαθέσθαι.

γραμμάτων διδάσκαλε τετριγώτων,
παῖ λόγων τε ῥηματίων τε πτώσεων,
λίσσομαί σ' ἐὰν συνιῇς μ' ἄμουσον,
δέσποτ', ἄπερρε.

ἀγαθῇ τύχῃ

Dennis, Floyd, Gail, Hardy, Jack,
Joel, John, Karen-edis, Ken, Rita,
Roberta, Ron, Seth, Stephanie, Tony

ΠΡΩΤΗ ΠΕΡΙΟΔΟΣ

παντοδαπὰ παροψωνήματα ὡς ἔχει

ἐκπώματα τοῦ προπίνειν ἕνεκα
(οὐκ ἀπριάτην)

ΔΕΥΤΕΡΑ ΠΕΡΙΟΔΟΣ

κυλίκιον νεωστὶ δρεφθέντων καρπῶν

ΤΡΙΤΗ ΠΕΡΙΟΔΟΣ

σαββατικὸς νεοττὸς τρωκτοῖς τε φύλλοις
καὶ πλακοῦντι φοίνικος κεκοσμημένος

ΤΕΤΑΡΤΗ ΠΕΡΙΟΔΟΣ

γάλα κρυσταλλόπηκτον σταφίδες τ' οἰνοβαρεῖς
πραμνειοπομφολυγοπάφλασμα
πῶμα κυαμῶδες ἢ φύλλια βεβρεγμένα

ὦ τε πεπονθότες ἄλφα τε χῶσσα τὰ γράμματα μέσσα,

εἴπωμεν χαίρειν πολλὰ διδασκάλιον.

The Greek poem was the work of Jack Collins, who was highly regarded for his composition skills. Most significantly, Kurt Vonnegut employed him to render his 1986 *Requiem: The Hocus Pocus Laundromat* into Latin. Both poems celebrate the conclusion of the summer with warmth and humor and are read aloud as part of the ceremonies. As previously noted, the event is not a true graduation and is actually held the Friday before Monday's six-hour final exam. In addition to students and faculty, guests include friends and supporters of the Institute.

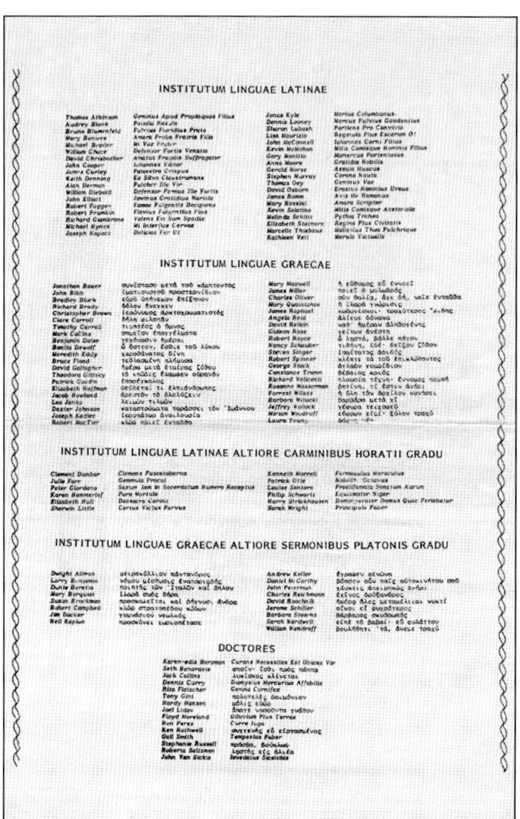

INSTITUTUM LINGUAE LATINAE

INSTITUTUM LINGUAE GRAECAE

INSTITUTUM LINGUAE LATINAE ALTIORE CARMINIBUS HORATII GRADU

INSTITUTUM LINGUAE GRAECAE ALTIORE SERMONIBUS PLATONIS GRADU

DOCTORES

Attendees have traditionally had their names listed both in English and as a Latin or Greek homophone or as a phrase that translates into their names (or into puns on their names). The name given to the author in the 1995 SLI, for example, was "Aspice nos fricantes," which means "look (at) us rubbing" (Lucas Rubin). Shown here are the final names for 1982 and a corresponding worksheet compiled by a program assistant. Faculty names remained consistent, with Moreland, Fleischer, and Hansen known respectively as Diluvium Plus Terrae, Gemma Carnifex, and μόλις εὐώψ. Spiritus Vini Lupa was the name given to Ethyle Wolfe.

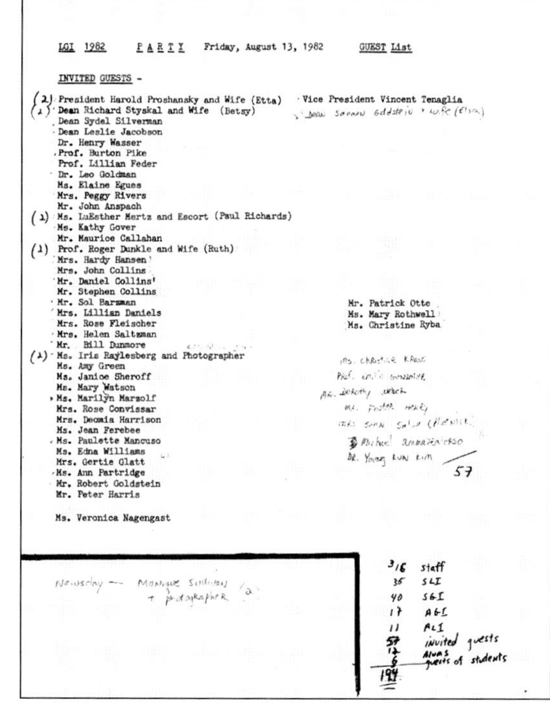

LGI 1982 PARTY Friday, August 13, 1982 GUEST List

INVITED GUESTS -

(2) President Harold Proshansky and Wife (Etta) Vice President Vincent Tenaglia
(2) Dean Richard Styskal and Wife (Betsy)
Dean Sydel Silverman
Dean Leslie Jacobson
Dr. Henry Wasser
Prof. Burton Pike
Prof. Lillian Feder
Dr. Leo Goldman
Ms. Elaine Egues
Mrs. Peggy Rivers
Mr. John Anspach
(2) Ms. LuEsther Mertz and Escort (Paul Richards)
Ms. Kathy Gover
Mr. Maurice Callahan
(2) Prof. Roger Dunkle and Wife (Ruth)
Mrs. Hardy Hansen
Mrs. John Collins
Mr. Daniel Collins
Mr. Stephen Collins
Mr. Sol Barzman
Mrs. Lillian Daniels
Mrs. Rose Fleischer
Mrs. Helen Saltzman
Mr. Bill Dunmore
(2) Ms. Iris Raylesberg and Photographer
Ms. Amy Green
Ms. Janice Sheroff
Ms. Mary Watson
Ms. Marilyn Marzolf
Mrs. Rose Convissar
Mrs. Deomia Harrison
Ms. Jean Ferebee
Ms. Paulette Mancuso
Ms. Edna Williams
Mrs. Gertie Glatt
Ms. Ann Partridge
Mr. Robert Goldstein
Mr. Peter Harris

Ms. Veronica Nagengast

Mr. Patrick Otte
Ms. Mary Rothwell
Ms. Christine Ryba

Dr. Young Kun Kim
57

Newsday — Monique Sullivan + photographer

16 staff
35 SLI
40 SGI
17 AGI
11 ALI
57 invited guests
12 Alums
6 guests of students
194

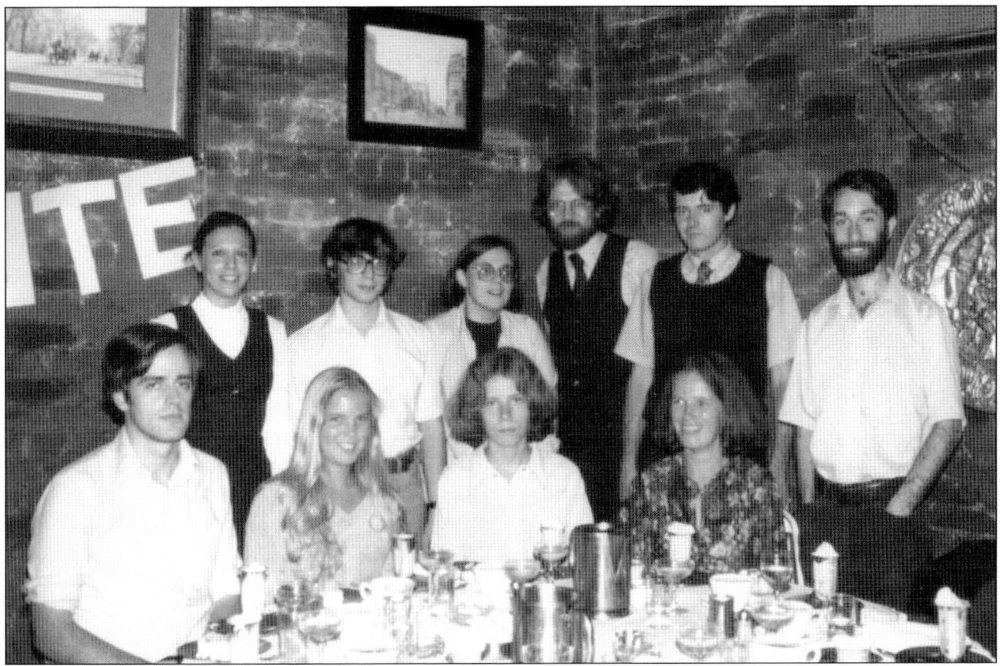

The party offers a rare opportunity for students and faculty to socialize in a relaxed setting, which Moreland specifically encouraged to help build a sense of community among soon-to-be-graduates. Here, Russell and Collins pose with students in 1979.

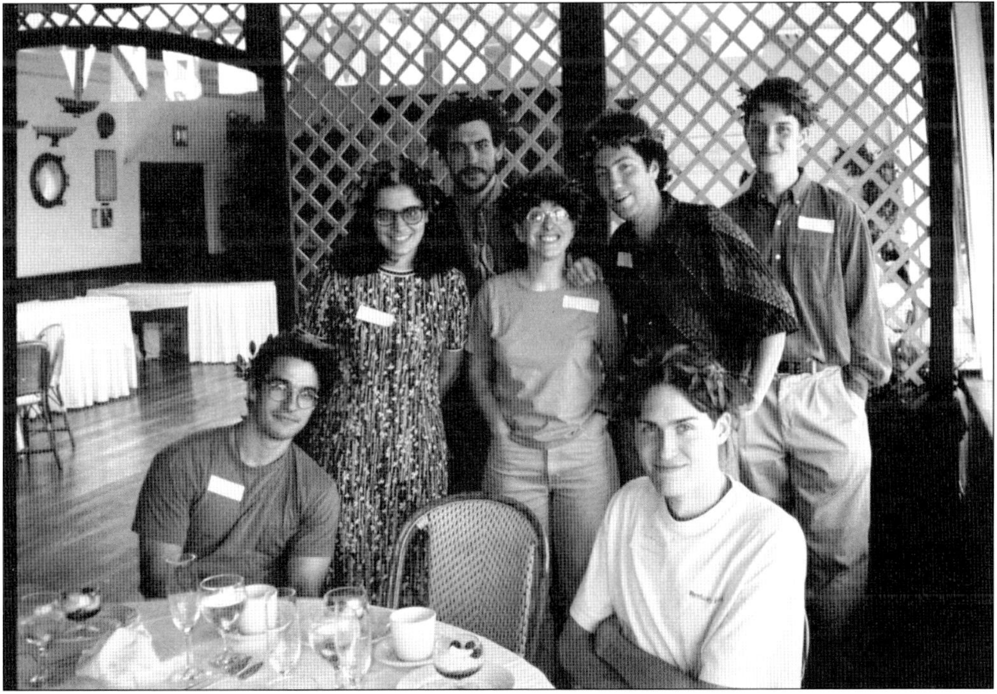

Alan Fishbone and Michelle Kwintner (middle, with glasses) pose for a photograph with SGI students in 1995. Both Fishbone and Kwintner went on to interesting post-Institute careers: he, as a sailboat captain, and she, after receiving an MSW at Smith College School for Social Work, as a psychoanalyst.

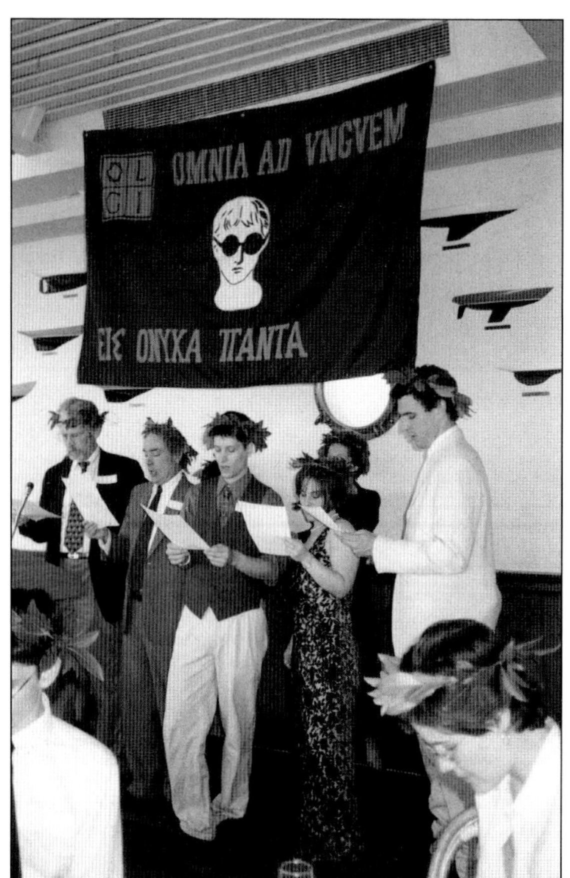

As part of the festivities, attendees sing *Gaudeamus Igitur*, a convivial 13th-century song that celebrates academic life. Its inclusion was a holdover from the Berkeley Latin Workshop where it was included at one of the program's weekly dinners and "allocutions." At the LGI, it evolved from a spontaneous performance to a formal component as seen here in 1998. The LGI version includes additional stanzas extolling the Institute (including one in Greek).

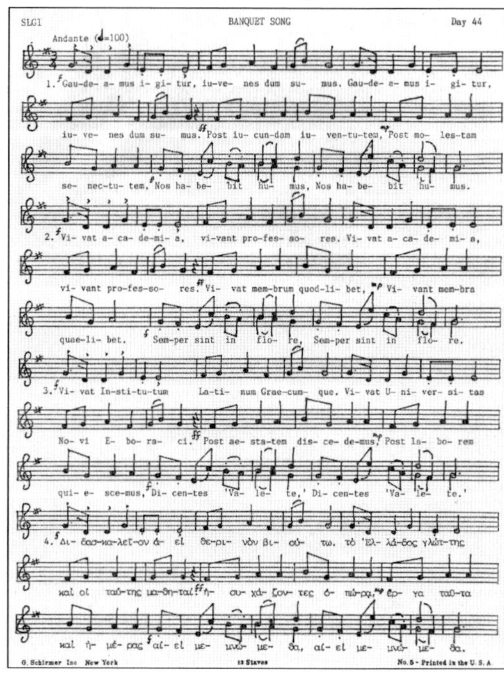

From the first impromptu gathering in 1973, students have attended in costume and/or performed skits. At the 1998 reception, SGI students Tova Friedman (standing), as Aphrodite, and Collomia Charles, in the guise of Sappho, performed Sappho's Fragment 1 (read in the Greek survey). Charles would later complete the SLI (in 2000) and teach in multiple LGI programs.

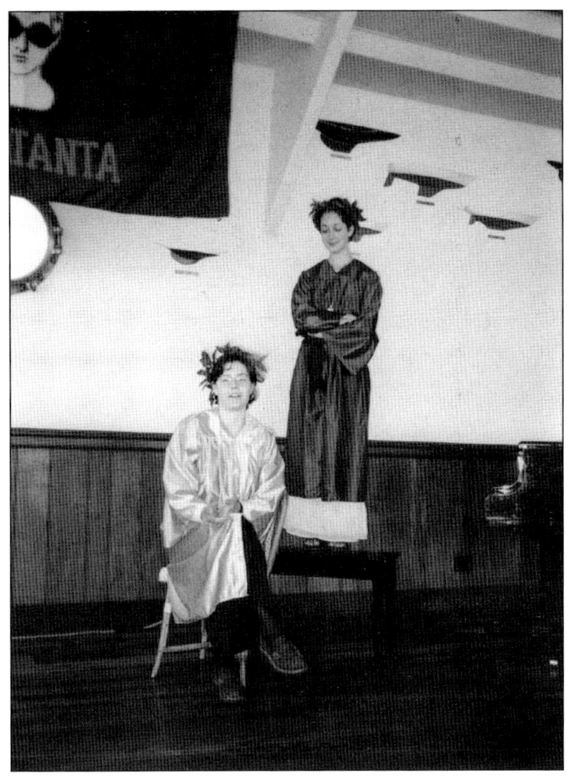

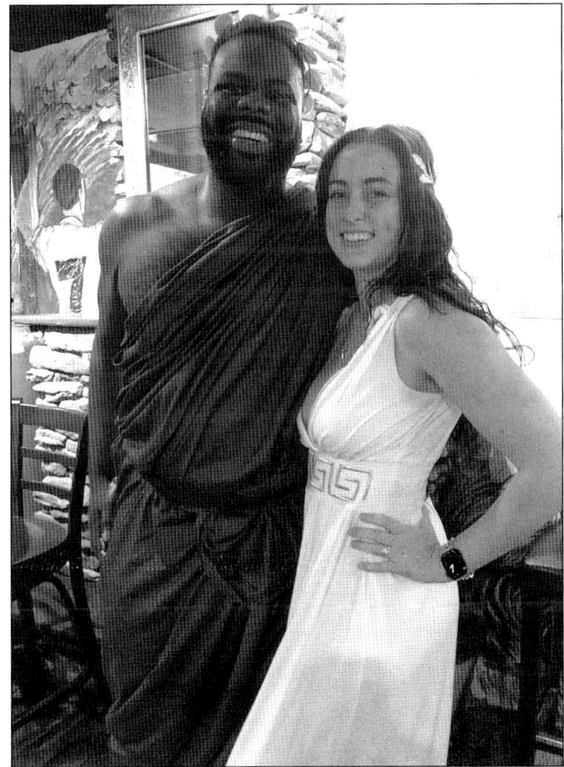

SGI students Marven Corrielus and Becca Tauscher continued the tradition of donning festive (and appropriately themed) attire in 2023. The LGI's *quinquagesima aestas* celebration was held in a private room at the Playwright Irish Pub, a callout to the host establishments of the early mid-1970s.

Omnibus notum sit

Nos, Praesidem, Professores, Curatores

Instituti Linguae Latinae Aestivi

Urbis Novi Eboraci Universitatis

quod Linguam Latinam apud nos

perdidicit et Litteras Humaniores coluit
titulo graduque

Socii Instituti Linguae Latinae Aestivi
adornavisse et distinxisse, et ei omnia privilegia
et honores ad hunc titulum pertinentia contulisse.

Datae Novi Eboraci
XVIII Kal. Sept.
MCMLXXXIX

INSTITUTI LINGUAE LATINAE AESTIVI PRAESES

COLLEGII ARTIUM HUMANIORUM BROOKLYNENSIS DECANUS

STUDIORUM GRAECORUM LATINORUMQUE UNIVERSITATIS PROCURATOR

On the final Tuesday (the day after the final exam), each graduate meets individually with Fleischer, a responsibility she inherited from Moreland in the late 1980s. In addition to their final grade, they receive a diploma. Though not a true standalone certificate-granting program, Moreland felt it important that graduates receive suitable recognition for their efforts. Originally hand-calligraphed, they have been generated by the GC's print services since the early 2000s. Both these examples date from 1989.

ἀγαθῇ τύχῃ

ἔδοξεν ἡμῖν τοῖς ἐν τῷ θερινῷ διδασκαλείῳ
τῷ Ἑλλάδος γλώττης διδάξασιν

διὰ τὸ τὴν γλῶτταν ἑλληνισθῆναι
καὶ τὰ γράμματα μεμαθηκέναι

εὖ καὶ καλῶς

θιασώτην καὶ ξυνουσιαστὴν τοῦ θερινοῦ
διδασκαλείου τελέσαι καὶ πασῶν τῶν τιμῶν
αἵπερ τοῖς οὕτω πεπαιδευμένοις
προσήκουσιν μεταδοῦναι

ΠΡΟΕΔΡΟΣ

δωδεκάτῳ ἐν θέρει

ΚΟΣΜΗΤΟΡ

ΠΡΥΤΑΝΙΣ

Faculty can award specific honors to graduates which are duly indicated on their diplomas: *cum laude* (SGI: εὖ), *magna cum laude* (εὖ καὶ καλῶς), and *summa cum laude* (ἄριστα). These are based on individual effort and in-class engagement and distinct from their final grade; accordingly, a student graduating with a "C" could in fact do so *cum laude.*

In the 1970s, the Institute sold iron-on transfers in the office. Beginning in the early 1980s, students also began making their own commemorative t-shirts. This example from 1996—before the widespread availability of editing and design software—is partially hand drawn. The quote is from Plato's *Ion* (section 539c): ζῳόν, ἔτ' ἀσπαίροντα ("alive, still gasping").

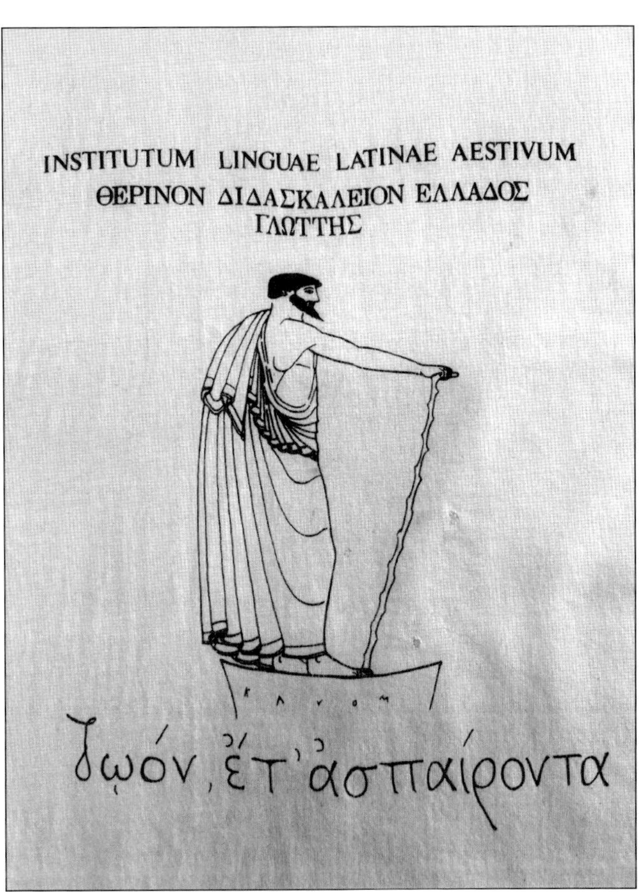

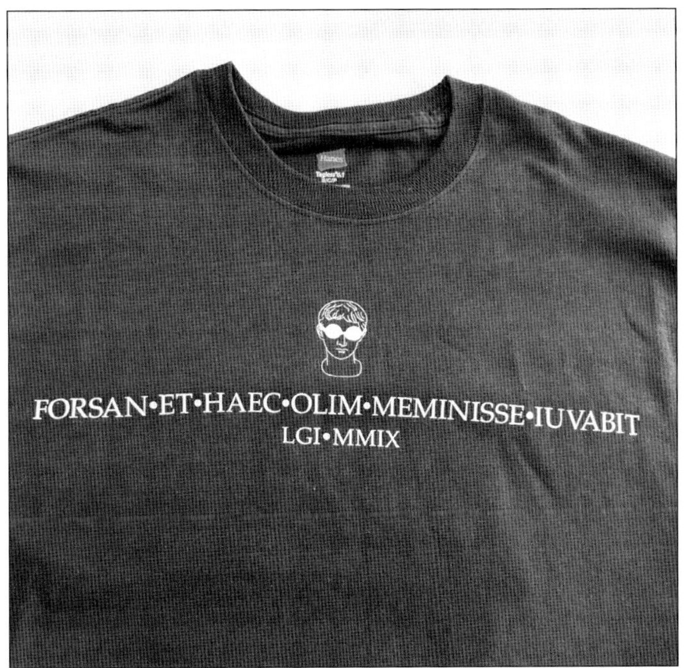

As with the previous quote, student-designed t-shirts often reference a work read that summer, and themes of challenge, struggle, and perseverance are quite frequent—an apt sentiment given the volume and rigor of the programs. *Aeneid* 1.203 ("perhaps someday it will be pleasing to remember even these things") has made a number of appearances, including on this simple design from 2009.

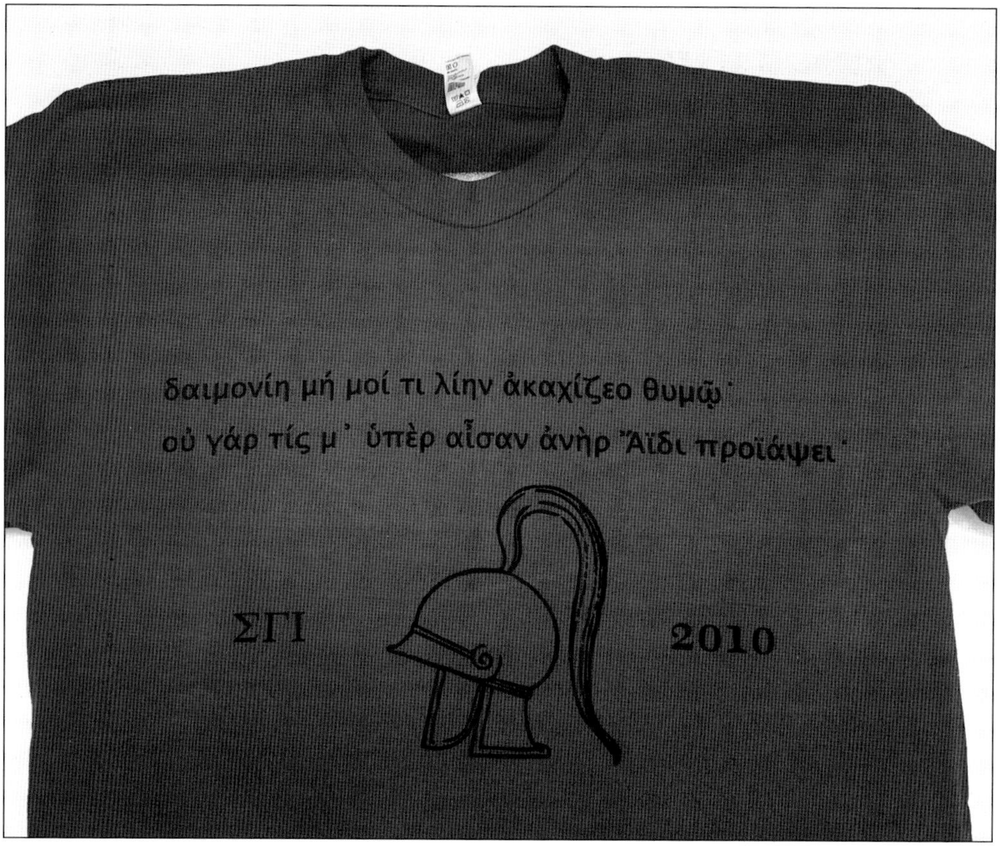

This 2010 SGI t-shirt is Hansen's favorite. The quote is from the *Iliad* 6.486-487, Hector's address to his wife, Andromache, before setting out for battle: "Strange one, don't grieve at heart too much, I beg you. No man will hurl me to Hades beyond my destiny."

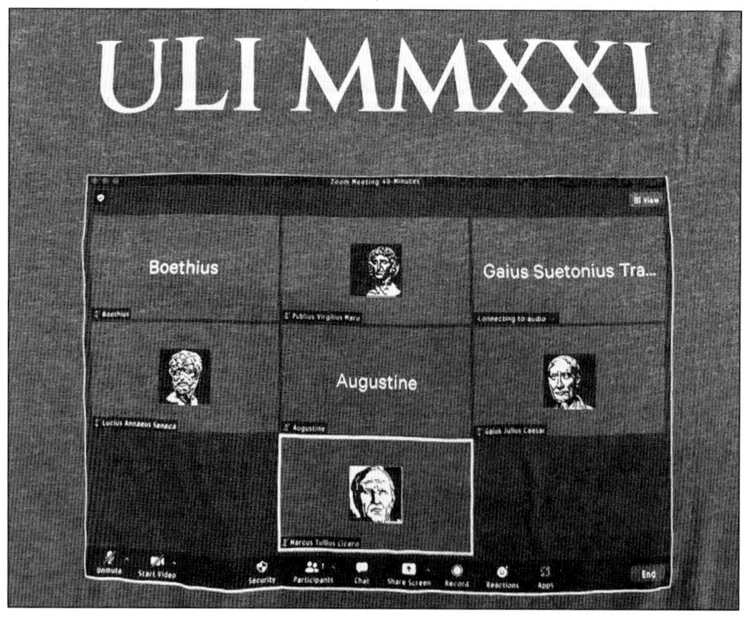

During the Covid pandemic, the Institute was restricted to online programs. In 2020, a section of online Upper Latin was offered, with both upper Latin and Greek mounted in the following summer. In 2021, the upper Latin students commemorated their summer by depicting the authors they had read as a Zoom screen.

SUMMER GREEK INSTITUTE — CLASS SCHEDULE FOR THE THIRD HALF

	8:30 optional	9:30 quiz and drill	10:40 drill	12:15 optional	12:45 optional	1:20-2:00	2:10-3:30	3:40-4:30
Monday August 21 day 49	Worry	Exam	More Exam	More Worry	Still More Exam	Still More Worry	Exhaustion and Despair	Relief and Incredulity (The exam didn't count.)
Tuesday August 22 day 50	η, The Noblest Letter JM	Newly Discovered Tenses of [illegible]ημι HH	ἐπί Parts 1, 2 EBH	The Genitive of Putative Origination CD	Plato's Letters to his Cousin RR	Verse Comp. 1 Choriambic Workout Routines BP	The ~~Seven~~ ~~Six~~ ~~Five~~ Three Sages of Boeotia CD	Beverage Stains in Early Medieval Manuscripts DS
Wednesday August 23 day 51	ει, The Upstart Pretende r EBH	The Aorist in Everyday Life: How to Live Gnomically BP	ἐπί Parts 3, 4, 5 HH	The Dative of Associative Affectation JM	High School Essays of Gorgias CD	Verse Comp. 2 Coping with Catalexis RR	Easy-to-Prepare Recipes from the Linear B Tablets HH	Semantically Significant Scratchings from Minoan Caves JM
Thursday August 24 day 52	εἴη: An Uneasy Alliance BP	How to Combat Correption CD	ἐπί Parts 6, 7, 8, 9 BP	The Accusative of Rebarbative Calumniation EBH	The Diaries of Aischines' Mother HH	Verse Comp. 3 Humorous Possibilities of the Resolved Dodrans CD	How to ϝαῦ Your Friends with Digammas RR	Hymnic Chants of the Cult of αἶξ ϝάνασσα AL
Friday August 25 day 53	Eh? HH	The Lurking Dangers of Hiatus JM	ἐπί Parts 10-35 CD	The Vocative of Performative Pontification RR		Disco Dancing to Dactyls and Spondees (required; begins at 1:00) CD, BP, HH*, EBH, JM, RR *spondees only		Refreshments (orthopedic help available)
Sat.-Sun. August 26-27	rest and counseling faculty available if you can reach us							
Monday August 28 day 54	ὦ... HH	Sibilants in Social Situations CD	ἀνακαθίστημι EBH	The Indicative of Insolent Asseveration BP	Product Placement in Pindar JM	Verse Comp. 4 Overcoming Anceps Anxiety RR	Navigating Laryngeals While Avoiding Glottal Stops HH	A Recently Discovered Love Poem by Narcissus CD
Tuesday August 29 day 55	ὦ! JM	Palatals, Plosives, and Propriety RR	ἐπανακαθίστημι BP	The Subjunctive of Instigative Instantiation EBH	Pastoral Poems of Αἰγίφιλος HH	Verse Comp. 5 Dionysiac Dances with Epitrites CD	Rhotacism: What You Need to Know JM	Tynnichos and his Μοῖσα (Got a problem with that?) RR
Wednesday August 30 day 56	ὦ; RR	Using Fricatives Responsibly BP	προεπανακαθίστημι HH	The Optative of Invidious Insinuation JM	Lyric Laments of Anakreon's Stylist CD	Verse Comp. 6 Teaching Siri to Recognize Caesuras EBH	Sentence Structure in Thucydides (2:10-midnight; refreshments available) HH	
Thursday August 31 day 57	..., ᾦ ... CD	Synizesis: Road to Ruin EBH	ὑποπροεπανακαθίστημι RR	The Imperative of Obnoxious Adjuration CD	Antiphony in Antiphon's Antitheses BP	Verse Comp. 7 The Metrics of Lamentation: Groans and Moans HH	Aristotle on the Happiness of Goats (αἰγιδαιμονίᾱ) EBH	Syllogistic Papyri from Tebtunis JM
Friday September 1 day 58	-ῶ! BP	Overcoming Psilosis HH	παρυποπροεπανακαθίστημι CD	The Infinitive of Obloquious Altercation RR	Great Thoughts of Isokrates (12:45-12:48) EBH	Verse Comp. 8 The Metrics of Lamentation: Howls and Screams JM	Final Final (3:15 – 3:30)	Scintillating Conversations Totally Unrelated to Greek
Sat.-Sun. Sept. 2 – 3	Trip to the Greek Islands (students treat faculty)							

In addition to their diploma, departing SGI students receive a "Class Schedule for the Third Half," filled with all manner of fanciful sight-reading opportunities (such as the "High School Essays of Gorgias") and highly suspect grammar ("The Optative of Invidious Insinuation"). If a humorous send-off, many departing students continue to read together in their groups—some of which have gone on for years.

In 1979, the Institute launched a newsletter to provide a way for the LGI community to stay in touch. The first edition, shown here, was edited by the ubiquitous Collins. As Fleischer transitioned to a more administrative role, she later assumed its responsibility. From several editions a year, it eventually became an annual production—and also lost the name *Postscript*.

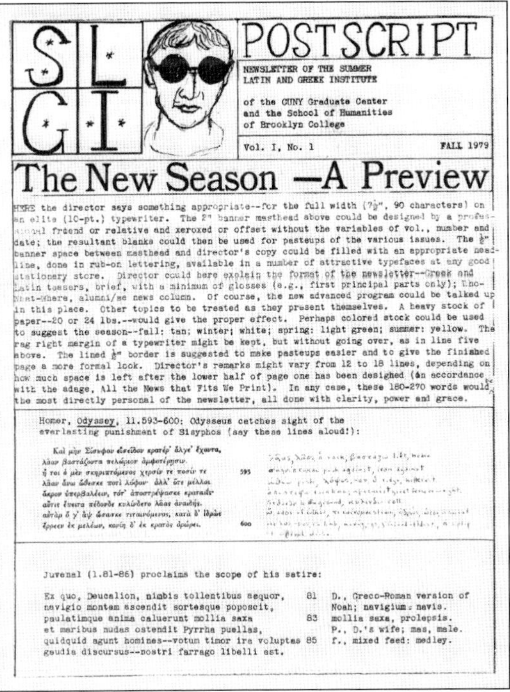

SLGI POSTSCRIPT

NEWSLETTER OF THE SUMMER LATIN AND GREEK INSTITUTE

of the CUNY Graduate Center and the School of Humanities of Brooklyn College

Vol. I, No. 1 — FALL 1979

The New Season —A Preview

HERE the director says something appropriate--for the full width (7½", 90 characters) on an elite (10-pt.) typewriter. The 2" banner masthead above could be designed by a professional friend or relative and xeroxed or offset without the variables of vol., number and date; the resultant blanks could then be used for pasteups of the various issues. The ½" banner space between masthead and director's copy could be filled with an appropriate headline, done in rub-on lettering, available in a number of attractive typefaces at any good stationery store. Director could here explain the format of the newsletter--Greek and Latin teasers, brief, with a minimum of glosses (e.g., first principal parts only); Who-What-Where, alumni/ae news column. Of course, the new advanced program could be talked up in this place. Other topics to be treated as they present themselves. A heavy stock of paper--20 or 24 lbs.--would give the proper effect. Perhaps colored stock could be used to suggest the season--fall: tan; winter; white; spring: light green; summer: yellow. The rag right margin of a typewriter might be kept, but without going over, as in line five above. The lined ⅛" border is suggested to make pasteups easier and to give the finished page a more formal look. Director's remarks might vary from 12 to 18 lines, depending on how much space is left after the lower half of page one has been desighed (in accordance with the adage, All the News that Fits We Print). In any case, these 180-270 words would be the most directly personal of the newsletter, all done with clarity, power and grace.

Homer, Odyssey, 11.593-600: Odysseus catches sight of the everlasting punishment of Sisyphos (say these lines aloud!):

Καὶ μὴν Σίσυφον εἰσεῖδον κρατέρ' ἄλγε' ἔχοντα,
λᾶαν βαστάζοντα πελώριον ἀμφοτέρῃσιν.
ἤτοι ὁ μὲν σκηριπτόμενος χερσίν τε ποσίν τε
λᾶαν ἄνω ὤθεσκε ποτὶ λόφον· ἀλλ' ὅτε μέλλοι
ἄκρον ὑπερβαλέειν, τότ' ἀποστρέψασκε κραταιΐς·
αὖτις ἔπειτα πέδονδε κυλίνδετο λᾶας ἀναιδής.
αὐτὰρ ὅ γ' ἂψ ὤσασκε τιταινόμενος, κατὰ δ' ἱδρὼς
ἔρρεεν ἐκ μελέων, κονίη δ' ἐκ κρατὸς ὀρώρει.

Juvenal (1.81-86) proclaims the scope of his satire:

Ex quo, Deucalion, nimbis tollentibus aequor, 81 — D., Greco-Roman version of
navigio montem ascendit sortesque poposcit, — Noah; navigium = navis.
paulatimque anima caluerunt mollia saxa 83 — mollia saxa, prolepsis.
et maribus nudas ostendit Pyrrha puellas, — P., D.'s wife; mas, male.
quidquid agunt homines--votum timor ira voluptas 85 — f., mixed feed: medley.
gaudia discursus--nostri farrago libelli est.

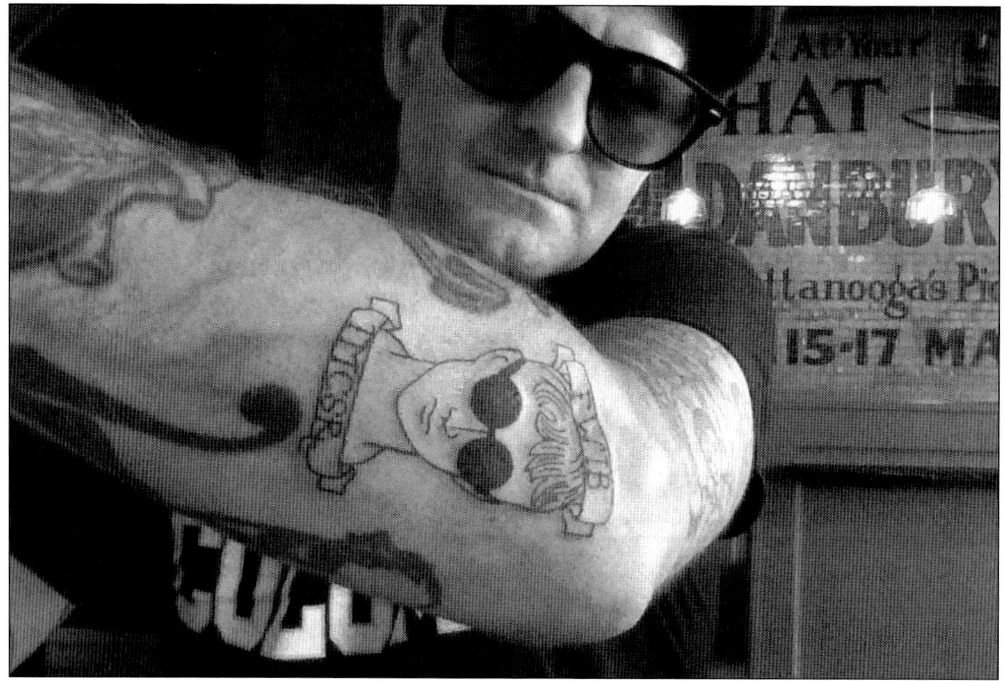

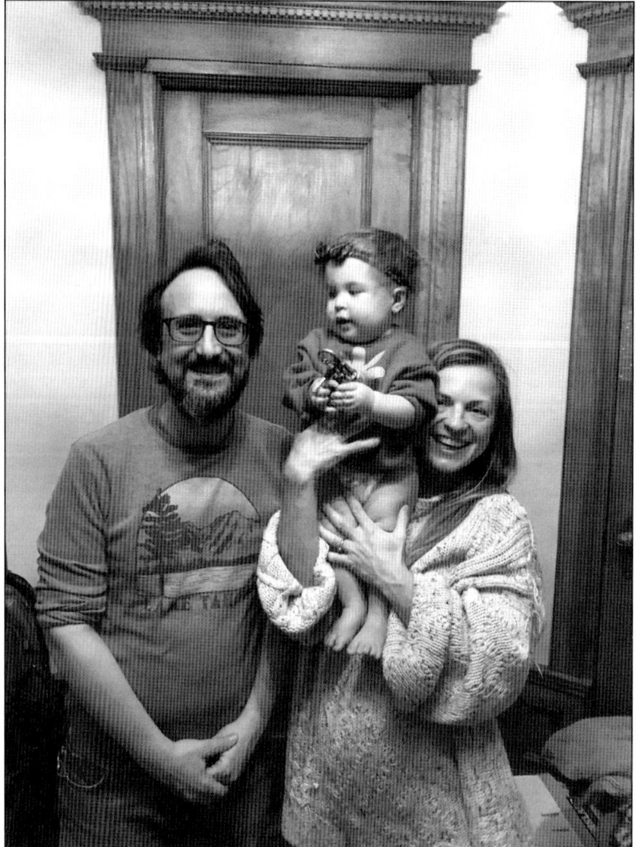

Though most alumni are content with a commemorative t-shirt, some have opted for other and, in some cases, more permanent memorialization. Several alumni now sport LGI tattoos. Here, Justin Colvin (UL 2021) displays his bust of Augustus surrounded by two well-known SLI acronyms: FWIB (the day one translation formula of the ablative) and TMCSRt (the five qualities of verbal syntax: tense, mood, construction, sequence, and relative time).

Since 2009, Katia Kosova-Krauss has taught in the Basic Latin, Basic Greek, and Upper Greek programs. Here, she introduces her daughter, born October 1, 2022, to the author. Her name is Hardy—in honor of the LGI's own Hardy Hansen.

Bibliography

Briggs, Ward W. Jr. "Frederic M. Wheelock (1902–1987)." *The Classical Outlook*, Vol. 80, No. 2 (2003), pp. 76–79.

Cantor, Gloria E. "VENI, VIDI & VICTA SUM: Thinking About Nothing but Latin." *Campus*, Series 1, No. 7 (1976), pp. 10–11.

Clayman, Dee L. "Ethyle R. Wolfe (1919–2010)." *The Classical World*, Vol. 103, No. 4 (2010), pp. 542–543.

Coulton, Thomas Evans. *A City College in Action; Struggle and Achievement at Brooklyn College, 1930–1955*. New York: Harper, 1955.

Davis, Derek S.B. "Revival of Latin Instruction Takes Hold in Schools." *Humanities Report*, Vol. IV, No. 4 (April 1982), pp. 4–8.

Gilder, Richard, and Judith P. Hallett. "Ovationes (Rita Fleischer)." *Classical World*, Vol. 101, No. 4 (2008), pp. 537–538.

Greene, Alexis. "Classics Reborn." *Change: The Magazine of Learning* (December 1978–January 1979), pp. 21–24.

Horowitz, Murray M. *Brooklyn College, the First Half-Century*. New York: Brooklyn College Press, 1981.

Kimmich, Flora "Of Catiline, Subjunctive Control & Complicated *Cum*-Clauses." *CUNY Matters: A Newsletter for the City University of New York* (Summer 1998), pp. 1, 8.

Moreland, Floyd L. "From Amo, Amas, Amat to Vergil in Ten Weeks. A Report on the 1967 Berkeley Summer Latin Workshop." *Northern California Foreign Language Newsletter*, Vol. 16, No. 65 (May 1968), pp. 8–9.

———, "Summer Latin." *The Classical Outlook*, Vol. 50, No. 9 (May 1973), pp. 100–101.

———, "An Intensive Approach to Latin and Greek: The Latin/Greek Institute of the City University of New York." *The Classical Outlook*, Vol. 58, No. 1 (October–November 1980), pp. 5–8.

———, *Strategies in Teaching Greek and Latin: Two Decades of Experimentation* (American Philological Association Pamphlets, 7). Chico, CA: Scholars Press, 1981.

Pari, Caroline. "Intensive and Beyond: The Foreign Language Institute & The Latin/Greek Institute." *The Graduate Student Advocate*, Vol. 1, No. 7 (May–September 1990), pp. 3, 19.

Consistent with our mission to preserve history on a local level, this book was printed in South Carolina on American-made paper and manufactured entirely in the United States. Products carrying the accredited Forest Stewardship Council (FSC) label are printed on 100 percent FSC-certified paper.

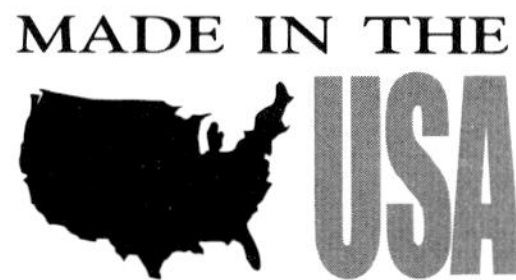